The Divided Dominion

The Divided Dominion

Social Conflict and Indian Hatred in Early Virginia

Ethan A. Schmidt

UNIVERSITY PRESS OF COLORADO

Boulder

Published by University Press of Colorado
5589 Arapahoe Avenue, Suite 206C
Boulder, Colorado 80303

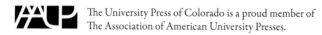 The University Press of Colorado is a proud member of
The Association of American University Presses.

The University Press of Colorado is a cooperative publishing enterprise supported, in part, by Adams State University, Colorado State University, Fort Lewis College, Metropolitan State University of Denver, Regis University, University of Colorado, University of Northern Colorado, Utah State University, and Western State Colorado University.

∞ This paper meets the requirements of the ANSI/NISO Z39.48–1992 (Permanence of Paper).

Library of Congress Cataloging-in-Publication Data

Schmidt, Ethan A.
  The divided dominion: social conflict and Indian hatred in early Virginia / by Ethan A. Schmidt.
    pages cm
  Includes bibliographical references and index.
  ISBN 978-1-60732-307-5 (cloth) — ISBN 978-1-60732-524-6 (pbk) — ISBN 978-1-60732-308-2 (ebook)
  1. Bacon's Rebellion, 1676. 2. Virginia—Social conditions—17th century. 3. Indians, Treatment of—Virginia—History—17th century. 4. Powhatan Indians—Virginia—History—17th century. 5. Powhatan Indians—Virginia—Government relations. 6. Virginia—Race relations—History—17th century. 7. Virginia—History—Colonial period, ca. 1600-1775. I. Title.
  F229.S245 2014
  975.5'02—dc23

                    2013050473

Cover photograph: detail from John Smith's *Map of Virginia*, Library of Congress, Geography and Map Division.

For my wife, Elizabeth, for believing in me.
For the late Edmund S. Morgan, for inspiring me.

Contents

    DECLINE OF SIR WILLIAM BERKELEY'S GOLDEN AGE, 1642–74   121

6. "TO RUIN AND EXTIRPATE ALL INDIANS IN GENERAL": THE
    REBELLION OF NATHANIEL BACON   149

EPILOGUE: WHITE UNITY AND INDIAN SURVIVAL   177

    Bibliography   187
    Index   201

Figures

Maps

Acknowledgments

I wrote the first words of the seminar paper that eventually became my dissertation and then this book more than ten years ago. Over the span of that decade, countless people have contributed to its journey. They are too numerous to mention, but a few deserve special recognition. I would first like to thank the organizations that provided the financial support necessary to conduct research from Chicago to London and parts in between. At the University of Kansas I twice received the Lila Atkins Creighton Scholarship for Graduate Research, as well as a dissertation fellowship (which I was fortunate enough to decline because I accepted my first tenure-track position). Two large fellowships from the Harry S. Truman Good Neighbor Foundation, the Eddie Jacobsen Memorial Award, and the Sherman and Irene Dreizeszun Award funded a significant portion of my research, as did the James B. Pearson Fellowship from the Kansas Board of Regents. The generous support I was given by Texas Tech University in general and the Office of the President, Vice-President for Research, College of Liberal Arts and Sciences, and Department of History in particular allowed me to conduct the additional research necessary to successfully convert my dissertation into this book. Without the monetary support of these organizations, this work would not have been possible.

I also thank the many educators who did so much over the years to encourage my intellectual and creative development. Faie Frederickson was the first teacher who told me I was intelligent. I have never forgotten that moment. During my undergraduate years at Emporia State University, Christopher Phillips ignited in me a love for Early American history (and introduced me to the work of Edmund Morgan), while Ron McCoy introduced me to ethnohistory. As I pursued my Master of Arts degree there, John Sacher and Karen Smith provided not only valuable guidance and mentorship but also friendship, which I value to this day. At the University of Kansas, I benefited from the expertise and advice of the perfect group of advisers for someone with as broad an array of methodological and theoretical interests as myself. Donald Worster, Theodore Wilson, Victor Bailey, and Luis Corteguera all contributed to this project both directly and indirectly, and I am eternally grateful to them for their time, patience, and dedication to furthering my research and career. My adviser Paul Kelton inspired me, challenged me, and has continued to support me every step of the way. Through thick and thin, the ups and the downs, Paul never doubted that this story was important and deserved to be told. Furthermore, he never doubted my ability to pull it off.

My graduate school colleagues at the University of Kansas continue to be some of my biggest supporters and greatest friends. Nicole Anslover, Brady DeSanti, Sally Utech, John Schneiderwind, Ryan Gaston, Kyle Anthony, Becca Anthony, Ryan Schumacher, Steven Sodergren, Christopher White, Dave Trowbridge, Emily Lowrance-Floyd, Tai Edwards, and Krystle Perkins became and remain permanent members of my extended family; I will always treasure our time together on Mount Oread.

Many colleagues both at Texas Tech University and at my new home at Delta State University have lent me their time, expertise, and most of all their friendship as I continued the long and sometimes seemingly impossible quest to publish this book. Miguel Levario, Karlos Hill, Saad Abi-Hamad, Zachary Brittsan, Paul Bjerk, Emily Skidmore, Richard Verrone, Manu Vimalassery, Allan Kuethe, Randy McBee, Jeff Mosher, and Jobi Martinez supported me through some rather difficult times with this manuscript and shared more than a few beers, meals, and laughs with me over the years. I value the time I spent with them as colleagues and friends. My newest colleagues, among them Chuck Westmoreland, Brian Becker, Paulette Meikle, Lynn Pazzani, James Robinson, David Hebert, Gavin Lee, Jerry Dallas, Vicki Tinnon, Mike Smith, Michael Ewing, Garry Jennings, and Michelle Johansen, have been most welcoming to me and my family as we embark upon our new adventure in the Delta. Here's to many more years of friendship and collaboration.

Many other scholars have lent their time and talents to the successful completion of this manuscript, and I have benefited immensely from their critiques and advice. I thank Helen Rountree, Robbie Ethridge, Donald Fixico, Woody Holton, Philip Levy, Margaret Huber, Theda Perdue, Martin Gallivan, and the anonymous readers for the University Press of Colorado for their comments, critiques, and helpful suggestions. Any deficiencies in this book are entirely my own, despite their best efforts.

The staffs of the various research repositories I visited while researching this book also deserve special mention. The staffs of the Spencer Research Library at the University of Kansas, the Rockefeller Library at Colonial Williamsburg, the Library of Congress, the Library of Virginia, the Newberry Library, the National Archives of the United Kingdom, the British Library, and the Texas Tech University Library were all instrumental in the completion of this project.

The staff members of the University Press of Colorado deserve special thanks for their unflinching belief in this project. Darrin Pratt first approached me about publishing with them not long after I finished my PhD. I was not interested in his press at that point, but he kept with it. When I came to his press a few years later after rethinking my initial decision, he did not turn his back on me, though it may have been what I deserved. Jessica d'Arbonne has fought continually on my and my project's behalf. She has been a joy to work with and is a shining example of the best the academic publishing world has to offer. I will never forget the faith both Darrin and Jessica have shown in me, and I am forever in their debt.

Finally, my family has played the largest part in making my dream of becoming a historian come true. Ryan Morris deserves special recognition for his amazing maps. To my extended family of Pierces and Schmidts, I say thanks for providing such a nurturing and intellectually active family in which to grow up. Tom and Susie Schmidt are simply two of the most caring, thoughtful, and nurturing people I have ever encountered. What a bonus that they also happen to be my parents. This project (and my entire future career) is dedicated to giving voice to the voiceless, whether they are poor and working-class Englishmen and Virginians or Native Americans. I became a social historian because my parents taught me to care about people who struggle outside the mainstream of society and to do my part to make this a more just, understanding, peaceful, and communal world. Mom and Dad, thank you for your help, encouragement, and your commitment to social justice and peace in the midst of a place that often doesn't seem to care about those things.

My older son, Connor, is roughly as old as this project. He has grown from a toddler into a well-rounded, thoughtful adolescent as this book has developed. My younger son, Dylan, likewise has spent his entire life with the thought of publishing this book ever-present in his father's mind, and I have often drawn inspiration from his extremely creative persona. My daughter, Brianna, is still of an age where she is largely unaware of what it is that Daddy does when he has to work on the computer instead of playing dress-up. Would this book have been published sooner had they not come along? Maybe, but its publication would have been much less satisfying and my life so much less fulfilling without the snuggles, hugs, story times, pick-up basketball games, games of catch, cartoons, Lego construction sessions, dress-up games, and dolly feedings. Other historians may experience greater success than me, but none will experience greater happiness.

My wife, Elizabeth, possesses a grace and patience beyond anything I can conjure. It has served her very well as an elementary school teacher and I am sure also as the wife of an academic. I remember the day I came home from work and told her I wanted to forgo a potentially lucrative career as a fundraiser, take a 70 percent pay cut, and pursue a graduate degree in history. She responded that if doing that made me happy, it was fine with her. She worked full-time (sometimes holding down two jobs) to support our growing family. From serving as my unpaid research and editorial assistant to picking me up when the bumps in the road knocked me down, she has always been there for me. Over the years, I have gone through considerable ups and downs with this manuscript. I have come close on many occasions to chucking the whole thing. Her faith in the project and in me has never wavered. Despite her impressive dedication to her own highly successful and very demanding career, she has always supported my efforts to conduct research and to write and exhibited so much love and caring for our children as well. Whenever my education and career have necessitated sacrifices beyond what I could reasonably expect another human being to make on my behalf, she has accepted them without the slightest hesitation. None of this would have been possible without her. Elizabeth, I love you and I am in awe of you. Thank you from the bottom of my heart.

The Divided Dominion

INTRODUCTION

A Tale of Two Uprisings

In January 1674, Roger Delke was incarcerated in Surry County, Virginia, for his participation in a December 1673 meeting at the Lawne's Creek Parish church in which he and thirteen other Surry County residents had discussed a plan to encourage their neighbors to resist paying a recently enacted tax levy. The available evidence suggests that the fourteen conspirators were certain that their fellow Virginians would rise up beside them if the government attempted to stop them. Furthermore, they were prepared for a violent uprising should that occur. According to his jailors, Delke stated as much: "It is apparent that the said Delk [*sic*] . . . did this day discourseing of that meeting, Justifye the same and said we will burn all, before one shall Suffer."[1] Yet despite Delke's promises, his neighbors did not flock to the cause. In fact, three days after he uttered the threat, many of his co-conspirators (the record is unclear as to whether he was one of them), upon being lectured by the court as to the justice of the levy, "answered that they were exceeding well satisfied in the case, and were heartily sorry for what they had done."[2] Nothing burned and the Lawne's Creek plot remained just that, a plot that failed much as had previous attempts to ignite a broad-based social rebellion in Virginia during the 1660s and 1670s.[3]

Two years later, during the spring and summer of 1676, Virginia famously exploded in the violent uprising known as Bacon's Rebellion. During this period an army made up of Virginians from all levels of society attempted, according to their leader Nathaniel Bacon, to "ruine and extirpate all Indians in Generall." When the leaders of the colony led by the Royal Governor, Sir William Berkeley, branded them

DOI: 10.5876/9781607323082.c000

as rebels and attempted to apprehend Bacon before he could achieve his genocidal aims, Bacon and his followers proceeded to loot their estates and terrorize their families. The ensuing four months of warfare between loyalist and rebel Virginians remained a particularly terrifying and potent memory for Virginians into the era of the American Revolution.[4]

Less than thirty months separated the Lawne's Creek plot and Bacon's Rebellion, yet while one produced widespread social rebellion, the other fizzled because of a lack of support from the populace and a lack of commitment among the leadership. Understanding the reasons why Bacon's Rebellion succeeded in garnering broader support and commitment while the Lawne's Creek plot failed is the central question of this study. Specifically, in this book I argue that while the Lawne's Creek plot stemmed from many of the same social conflicts that later fed Bacon's Rebellion, it lacked the ability to break the powerful bonds of dependence that bound the various groups of disgruntled Virginians to the wealthy and powerful planters who controlled the colony's government. A call for the extermination of all Indians constitutes the critical element missing from the Lawne's Creek rising, but that call was so powerfully present in Bacon's Rebellion, so compelling in fact, that it helped unite enough of the disparate strands of disaffection in the colony to forge a widespread social rebellion. The differences in the two incidents demonstrate that the imbalance in political power and the burdens of regressive taxation were not enough in and of themselves to spark an uprising in Virginia. Something or someone needed to unite dissatisfied Virginians across class, geographic, political, and social boundaries. I contend that that something was a desire to violently displace Indians, and the man who exploited that hatred most effectively was Nathaniel Bacon.

In addition, whereas it may be tempting to view Bacon's Rebellion as a sudden and violent eruption that, in the words of Edmund Morgan, "produced no real program of reform" and espoused no defined principles, when we examine the rebellion as the logical outgrowth of the social relations established in the early decades of the colony, we can begin to see both the principles and the reform program dismissed by previous scholars.[5] In short, we must view Bacon's Rebellion not as a precursor to eighteenth-century colonial America but instead as an incident created by and representative of an earlier social matrix and the interaction of that social matrix with Native societies. Homicidal tendencies toward Virginia Indians represent much more than an unimportant symptom of Bacon's Rebellion. They embody both the rebellion's primary cause and its ultimate goal or program. Therefore, the relationships and ideas that produced the rebellion deserve study in their own right, as much as those resulting from it.[6]

The class relationships of seventeenth-century Virginia exemplify the scenario best expressed by E. P. Thompson in his famous "field of force" analogy that compared the various orders of English society to a science experiment in which "an electrical current magnetized a plate covered with iron fillings." When magnetized, most of the fillings attached themselves to whichever pole they happened to be closest to, but the fillings in the middle of the plate wound up caught between the magnetic fields of both poles. Thompson argued that one pole represented the elite classes of gentry and aristocracy while the other symbolized the plebeian classes. The paralyzed shavings in the middle represented the middling orders of tradesmen, artisans, and lesser gentry who were, in Thompson's words, "bound down by lines of dependency to the rulers."[7]

The analogy best applies to seventeenth-century Virginia during the thirty years preceding Bacon's Rebellion. During that time period, which according to historian Edmund Morgan was "a golden fleecing," the attempts at aggrandizement by Virginia's social and economic elite grew evermore brazen. In the words of historian Anthony Parent, during this period "an elite evolved, consolidated its power, and fixed itself as an extensive land- and slaveholding class." Parent places this development in the era immediately following the end of the Anglo-Powhatan Wars, largely because of his conclusion that the switch to African slavery occurred in the 1670s and 1680s. However, John Coombs places the transition much earlier. Specifically, he locates the conversion to race-based slavery in Virginia as early as the 1650s, with slaves outnumbering indentured servants by the 1680s. If Coombs is correct, the colony's elites would have to have acquired the massive landholdings required for a slave society by that period. Therefore, the period between the beginning of the Second Anglo-Powhatan War in 1622 and the arrival of Sir William Berkeley as governor in 1641 represents the critical period for examining the rise of this planter elite.[8]

By the 1670s, elite Virginians' self-serving manipulation of the colony's legal, political, and judicial structures had combined with other issues beyond their control to create a situation in which middling planters, westerners, and others outside the small circle of power that surrounded Virginia governor William Berkeley broke away from the force exerted on them by Virginia's elite. When this occurred, the balance of the field of force tilted in favor of non-elites, and they exploited the opportunities this presented to unleash violence against all Indians in Virginia as a way of gaining the land they felt was both their birthright and their best hope for checking the growing power of their elite counterparts. Specifically, the issue of carte blanche permission for all-out war on all Indians in Virginia divided the colony's planter classes to the point that many of them joined with landless freedmen, former indentured servants, middling and small landholders, and others outside the small inner circle of men who controlled Virginia's government to plunge the Old Dominion into months of violent chaos.[9]

This book asserts that Bacon's Rebellion resulted from myriad internal and external factors, building in Virginia since its earliest days, that drove Virginians to increasingly interpret their disputes with one another along class lines. Disputes over access to political power, taxation, land, and defense policies that seemed to favor the well-connected at the expense of those outside the inner circle of power; failed attempts to diversify the colony's economy; restrictions on access to the lucrative Indian trade; the reverberations of wars between Indian groups outside Virginia; English conflicts with the Dutch during the 1660s; the effects of the transition from indentured servitude to slavery; the ups and downs of the tobacco economy; and tensions resulting from increased Crown intervention in the governance of the colony all played a significant role in driving Virginia to the 1676 upheaval. In the end, though, only a call for the annihilation of all Indians in Virginia could unite the different factions arising from these issues and mold them into a widespread social rebellion.

The concept of class is fraught with multiple interpretations and connotations. In using the term in a pre-industrial context such as seventeenth-century Virginia, I have employed the definition used by Gary Nash in *The Urban Crucible*. According to Nash, Americans, "living amid historical forces that were transforming the social landscape, came to perceive antagonistic divisions based on economic and social position; they began to struggle in relation to these conflicting interests; and through these struggles developed a consciousness of class."[10] In other words, to paraphrase E. P. Thompson, classes come into existence through conflict over differing interests. Those interests may be defined by the classic relationship to the ownership of the means of production, or they may not.[11]

In this case, access to land, servants, and political power came to define the class interests of seventeenth-century Virginians. Class antagonism stemming from these interests roiled throughout the first seventy-five years of Virginia's existence. For much of that same period, unremitted violence against Virginia's Indian peoples also constituted the norm. Bacon's Rebellion in 1676 represents a unique historical moment in which both class conflict and violence against Indians became enmeshed, with terrifying and long-lasting consequences. Therefore, the role of class-based disputes over who could and who could not authorize violence against Virginia's Indian peoples represents a critical element of Bacon's Rebellion heretofore understudied by scholars of seventeenth-century Virginia in general and of Bacon's Rebellion in particular. Whereas other studies of Bacon's Rebellion assign Virginia's Native people to a relatively minor role as unwitting instigators of its outbreak, this study argues that Indians were crucial to the rebellion's beginning, progress, and, ultimately, its resolution.[12] That resolution not only hastened the spread of African slavery and the development of patriarchal gender relations in Virginia but also forever altered the relationships among Native Americans, Virginia colonists, and the Virginia government in ways fundamental to our understanding of the later history of Virginia and the relationship between Native Americans and whites, as well as class and race in the future United States.

Specifically, the violent confrontations between colonists and the Powhatan chiefdom during the first thirty-five years of the colony, while necessary for the consolidation of elite power, also inculcated in the minds of many Virginians a belief that unrestrained violence against Indians by any member of white Virginia society for land acquisition purposes represented the normative state of Virginia-Indian relations.[13] When the end of the Cromwellian Protectorate in 1660 returned Sir William Berkeley to the governorship of Virginia, he used the opportunity to embark upon what one historian has termed "the boldest state-building program the colony had yet seen."[14] The key components of this program were a lucrative trading relationship based on peaceful coexistence with Indians, both in Virginia and beyond its borders; securing the loyalty of property-owning Virginians; checking the potential for disorder among the colony's landless, servant, and enslaved populations; and diversifying Virginia's economy. For various reasons, many of which were beyond his control, Berkeley's state-building program ultimately failed. The repercussions of that failure, including the imposition of higher taxes, the abridgement of political rights, and attempts to protect the Indian trade by upholding the rights of Indians at the same level as those of whites, led to Bacon's Rebellion. While Virginians held grievances against the Virginia government before this time, it took Berkeley's reluctance to allow the indiscriminate killing of Indians by frontier whites to finally bring about the rebellion.

This study differs from many previous works in ways intended to augment rather than replace their conception of seventeenth-century Virginia society. Specifically, my aim is not to explain the role of Bacon's Rebellion in hastening the onset of African slavery, hardening the patriarchal gender system in Virginia, or demonstrating the rebellion's connection to either King Philip's War (which was raging in New England at the same time) or the American Revolution 100 years later. Instead, I seek to examine the social struggle that created the rebellion and to place a dispute among Virginians over the permissibility of eradicating Indians for land at the forefront of our understanding of this pivotal event.[15]

In addition, other works that examine the social and political structures of seventeenth-century Virginia often fail to treat Virginia Indians with the same complexity they apply to whites.[16] Many works that focus on Virginia Indians do the exact opposite.[17] One of the overriding goals of this study has been to present whites and Indians in Virginia as equally sophisticated participants in the making of their shared history.

Finally, as alluded to earlier, much of the scholarship that focuses solely on Bacon's Rebellion has long been preoccupied with whether the rebellion represented the first stirrings of the liberal democratic ideals often associated with the American Revolution. Therefore, those interpretations have generally sought to explain the events of 1676 in light of the events of 1776. They therefore provide little in the way of explaining how seventeenth-century Anglo and Indian Virginians understood the world in which they lived.[18] My work seeks to understand this period in terms the participants themselves would have understood, not in light of a revolution 100 years later that none of them could have foreseen. To do so, we must begin at the beginning, so to speak, by examining the various attitudes and assumptions Virginians and Indians brought with them to their encounter and the ways those assumptions started them on the path toward the momentous events of 1676.[19]

At the dawn of the seventeenth century, Virginia, or Tsenacommacah as its Algonquian inhabitants referred to it, stood on the cusp of what historian Elliot West has referred to as one of those times when "events line up to produce explosions of imagination." For West, the contact between previously separate peoples constitutes one of the most dynamic instances in which we can glimpse the "human envisioning of new lifeways and routes to power, the effects of that search on physical and social environments and the dilemmas and disasters that so often follow."[20] While West was referring to the meeting of Native Americans and whites on the Great Plains, the contact era in Virginia also fits this model. First, the Algonquians of Virginia fashioned a powerful chiefdom out of smaller, tangentially connected settlements. They did so not simply to accumulate temporal political gains or in response to environmental stimuli, though both of these were factors, but, most important, for the accretion of, and in accordance with, their understanding of powerful spiritual forces that guided their actions through ritual, ceremony, and vision. Almost as soon as this spiritually ordained "empire" came into existence, the Europeans arrived in the midst of the "new world" the Powhatans of Virginia had created for themselves.

Having only recently broken the bonds of ignorance and superstition that had circumscribed their movements for a millennium, Europeans likewise began to re-imagine the world and their place in it. Spurred on by the developments of the Renaissance and the Scientific Revolution, Europeans quickly re-engineered old religious, societal, economic, and governmental structures such that, by the late six-teenth and early seventeenth centuries, the idea that humans could understand and control all things in the world had become commonplace. Furthermore, the notion that groups of people, organized into governments and nations, were in competi-tion with one another for the world's wealth spurred Europeans to spread out across the globe in an effort to dominate the lands, peoples, and resources of distant shores.

This process brought the Algonquians of Virginia face to face with English invad-ers in 1607. The meeting of Algonquian and English cultures in seventeenth-century Virginia opened in the minds of many on both sides new paths to power and new opportunities to strengthen their respective societies. To again cite Elliot West, "Above all the merging of worlds was a revelation of routes to power in its largest sense."[21] So rather than a conservative clash in which each side sought to impose its traditional ways of doing things on the other, both Virginia Algonquians and English colonists developed particular visions for the future of Virginia that involved the merging of their cultures to a certain extent. Eventually, English colonists envisioned two different and competing scenarios that they attempted to impose on the region's Native inhabitants. Many of Virginia's leaders envisioned a well-ordered colony based on a hierarchical social structure. Whether such a schema was designed to enrich them personally or represented the best means for securing the good of the entire population is less important than the undeniable fact that they prized an ordered society in Virginia above all things. Regardless of what motivated their desire for said order, challenges to it would be met with swift and severe resistance.

In addition, many outside the colony's leading families came to perceive this desire for order on the part of the elite as motivated solely by a desire to enrich the few at the expense of the many, and they thus began to struggle against their leaders. Many Virginians—particularly those who possessed less wealth and political power than those who controlled the colony's government but also wealthy men who by the 1670s, as a result of geography, political ideology, or temperament, found themselves outside Sir William Berkeley's increasingly small inner circle—sought opportunity above all else. Having left a homeland in which the combination of a small amount of land and a growing population had virtually destroyed any hope they may have had of improving their economic life and, by extension, gaining for themselves some small measure of political power, many poor Englishmen were easily lured to Virginia by promotional literature that portrayed the colony as a veritable land of milk and honey. Being worked to death for the purpose of enriching someone else was decidedly not what they had in mind.

Increasingly, as the seventeenth century wore on, Indian land in the West came to represent their last opportunity for improvement. Likewise, smaller property holders looking to maintain or increase their social position and wealthier individuals denied access to the inner sanctum of power in the colony also looked to the Indian lands in the western portions of the colony as both a sort of birthright and a gateway to the lucrative Indian trade beyond. As mentioned, seventeenth-century Virginia society was not one of static classes defined by an unchanging relationship to a sort of pre-industrial "means of production"; instead, class in Virginia was a lived and changeable relationship defined by many things, some economic in nature but many not. At times, class consciousness in Virginia was defined by tobacco wealth, land ownership, political power, occupation, and various other means by which seventeenth-century Virginians differentiated themselves. By 1676,

the essential division within Virginia society had become the fundamental importance of Indian land to one's future and the access to the political power needed to
make the acquisition of that land possible.[22]

Finally, though he had created an extremely powerful chiefdom, the Algonquian
leader Powhatan was not content to sit back and rest. Powerful non-Algonquian
groups to his north and west, as well as the rebellious tendencies of some members
of his own chiefdom, created a powerful need to seek new alliances in the physical
world and new avenues of power in the spiritual world. As such, the Algonquian
peoples of Virginia possessed their own vision of Virginia's future, and all newcom-
ers to the area would be dealt with according to their perceived ability to help or
hinder the realization of that vision.

During the first thirty-five to forty years of the colony's existence, these competing visions of Virginians and Virginia Algonquians spawned three separate conflicts known collectively as the Anglo-Powhatan Wars. It was during those wars that
many Virginians first came to believe that violence against Indians for the purpose
of obtaining land needed no sanction beyond that of the individual engaged in it.
In seeking to win those wars, Virginia's leaders unwittingly encouraged this idea to
develop. By the end of the Anglo-Powhatan Wars in 1646, the roots of the conflict
that would become Bacon's Rebellion were well entrenched; despite the defeat and
dissolution of the Powhatan chiefdom, Indian hatred constituted the critical element around which all other disaffection in Virginia coalesced.

Beyond this introduction, this book is divided into six chapters and an epilogue. The first chapter describes the early relationship of the Virginians and the
Powhatans at Jamestown. In these early years, best remembered for the incidents
involving John Smith and Pocahontas, one can see the early stirrings of the conflicts
that would bedevil the Anglo-Powhatan relationship for the next thirty years.

Chapter 2 locates the early origins of the belief in unrestrained violence against
Native people that eventually spawned Bacon's Rebellion in the First Anglo-
Powhatan War. It was during this conflict that Virginia's leadership first encouraged violent retribution against Native people by all levels of society as a means of
establishing full control over the colony. Sixty years later, Nathaniel Bacon and his
followers would employ much of the language and rationale used during this period
in their own campaign against Virginia's Indian people.

The third chapter covers the years 1614 to 1646, with particular emphasis on the
role of the Second Anglo-Powhatan War and the tobacco boom in the creation of
a group I refer to as the "planter elite." Virginia colonists, like their brethren back
in England and in other colonies, understood that society was organized along the
lines of hierarchy and inequality. However, if it had ever been their purpose, the
early leaders of the colony proved unable to completely replicate the social structure

of England on the banks of the James River. Specifically, the opportunity for land ownership was certainly more widespread. However, as we will see, this did not necessarily mean land ownership *was* widespread. In addition, owning land did not necessarily convey the same degree or level of social and political status it did in England. Instead, one's ability to own the labor of other human beings, be they indentured servants or slaves, became the basis for the major social distinctions in seventeenth-century Virginia. Because these social distinctions were based on one's ability to control the distribution of servants and slaves and, to a lesser extent, land and not on hereditary distinctions, the social hierarchy in Virginia remained quite volatile throughout the seventeenth-century, with many individuals moving in and out of the various rungs of the social ladder. However, through their membership on the Council of State and service in the House of Burgesses as well as the local county bench, a relatively small group of people came to dominate Virginia society and politics during the period between the end of the First Anglo-Powhatan War in 1614 and the end of the Third Anglo-Powhatan War in 1646.[23]

These people were the "winners" in the scramble set off by the tobacco boom and the head-right system. Specifically, they wanted to create social stability, which meant they desired to end the wars against the Powhatans as soon as possible, as long as the Powhatans would either relocate or accept the role prescribed for Indians in their vision of the colony's future. They also wanted to limit competition from new arrivals and non-elites, such as middling and small planters, artisans, and landless freeman. Finally, elites wanted order above all things. Whether that desire stemmed from Renaissance Humanist sources, from the Metropole's (Crown, company, far-away decision makers) need for profit, or from racialist notions first espoused to justify the subjugation of Ireland in the end matters little. Order, to allow for the maximization of personal profit or of what they termed the greater good, constituted the overriding goal of Virginia elites.[24] Eventually, this group became divided against itself as a result of factors relating to geography, length of time in the colony, political opinion, and general temperament. The call for an extermination campaign against all Indians in 1676 represents the issue that brought all of these divisions to the fore and spawned Bacon's Rebellion.

Chapter 4 describes the disappointing experience of many immigrants to Virginia during the first half of the seventeenth century. While many of these immigrants eventually became landholders and a few even obtained planter elite status, the majority came from groups beneath the great planters. According to historians Warren Billings, John Selby, and Thad Tate, these groups included servants, slaves, and freemen. The latter were further subdivided into the categories of the landless underclass, small planters, and middling Virginians. The Virginia underclass consisted of former servants, slaves, failed planters, and others of the dispossessed. Their most distinguishable characteristics were their landlessness and their lack of a tie to any particular locale. Small planters stood one level removed from the underclass and had been only marginally successful at attaining enough land to make a go of tobacco planting. In addition, they rarely, if ever, held even the most insignificant political office. Middling planters included tobacco planters as well as most artisans. These individuals owned enough property and, therefore, sufficient tobacco profits to allow them to own a small number of servants or, more rarely, slaves. In addition, Billings, Selby, and Tate found that many of them brought powerful connections to the English mercantile sector that allowed them to diversify their economic activities and avoid sole dependence on the tobacco trade. Members of this group were often successful at obtaining political office, particularly at the county level, and many of the most adroit of their number managed to attach themselves to elites in a burgeoning client-patron system so that they often managed to leave their children in a higher social position than the one they had originally occupied.[25]

My collective labeling of this group is not meant to indicate unanimity of thought, opinion, or action among them. In fact, many of these groups found themselves at odds with each other as often as not. Middling and small planters nearly always aspired to join the ranks of those who were above them in the social hierarchy and therefore were often less inclined to support the grievances of those within or below their station so they would not damage their standing with their more elite patrons. However, in 1676 circumstances aligned to drive them into an alliance with one another against the leadership of the colony. Despite their differences, these groups did share one basic commonality: they came to Virginia expecting opportunity. They were promised it in the promotional literature in general and by those who either paid their way or recruited them to undertake the journey. Therefore, their vision of Virginia's future was one in which they expected to enjoy more economic success and political power than they had in England. Instead, many small planters and members of the underclass found themselves exploited by elite planters looking to capitalize on the tobacco boom. Likewise, many middling planters and artisans found their road to political and social advancement increasingly blocked by the growing concentration of power in the hands of the planter elite as the seventeenth century wore on.

Chapter 5 examines the period from the outbreak of the Third Anglo-Powhatan War in 1644 to the eve of Bacon's Rebellion more than thirty-five years later. During this period, particularly after the Stuart Restoration, many of Virginia's leaders, Sir William Berkeley chief among them, came to believe they had succeeded in establishing the colony and their government on a firm footing of authority sufficient to unleash a period of peace and prosperity unrivaled in the English Atlantic world. In many ways, Berkeley was correct. The thirty years between his capture of Opechancanough and the outbreak of Bacon's Rebellion brought unprecedented peace, wealth, and stability to many in Virginia. However, this reality led Berkeley and his closest associates to attempt a series of sweeping reforms of Virginia's economy and society that ultimately failed, thus endangering this period of stability. In addition, a much more hands-on approach by restored Stuart officials in England intent on using the colonies to forge a lasting mercantile empire, the repercussions of Iroquois aggression to the north, warfare with the Dutch, as well as a growing perception among many frontier residents that Berkeley's government had increasingly come to favor the fortunes of a small inner circle of longtime friends and councilors to the detriment of the rest of the population initiated much of the unrest that culminated in Bacon's Rebellion.

In this chapter, I return to the events of the Lawne's Creek Uprising. The standard interpretation is that the uprising never got off the ground because of the low social standing of those who led it and that it would take people much higher up in the social hierarchy to build a movement broad enough to truly threaten Virginia's ruling elites. I complicate this by arguing that the missing element is Indians. While I do not believe scholars such as Edmund Morgan are wrong to say that the missing element is the leadership of someone like Bacon, the key issue for Bacon was the permissibility of the violent acquisition of Indian land. Therefore, it took both leadership from the middling planter–frontier elite strata of society and the issue of violence against Indians to unite the heretofore separate streams of unrest into a cohesive rebellion.

The next chapter examines the rebellion itself. I place particular emphasis not only on the role of violence toward Indians in the outbreak and progress of the conflict but also on the way the rebellion transitioned from a war against Indians to an excuse to terrorize and loot the estates of Berkeley's elite supporters. When this occurred, those elites whose support was so critical to Bacon's Rebellion largely deserted him, thus dooming his uprising to failure.

The final chapter is an epilogue that outlines the ways Virginia was irrevocably changed by the experience of Bacon's Rebellion. It does so in two primary ways. First, it examines the post-rebellion era in which the right of all Virginians, regardless of social standing, to violently wrest land from Native Americans was affirmed and, among other things, helped to forge a heretofore missing unity between the House of Burgesses and the general population in the colony that became increasingly important to understand the conflicts between the royal governors and the Council of State on one hand and the burgesses on the other that characterized their eighteenth-century relationship. I conclude with a discussion of the way that, despite the increasing desperation of their situation, Virginia Indians managed to ensure their continued existence in Virginia by manipulating English legal structures in the 1677 Treaty of Middle Plantation.

Bacon's own actions sufficiently support the arguments outlined here. In his drive to clear the backcountry of those he referred to as "Robbers and Theeves and

Invaders of his Majesties Right and our Interest and Estates," Bacon gave no quarter. He reportedly tortured and killed prisoners as well as combatants. According to one account, Bacon indiscriminately "fell upon the Indians and killed some of them who were our best Friends."[26]

Perhaps the best evidence of the primacy of Indian hatred for Bacon and his followers comes not from Bacon but from one of his lieutenants. With his last words Thomas Hansford, the first of Bacon's followers to be executed as part of Governor Berkeley's campaign to reassert his control over Virginia, cited only one reason he took up arms against the government: "Dureing the short time he had to live, after his sentance, he approved to his best advantage for the well fare of his soule, by repentance and contrition for all his Sinns, in generall, excepting his Rebellion, which he would not acknowledg; desireing the People, at the place of execution, to take notis that he dyed a Loyall Subject, and a lover of his Countrey; and that he had never taken up arms, but for the destruction of the Indians, who had murthered so many Christians."[27]

We now turn to an examination of the cultures that met in Virginia during the seventeenth century to determine what assumptions about the world and their place in it they brought to that meeting. It is hoped that this examination will lead us much closer to understanding Nathaniel Bacon, Thomas Hansford, their followers, their opponents, and their Algonquian victims.

NOTES

1. Warren Billings, "The Warrants for the Arrest of the Dissidents January 3, 1674," in *The Old Dominion in the Seventeenth-Century: A Documentary History of Virginia, 1606–1689,* ed. Warren Billings (Chapel Hill: University of North Carolina Press, 1975), 263–64.

2. Warren Billings, "The Surry County Court's Verdict, January 6, 1674," in *Old Dominion in the Seventeenth-Century,* 265.

3. Other instances of unrest occurred in York County in 1661 and in 1663 in Gloucester County. See York County Court, "Proceedings in York County Court," *William and Mary Quarterly* 11, no. 1 (July 1902): 34–27; Virginia State Historical Society, "Virginia Colonial Records (Continued)," *Virginia Magazine of History and Biography* 15, no. 1 (July 1907): 38–43.

4. Nathaniel Bacon, "Manifesto Concerning the Present Troubles in Virginia," *Virginia Magazine of History and Biography* 1 (1894): 55–58; Wilcomb Washburn, *The Governor and the Rebel: A History of Bacon's Rebellion in Virginia* (Chapel Hill: University of North Carolina Press, 1957), 43; "Commissioners' Narrative," in *Narratives of the Insurrections, 1675–1690,* ed. Charles McLean Andrews (New York: Charles Scribner's Sons, 1915), 112; Edmund S. Morgan, *American Slavery, American Freedom: The Ordeal of Colonial Virginia* (New York: W. W. Norton, 1975), 384–85.

5. Edmund S. Morgan, "Slavery and Freedom: The American Paradox," *Journal of American History* 59, no. 1 (June 1972): 22.

6. The National Archives (TNA), Public Record Office (PRO) CO5/1371 Colonial Office: Proceedings and Reports of the Commissioners for Enquiring into Virginian Affairs and Settling Virginian Grievances, British National Archives, Kew, England; Edward D. Neill, *Virginia Carolorum: The Colony under the Rule of Charles the First and Second, A.D. 1625–A.D. 1685* (Albany, NY: Joel Munsell's Sons, 1886), 355; Lieutenant Governor Herbert Jeffreys, "Declaration. Swans Point. April 27, 1677," Bacon's Rebellion, Miscellaneous Papers, 1676–1677, Rockefeller Library, Williamsburg, VA. The emergence of nationalism in the aftermath of the American Revolution led to one of the most significant alterations in the way Americans conceptualized the events of 1676. In 1804 the Richmond, Virginia, *Enquirer* printed a previously forgotten firsthand account of Bacon's Rebellion. Along with the document, only recently obtained by Thomas Jefferson, the *Enquirer* printed an anonymous prefatory statement that recast Bacon and his contemporaries as the forerunners of Jefferson and his fellow revolutionaries. From that moment until the publication of Edmund Morgan's article "Slavery and Freedom: The American Paradox" in 1972 and his subsequent book-length study of colonial Virginia, *American Slavery, American Freedom*, published in 1975, all interpretations of Bacon's Rebellion operated within this paradigm. See *Tracts and Other Papers Relating Principally to the Origin, Settlement, and Progress of the Colonies in North America, from the Discovery of the Country to the Year 1776*, ed. Peter Force (Washington, DC: Peter Force, 1835), 3–4; Morgan, "Slavery and Freedom," 5–29; Morgan, *American Slavery, American Freedom*; Mary Newton Stannard, *The Story of Bacon's Rebellion* (Washington, DC: Neale, 1907); Thomas Jefferson Wertenbaker, *Torchbearer of the Revolution: The Story of Bacon's Rebellion and Its Leader* (Princeton, NJ: Princeton University Press, 1940); Washburn, *The Governor and the Rebel*.

7. E. P. Thompson, *Customs in Common: Studies in Traditional Popular Culture* (New York: New Press, 1993), 73.

8. Anthony Parent, *Foul Means: The Formation of a Slave Society in Virginia, 1660–1740* (Chapel Hill: University of North Carolina Press, 2003), 3; John C. Coombs, "Building 'the Machine': The Development of Slavery and Slave Society in Early Colonial Virginia" (PhD diss., College of William and Mary, Williamsburg, VA, 2004); John C. Coombs, "Beyond the 'Origins Debate': Rethinking the Rise of Virginia Slavery," in *Early Modern Virginia: Reconsidering the Old Dominion*, ed. Douglas Bradburn and John C. Coombs (Charlottesville: University of Virginia Press, 2011), 239–78.

9. The idea that Indian hatred was vital to the development of ideas of whiteness, American identity, and even irregular warfare is not in itself a new rise of Early American historiography. However, the trend has been applied less often to the American South. See Francis Jennings, *The Invasion of America: Indians, Colonialism, and the Cant of Conquest* (New York: W. W. Norton, 1975); Jill Lepore, *The Name of War: King Philip's War and the*

Origins of American Identity (New York: Vintage Books, 1999); Alfred Cave, *The Pequot War* (Amherst: University of Massachusetts Press, 1996); Kevin Kenny, *Peaceable Kingdom Lost: The Paxton Boys and the Destruction of William Penn's Holy Experiment* (New York: Oxford University Press, 2009); John Grenier, *The First Way of War: American War-Making on the Frontier, 1607–1814* (New York: Cambridge University Press, 2008).

10. Gary B. Nash, *The Urban Crucible: The Northern Seaports and the Origins of the American Revolution* (Cambridge: Harvard University Press, 1986), xii.

11. E. P. Thompson, "Eighteenth-Century English Society: Class Struggle without Class?" *Social History* 3 (1978): 149. In addition to my reliance on the Marxian theoretical stance of scholars such as Thompson and Nash, I have also drawn much inspiration from other practitioners in this historiographical tradition such as Peter Linebaugh, Marcus Rediker, Alfred Young, and Woody Holton. See Peter Linebaugh and Marcus Rediker, *The Many-Headed Hydra: Sailors, Slaves, Commoners and the Hidden History of the Revolutionary Atlantic* (Boston: Beacon, 2000); Marcus Rediker, *The Slave Ship: A Human History* (New York: Penguin, 2008); Peter Linebaugh, *The London Hanged: Crime and Civil Society in the Eighteenth Century* (New York: Verso, 2006); Alfred F. Young, *The Shoemaker and the Tea Party: Memory and the American Revolution* (Boston: Beacon, 2000); Woody Holton, *Forced Founders: Indians, Debtors, Slaves and the Making of the American Revolution in Virginia* (Chapel Hill: University of North Carolina Press, 1999).

12. For example, Wilcomb Washburn's *The Governor and the Rebel,* while certainly not the first but one of the most lasting treatments of the events in question, characterizes both Indian hatred and resistance to taxation in Virginia as symptoms of a larger dispute over the location of authority in the colony. "The locus of significant power in Virginia was not in the governor, but in the individual Englishman, made a superman by his possession of firearms. Neither the Indian in front of him nor the government behind him had the power to curb his desires except in a limited fashion . . . The resulting confusion is what we know as 'Bacon's Rebellion'" (Washburn, *The Governor and the Rebel*, 21). While Indians play a larger part in the beginning stages of Edmund Morgan's assessment of Bacon's Rebellion than they do in many other studies before or since, in the end he concludes that Bacon's Rebellion offered an opportunity for "discontent with upper-class leadership" to be "vented in racial hatred" (Morgan, *American Slavery, American Freedom,* 257). Kathleen Brown also views the role of Indians as merely a manifestation of a long-standing conflict between white Virginians. She states: "Questions about who constituted legitimate political authority in the colony and about what it meant to be a male citizen came to a head during the 1670s as ordinary men faced mounting impediments to their performance of male social roles." Furthermore, "Skirmishes with Indians undermined the security of those who did have families and property, eroding the local and domestic foundations of patriarchal power . . . Chafing under these burdens, ordinary men became unwilling to defer to the gentlemen who were supposed to be their leaders and demanded redress

through armed resistance" (Brown, *Good Wives, Nasty Wenches, and Anxious Patriarchs: Gender, Race, and Power in Colonial Virginia* [Chapel Hill: University of North Carolina Press, 1996], 139). For Stephen Saunders Webb, while the repercussions of Indian warfare to the north of Virginia sparked the violence, the ultimate program of Bacon and his followers was nothing less than the establishment of a republican government along the lines of that established in America 100 years later (Webb, *1676: The End of American Independence* [New York: Alfred A. Knopf, 1984], 3–9). Much of Michael Leroy Oberg's overall argument is similar to my own, but key differences do exist. Oberg's bipolar classification system for English colonists that consists of the binary of "metropolitans" and frontier residents is often vague and tends to ignore the role of class as well as other forms of social difference in favor of a kind of geographic means of social categorization that obscures as much as it reveals. In addition, my study places more emphasis on the active role of Indians in this process, which I achieve through a heavier reliance on ethnohistorical methods. Finally, Oberg's work is a comparison of seventeenth-century relationships between English colonists in Virginia and New England and as such, in an effort to provide a common thread between them, often overlooks critical differences between the two regions. This study, by contrast, focuses solely on the Virginia experience (Oberg, *Dominion and Civility: English Imperialism and Native America, 1585–1685* [Ithaca, NY: Cornell University Press, 1999]). Both Warren Billings and his colleagues and Alexander Haskell place Bacon's Rebellion within the context of a failure of Virginia elites to assure small and middling planters that the Virginia government truly had their best interests at heart; therefore, the government's unresponsiveness to the Indian raids that sparked the rebellion again represents only a symptom of a larger issue (Warren Billings, Thad Tate, and John Selby, *Colonial Virginia: A History* [White Plains, NY: KTO, 1986]; Warren Billings, *Sir William Berkeley and the Forging of Colonial Virginia* [Baton Rouge: Louisiana State University Press, 2004]; Alexander B. Haskell, "'The Affections of the People': Ideology and the Politics of State Building in Colonial Virginia, 1607–1754" [PhD diss., Johns Hopkins University, Baltimore, MD, 2004]). The year 2010 brought three more treatments of Bacon's Rebellion that all subsume the role of Indian hatred within the context of other forces affecting white Virginia society. Lorena Walsh, while not discounting many of the motivations listed earlier, argued that "the economic hardships wrought by new imperial policies and by commercial disruptions caused by international warfare in the mid-1660s and again in the mid-1670s surely contributed to widespread popular discontent" (Walsh, *Motives of Honor, Pleasure and Profit: Plantation Management in the Colonial Chesapeake, 1607–1763* [Chapel Hill: University of North Carolina Press, 2010], 126–27). At roughly the same time, legal historian Christopher Tomlins at least partially returned the scholarship on Bacon's Rebellion back to Edmund Morgan's familiar conclusion by locating its roots in "the social instabilities inherent in importing thousands of young single males for years of hard labor while simultaneously frustrating the survivors' ambitions to acquire land by engrossing what was available, forcing the land-hungry to the most dangerous margins of settlement" (Tomlins, *Freedom Bound: Law, Labor, and Civic Identity in Colonizing English America, 1580–1865* [New York: Cambridge University Press, 2010], 269). Finally, Lauren Benton argues very similar to Oberg that Bacon's Rebellion is best understood within the context of "geographical distinctions between coastal regions and upriver country" (Benton, *A Search for Sovereignty: Law and Geography in European Empires, 1400–1900* [New York: Cambridge University Press, 2010], 96).

13. For a discussion of the importance of Powhatan land to the emergence of the Virginia planter elite, see Parent, *Foul Means*, 9–53.

14. Haskell, "Affections of the People," 179.

15. Morgan, *American Slavery, American Freedom*; Brown, *Good Wives, Nasty Wenches and Anxious Patriarchs*. See also Bernard Bailyn, "Politics and Social Structure in Virginia," in *Seventeenth-Century America: Essays in Colonial America*, ed. James Morton Smith (New York: Norton, 1959), 90–115. Bailyn sees three shifts in Virginia elite leadership over the course of the seventeenth century and argues that ultimately the third group of leaders (those who arrived in the 1660s) exerted the most influence on both the future of the colony and the outbreak of Bacon's Rebellion. I differ slightly with Bailyn in that I argue for more continuity among the elite leadership throughout the century, if not in membership, then in sentiment and practice.

16. Works that treat white Virginians as a complex and differentiated group while failing to do so for Virginia Indians include April Lee Hatfield, *Atlantic Virginia: Intercolonial Relations in the Seventeenth Century* (Philadelphia: University of Pennsylvania Press, 2003); Oberg, *Dominion and Civility*. To be fair, Hatfield's stated purpose is to demonstrate the extent to which Virginia existed as part of a larger Atlantic trading and political network, so therefore an in-depth examination of Anglo-Indian relationships is not central to her study.

17. Works that provide an in-depth portrait of Virginia Indians but present whites as one monolithic entity include Helen Rountree, *Pocahontas, Powhatan, Opechancanough: Three Indian Lives Changed by Jamestown* (Charlottesville: University of Virginia Press, 2005); Frederic W. Gleach, *Powhatan's World and Colonial Virginia: A Conflict of Cultures* (Lincoln: University of Nebraska Press, 1997); Margaret Holmes Williamson, *Powhatan Lords of Life and Death: Command and Consent in Seventeenth Century Virginia* (Lincoln: University of Nebraska Press, 2003).

18. These works include Wertenbaker, *Torchbearer of the Revolution*; Washburn, *The Governor and the Rebel*; Webb, *1676: The End of American Independence*.

19. Alfred Cave's *Lethal Encounters: Englishmen and Indians in Colonial Virginia* (Santa Barbara, CA: Praeger, 2011) is currently the most recent treatment of the Anglo-Indian encounter in seventeenth-century Virginia. However, Cave's work is solely focused on proving whether the actions of Englishmen in Virginia constituted genocide or ethnic cleansing. While I do not dispute Cave's basic argument that Virginians were certainly guilty of the

latter and oftentimes of the former, my purpose is to analyze the topic in terms that would have been understandable to seventeenth-century Virginians themselves.

20. Elliot West, *The Contested Plains: Indians, Goldseekers, and the Rush to Colorado* (Lawrence: University Press of Kansas, 1998), xxii–xxiii.

21. Ibid., xxii.

22. I rest this particular formulation of class and class consciousness in Virginia on the theoretical model of E. P. Thompson, as expressed in numerous of his major works but best stated in his seminal work *The Making of the English Working Class* (New York: Vintage Books, 1966), 9–10.

23. See Billings, Selby, and Tate, *Colonial Virginia*, 55. Christopher Tomlins disputes this on the basis that his calculations show fewer indentured servants in the colony than previous scholars claimed; however, the fact that the overall number of servants was lower need not negate the fact that owning the labor of others still represented the marker of social success in the colony. In addition, Anthony Parent recently argued rather effectively that Virginians transitioned to slavery much earlier than previously assumed. Even by the 1630s and 1640s, he found a preference for African slaves over indentured servants among Virginia planters. If this is the case, then the basic argument outlined by Billings, Selby, and Tate remains. See Tomlins, *Freedom Bound*; Parent, *Foul Means*.

24. Alexander Haskell has argued that Virginia elites were concerned "that the only way that they would ever succeed in creating the order and obedience that they considered necessary for transforming Virginia into a civilized 'commonwealth' was by winning and maintaining the 'affections of the people.'" While this might have been the case for many, it seems just as plausible that a deep concern for establishing authority could have derived from a desire to both win the people's allegiance and maximize one's own profit (Haskell, "Affections of the People," 8). For more on the general idea of what exactly the English hoped to establish in Virginia, see Andrew Fitzmaurice, *Humanism and America: An Intellectual History of English Colonization, 1500–1625* (New York: Cambridge University Press, 2003); Ethan A. Schmidt, "The Well-Ordered Commonwealth: Humanism, Utopian Perfectionism, and the English Colonization of the Americas," *Atlantic Studies* 7, no. 3 (September 2010): 309–28; Oberg, *Dominion and Civility*; Nicholas Canny, "The Ideology of English Colonization: From Ireland to America," *William and Mary Quarterly* 30, no. 4 (October 1973): 575–98.

25. Billings, Selby, and Tate, *Colonial Virginia*, 58–59.

26. Bacon, "Manifesto Concerning the Present Troubles in Virginia," 55–58; Washburn, *The Governor and the Rebel*, 43; "Commissioners' Narrative," in *Narratives of the Insurrections*, 112.

27. "The History of Bacon's and Ingram's Rebellion, 1676," in *Narratives of the Insurrections, 1675–1690*, 80.

Virginia Algonquians in 1607

MAP 1.1. Virginia Algonquians, 1607. Map by Ryan Morris.

1

Being All Friends and Forever Powhatans

The Early Anglo-Powhatan Relationship at Jamestown

In 1570 a group of Spanish Jesuits attempted to establish a mission among the Algonquian-speaking peoples of Tsenacommacah in the area now referred to as the Virginia coastal plain.[1] An Algonquian captured nearly ten years before by other Spanish invaders had guided them to the area. The man's Algonquian name is lost to us, but his captors renamed him Don Luis. Don Luis had spent most of the previous decade living as a servant in the households of many of the most important military and spiritual leaders of the Spanish Empire, in places such as Madrid, Havana, and Mexico City. When approached first by a group of Franciscans and then by the group of Jesuits to assist them in their endeavor to establish a mission among his people, he readily accepted.[2]

Eventually, the Jesuits decided to settle in the York River area to be near the increasingly powerful leader of the local Algonquian groups. At that time, Don Luis made the decision to leave the Jesuit camp and return to his people. Despite the Jesuits' assumption that during his years of captivity Don Luis had completely shed his Algonquian life for that of a lowly Spanish servant, he almost immediately reconnected with his family (who thought he had returned from the dead) and determined to live up to his kinship responsibilities to them by staying to help them weather the effects of a six-year drought that had plagued their homeland. The Jesuits responded by demanding that Don Luis return to them and use his connections to local Algonquians to procure food for the progressively famished mission. According to the account of a Spaniard named Alonso, a child witness to the

DOI: 10.5876/9781607323082.c001

events, Don Luis did return to the mission after a party of three Jesuits had been sent to retrieve him.[3]

> On the Sunday after the feast of the Purification, Don Luis came to the three Jesuits who were returning with other Indians. He sent an arrow through the heart of Father Quirós and then murdered the rest who had come to speak with him. Immediately Don Luis went on to the village where the Fathers were, and with great quiet and dissimulation, at the head of a large group of Indians, he killed the five who waited there. Don Luis himself was the first to draw blood with one of those hatchets that were brought along for trading with the Indians; then he finished the killing of Father Master Baptista with his axe, and his companions finished off the others.[4]

In 1571, Spain and its empire were in the midst of a period often referred to as the Siglo de Oro, or the Golden Century. During the past eighty years, the Spanish had completed the Reconquista, landed in the Caribbean, destroyed and subjugated the Aztec and Incan civilizations, and circumnavigated the globe. Yet they had failed to extend their conquests to Tsenacommacah. To be fair, beyond the opportunity to extend the Catholic religion to the Native people of the area, there was little in Virginia to entice any but the most devout Spaniards to attempt such an enterprise. In addition, in recapturing the boy Alonso from Don Luis's people in 1572, the Spanish reportedly killed at least 20 Algonquians in retribution for Don Luis's attack. However, the Spanish never again attempted to penetrate as far north as the territory of the Virginia Algonquians. Furthermore, the 20-odd Algonquians they did manage to kill represented but a fraction of the approximately 14,000 people already engaged in the process of coalescing into a vast paramount chiefdom under the control of a man known as Powhatan. Contrary to the archetypal story of European colonial expansion, in this case (and in others) Indians clearly held the upper hand in the relationship.[5] In the case of the Powhatans of Virginia, they did so for the first twenty to thirty years of the English colony that followed the Spanish mission.

At the turn of the seventeenth century, Virginia Algonquians found themselves in the midst of a vast reordering of their world that had little to do with the small groups of Europeans who sometimes appeared on the fringes of their territory. The process by which Powhatan transformed his initial inheritance of six villages into a great chiefdom that controlled the entire eastern half of what is now Virginia was well under way by the time Don Luis destroyed the Spanish Jesuit mission in 1571. Powhatan's, and his chiefdom's, power and stature only continued to grow after that incident, to the point that their command of both spiritual and temporal power reached heights never seen by their predecessors.[6] On the eve of the Jamestown landing in 1607, Powhatan and his chiefdom, while acutely aware of the threats

FIGURE 1.1. *The Killing of Father Segura and His Companions,* by Melchior Kusell. From Mathias Tanner, *A History of the Lives and Deaths of Those Jesuits Who Suffered Martyrdom for the Faith* (Prague: Typis Universitatis Carolo-Ferdinandeae, 1675); at http://reader.digitale -sammlungen.de/resolve/display/bsb10637121.html.

they faced both internally and externally, rested securely in the knowledge that they were the masters of the Virginia coastal plain and that their access to powerful spiritual forces had made them so. Thus, they approached European invaders, both temporary and permanent, with an attitude of superiority and an expectation that only those willing to accept Powhatan's leadership and prove themselves useful to his chiefdom would be suffered to remain.

There is general agreement that Indians have inhabited Virginia since the end of the last ice age nearly 10,000 years ago. Whether these early peoples represent direct ancestors of the people the English called Powhatans is harder to pinpoint.[7] However, the anthropological and archaeological literature agrees on at least two basic facts. The first is that the Algonquian cultural and linguistic characteristics shared by the Indians of the Virginia coastal plain in 1607 did not originate there but instead in the Great Lakes region. Second, the mass migration of Algonquian peoples and cultural traits into the area occurred either toward the end of the Middle Woodland period (100–200 CE) or during the beginning of the Late Woodland period (500–1000 CE).[8]

Whatever the case, we do know for certain that sometime during the mid- to late sixteenth century the man known as Powhatan came into his inheritance of six villages located near present-day Richmond. Throughout the rest of the century he added to his territory using a mixture of alliance, intimidation, and outright force. We know very little specific information about this process, especially regarding the groups he added to his domain during the early years of his leadership. However, two instances—the destruction of the Kecoughtans and the Chesapeakes—both of which occurred in the period just before the English landing at Jamestown, provide excellent examples of his methods.[9]

In the mid-1590s Powhatan assaulted the village of Kecoughtan, located at the extreme southeastern tip of the peninsula between the James and York Rivers. The Kecoughtans' refusal to willingly place themselves under his orbit seems to have sealed their fate. Powhatan seized the opportunity presented by the death of their *weroance*, the Powhatan term for a village or district chieftain, to make an example of them. In 1612 William Strachey included the event in his *History of Travel into Virginia Britannia*: "Upon the death of an old Weroance of this place some 15 or 16 years since (being too powerful neighbors to side [with] the great Powhatan) it is said Powhatan taking the advantage subtly stepped in, and conquered the people killing the Chief and most of them." To ensure the complete integration of the Kecoughtan survivors, Powhatan relocated them to villages intensely loyal to him.[10] By 1608, the strategy seems to have worked. When Powhatan destroyed another recalcitrant Algonquian group, this time the Piankatanks, he allowed the remnants of the Kecoughtans to resettle their lands.[11]

Just before the arrival of English colonists at Jamestown, Powhatan completely wiped out the Chesapeakes, who had occupied the territory south and east of the James River near what is now Virginia Beach. The Chesapeakes had never been a part of Powhatan's chiefdom and were traditionally regarded as enemies. Furthermore, this particular act also seems to have been religiously based. Strachey mentioned a prophecy told to Powhatan by his chief priests. According to the prophecy, "From the Chesapeake Bay a Nation should arise, which should dissolve and give end to his Empire." The Chesapeakes' long-standing refusal to succumb to his rule, coupled with the coincidence of their location and that mentioned by the prophecy, sealed their doom. Therefore, Powhatan "destroyed and put to the sword, all such who might lie under any doubtful construction of the said prophecy."[12] Through tactics such as these, as well as less violent methods of coercion and negotiation, Powhatan managed to bring all of the Algonquian groups of the coastal plain under his nominal control by 1607. In a period of approximately forty years, he had fashioned a powerful chiefdom out of a collection of loosely connected villages. The Algonquian leader the English encountered upon their arrival was a man at the height of his power. However, that power was threatened from within and without. Furthermore, it was rooted in a spiritual worldview the English had very little basis for understanding.

While the paramount chiefdom headed by Powhatan represented the largest group in the area, an examination of the group in relation to its neighbors reveals that the Powhatans were neither monolithic nor unchallenged. Specifically, internal conflict between Virginia Algonquians themselves combined with the external threats of Siouan and Iroquoian invaders to create a pre-contact Virginia characterized by warfare, uneasy truces, and shifting alliances. Even within his own domain, Powhatan did not exercise full control over the various sub-chiefdoms, and beyond the borders of Tsenacommacah lurked various Iroquoian and Siouan enemies who often encroached upon their territory. Aid in the form of guns, metal, and soldiers could easily tip the balance in favor of the *mamanatowick,* or Great Chief as Powhatan was known, in his struggle not only to preserve the unity of his organization but also to defend it against encroachment from outsiders. In light of this pre-contact reality, Powhatan's post-contact actions toward the English reflect a level of sophistication and diplomatic savvy the English failed to recognize.

The nature of military and foreign relations between the peoples of pre-contact America provides useful insights for unraveling Powhatan's motivations regarding the English. Early observers of Indian warfare in North America dismissed it as motivated only by a desire for flamboyant displays of bravado. According to one early Spanish observer, "Their enmity and hatred spring primarily from a desire for ostentation . . . and to gain experience in military science rather than from a desire to obtain the property and estate of another." Such shortsighted early accounts established a tradition in which scholars often viewed Native warfare as largely pointless, personal, and disconnected from the welfare of the larger group.[13]

With the advent of ethnohistory during the mid-twentieth century, scholars began to reexamine these assumptions about warfare in the late prehistoric period. While the desire for revenge, personal status, or military knowledge all remain valid reasons for individual warriors to join a war party, they fail to explain the strategic reasons why the leaders of the group would want to commence such a war party in the first place. For example, soldiers in the US armed forces often cite a desire to serve one's country, gain certain training, earn money for college, or see the world as their motivations for enlistment, but those reasons do not explain why they are sent to specific locations to conduct specific missions. Only the interests of the nation expressed (accurately or inaccurately) through the various levels of the US government can explain the reasons. Similarly, Native American groups in late pre-contact America went to war with one another for a variety of reasons, many of which corresponded with European reasons for warfare.[14]

Therefore, these multiple motivations for warfare—some personal, some societal, and even some derived from environmental stimuli—necessitated a very dynamic and fluid sociopolitical landscape.[15] New alliances, polities, conflicts, and enemies appeared and reappeared on a regular basis. Powhatan's paramount chiefdom constitutes a prime example of this phenomenon. As discussed previously, Powhatan did not inherit the paramount chiefdom but rather created it by enhancing his original inheritance of six districts split between the York and James Rivers. The chiefdom Powhatan led in 1607 represented a recent creation forged through the crucible of tensions and conflict that surrounded his initial inheritance.

Elements of the Powhatan cosmology and religion support this notion. In one creation account, the relationship between the primary deity (who appears as a "great hare") and the four gods representing the cardinal directions is one of animosity, jealousy, and conflict. The four deities attempt to eat the men and women created and protected by the great hare. After the hare repulses their initial attack and creates the "great deer," they return in a jealous rage and kill the deer. Finally, at the end of the story, the great hare releases the men and women from his immediate protection and scatters them in different countries, presumably those from whence came the various tribal groupings. Another Virginia Algonquian creation account tells a similar tale in which the great hare protected the first men and women from a great serpent that came into their country to destroy them, after which they were dispersed in the same manner as the people in the previous creation story. These creation accounts seem to parallel the creation of Powhatan's chiefdom itself, which had occurred not long before the arrival of the English.[16]

The *huskanaw,* the only Powhatan ritual about which we have credible information, reveals the contested and violent nature of pre-contact Virginia as well. Violence, abduction, pain, captivity, and wilderness represent repeated themes in the performance of the ritual. According to anthropologist Helen Rountree, "The Powhatan *huskanaw* was a product of chiefdom-level societies living in a state of war with their neighbors." Groups not immediately threatened by their neighbors or European invaders seem to have lacked rituals such as the huskanaw.[17]

Beyond the realm of religious symbolism, the political relations among Virginia Algonquians located in different geographies also support the idea of disunity in the immediate pre-contact period. The Indians of the Eastern Shore shared basic Algonquian characteristics with Powhatan's mainland chiefdom. However, their geographic isolation created significant political and cultural fissures between them and their mainland kinsmen. At the time of the Jamestown expedition, Eastern Shore Algonquians only nominally recognized Powhatan's authority.[18]

In addition, the Eastern Shore groups exhibited distinct cultural and political traits that distinguished them from the mainland Algonquians. None of the Eastern Shore groups practiced the huskanaw ritual. Their subsistence systems and political structures differed in many ways from those of the Powhatans. For example, no evidence exists to suggest that the priesthood operated the same on the Eastern Shore as it did on the western side of the Chesapeake. Furthermore, according to both Rountree and Thomas Davidson, some Eastern Shore groups used a political system in which the district weroances ruled together as equals, while others reproduced the Powhatan system in which district weroances remained subordinate to an overall paramount chief. Finally, only the paramount chief who governed the Accomack and Occohannock people swore allegiance to Powhatan.[19]

The various Algonquian groups living in the northern reaches of Virginia near the Potomac River also frequently resisted Powhatan's rule. Their relationship to Powhatan evokes comparisons to the Germanic and Gallic "barbarians" of the Roman Empire. Particularly after the English arrived, these groups' loyalty tended to decline. For example, in 1610 Henry Spelman, a young Englishman who lived among the Powhatans for a time, began to sense that the deteriorating relationship between his countrymen and the Powhatans had placed him in a dangerous position, and he feared for his life. It would seem that his intuition was correct, as Powhatan had decided to kill him. Ultimately, Spelman survived by exploiting one of the existing divisions within the paramount chiefdom. In an act of open defiance, the Patawomecks, one of the Potomac River groups, helped Spelman escape and sheltered him from Powhatan's wrath.[20] According to archaeologist Stephen Potter, "The Patawomecks were the largest and most powerful of the northern Virginia Algonquian chiefdoms and had been key players in the Native trade network before the English invasion." Potter estimates their population at around 1,000.[21] Their considerable distance from Powhatan's seat at Werowocomoco, their military strength, and the considerable wealth derived from their trading activities allowed them to follow Powhatan's directives only when it suited their interests. As English power in the region grew, the Patawomecks increasingly cast their lot with the new-comers and began to defy Powhatan more often.[22]

The Chickahominies provide another excellent example of the challenges to Powhatan's power and thus of the fragmented unity of his chiefdom. Powhatan governed his chiefdom using a three-tiered, feudal-like system of leadership. He, as mamanatowick, or Great King, represented the top level. Below him, regional vassals called weroances, sworn to loyally serve the mamanatowick, governed the individual satellite villages. Lesser weroances then governed the various towns within those regional chiefdoms. However, the Chickahominies, described by Strachey as a "warlike and free people," insisted on an equal relationship with Powhatan. While they paid "certain duties to Powhatan," they nonetheless insisted that they govern themselves. They did so through a council of elders as opposed to a weroance. The payments they made to Powhatan were not the normal tribute subject chiefdoms owed him but more a diplomatic exchange designed to buy his friendship. For his part, Powhatan could not order the Chickahominies to participate in any of his military campaigns. Instead, if he wanted to utilize Chickahominy warriors, he was forced to hire them and pay for their services with copper. Much like the Patawomecks, the military strength of the Chickahominies allowed them to dictate these terms to Powhatan. The Chickahominies, however, seem not to have embraced an alliance with the English like the Patawomecks did. After the arrival of the English, they maintained their independence but entered into an official alliance with Powhatan against the English and other mutual enemies.[23]

In addition to these variations and conflicts among Virginia's Algonquian-speaking peoples, the Iroquoian and Siouan speakers who represented the primary (non-English) threats to Algonquian domination also weighed heavily on Powhatan's mind. A Siouan-speaking Mannahoac, captured by John Smith on one of his exploratory expeditions in 1608, provided the Englishman with a glimpse of Virginia's pre-contact realities. According to Smith's account, the Englishman asked the captive "how many worlds he did know, he replied, he knew no more but that which was under the sky that covered him, which were the Powhatans, with the Monacans, and the Massawomecks, that were higher up in the mountains." Rather than a landscape dominated by an all-powerful Algonquian polity (the Powhatans), the Mannahoac captive provided the English, had they been willing to listen, with a clear explanation of the triagonal struggle they had landed within. The Iroquoian groups, represented by the Massawomecks in this case, and the Siouans (Monacans

Early Seventeenth Century Virginia Indian Foreign Relations

MAP 1.2. Early-seventeenth-century Virginia Indian foreign relations. Map by Ryan Morris.

and Mannahoacs) interacted and conflicted with one another and the Algonquians to form the basis of Virginia's Indian world.[24]

The Meherrin and Nottoway peoples who occupied what is today extreme southern Virginia and northern North Carolina constituted the closest Iroquoian groups to Powhatan's paramount chiefdom. The little evidence that exists suggests that relations between these groups and Powhatan were largely peaceful. However, the reason behind the peace is extremely suggestive of the precarious nature of relations among Virginia Native groups on the eve of English colonization. The Meherrins and Nottoways lived south of the James River in the interior of the coastal plain. This location placed them within 100 miles of the heart of Powhatan's territory, yet he never attempted to annex them to his chiefdom. Recent anthropological scholarship cites the Meherrins' and Nottoways' close relationship with and proximity to the Tuscaroras of North Carolina as the major factor preventing Powhatan from challenging them. In the early eighteenth century, the trader John Lawson cataloged the fighting strength of the Tuscaroras at 1,200, a number much lower than it would have been 100 years earlier. Therefore, the uneasy peace that existed in the early seventeenth century between the Powhatans and their Meherrin and Nottoway neighbors stemmed more from the fear generated by the combined strength of the Tuscarora, Meherrin, and Nottoway peoples than from any real harmony.[25]

Peace, uneasy or otherwise, did not exist between the Powhatans and the Iroquoian Massawomecks who attacked the chiefdom by way of the Potomac River from the north. According to John Smith, the Massawomecks greatly frightened the Powhatans. Not long after he arrived in Virginia, they attacked Smith himself on one of his exploratory voyages to the Potomac River area. Both Smith and Spelman noted that Massawomeck attacks had been particularly devastating to both the Kecoughtans and the Patawomecks. Early accounts (told to the English from the Algonquian point of view) largely characterized the relationship between the Powhatans and the Massawomecks as one in which the Iroquoians mounted unprovoked and unanswered attacks on the peaceful Algonquians. However, Rountree is inclined to believe otherwise. She observes, "Given the warlike and vengeful character of the Powhatans, it is likely that they returned the Massawomecks' raids with interest." After all, Strachey cited revenge as the principal reason for Algonquian warfare in early-seventeenth-century Virginia: "So vindictive and jealous they be, to be made a derision of, and to be insulted upon by an enemy." Therefore, Rountree's conclusion that the Powhatans must have engaged in similar attacks on the Massawomecks seems likely. Furthermore, if this was indeed the case, then the pressure exerted on his chiefdom by the Massawomecks could not have been far from Powhatan's mind in 1607 when he learned of the arrival of the English.[26]

While the Iroquoians to his north and south caused Powhatan sporadic difficulties, the Siouan groups to the west of his chiefdom presented a serious and constant threat. The Mannahoacs of the upper Rappahannock Valley, along with the Monacans of the upper James River, raided Powhatan's domain annually. The animosity between the Powhatans and their western Siouan neighbors must have weighed heavily in the Powhatans' councils. Strachey mentioned the conflict more than once: "Powhatan had many enemies, especially in the westerly countries . . . and those Monacans have been deadly enemies ever unto Powhatan." Later he wrote, "There was every Enmity, and open wars between the High-and Low Country, going by the names of *Monacans,* and *Powhatans.*"[27]

Furthermore, anthropological evidence suggests that the Monacans may have been larger and even more centralized than the Powhatan chiefdom. In other words, the most powerful and monolithic society in the pre-contact world may not have been the Powhatan chiefdom but instead the Monacans. However, since the English did not penetrate the western reaches of Virginia until much later in the century and the Monacans adopted a strategy of avoidance concerning European invaders, the historical accounts from the immediate contact period cite the Powhatans as the region's power.[28]

One study has found that the Monacans numbered as many as 15,000 at the time of English colonization. Throughout the Piedmont region, anthropologists have discovered a striking unity among the burial mounds that, in the words of anthropologist Martin Gallivan, indicates "physical evidence of a shared Monacan ideology." In the Blue Ridge and Shenandoah Valley regions (the other area of Monacan existence), similar studies have discovered evidence of specialized agriculture, trade, social stratification, and palisaded villages. The Monacans also lived in close proximity to various deposits of copper that were in much demand during the pre- and post-contact eras. The evidence suggests that when not at war, they traded the commodity with the Powhatans. These findings indicate a complex society of wealth, mobility, and military power. Once again, according to Gallivan, "These are precisely the archaeological attributes associated with a centralized political economy and social inequality that archaeologists have had difficulty identifying in the Coastal Plain and in the Piedmont." Whether the English fully recognized it, the Siouan-speaking Monacans represented a substantial threat to both the lives of Powhatan's people and to his hold on the leadership of the chiefdom. In light of both the external and internal conflicts outlined here, the idea that Powhatan needed to constantly cultivate new allies and reinforce his authority over his people makes tremendous sense. However, the geopolitics of maintaining the chiefdom's territorial control represents only part of the explanation for his actions.[29]

By the time the English arrived in 1607, Powhatan had managed to maintain his hold on the region for at least twenty years, if not longer. In doing so, he initiated a tradition among Virginia Algonquians of leadership that combined diplomatic, spiritual, military, and economic power with traditional Algonquian practices of consent, custom, and kinship. Neither a complete dictatorship nor a democracy, Powhatan used whatever means he found most effective to keep his chiefdom together. At times, that meant violence; at other times, it meant negotiation.

Powhatan sought to tie the fate and fortunes of his potentially rebellious male subjects to his own by emphasizing the need to protect the chiefdom from outsiders such as the Monacans and to feed the population. By inculcating in them a common belief in the need for military victory and success at hunting, both of which could only be achieved on a large enough scale through communal efforts, he sought to retain their loyalty. However, as important as Powhatan's military and political power was in keeping the various elements of the chiefdom loyal, it represents only part of the picture. To attribute Powhatan's status as paramount chief solely to his political and military prowess makes sense to the western mind, but additional perspective is needed to understand the Powhatans on their own terms.[30]

The political skill and military prowess that propelled Powhatan into the position of mamanatowick stemmed from spiritual rather than secular sources. Similar to most Native societies, coastal Algonquians such as the Powhatans recognized no line between the spiritual and physical worlds. In fact, they predicated their beliefs on the opposite premise: that every individual possessed a particular connection to the supernatural world. That connection, and therefore that individual's spiritual well-being, was a direct result of his or her particular relationship with spirits. Thus, all members of the group located their particular actions in the physical world within their own understanding of the requirements of the personal spiritual message they received, as opposed to a universal standard of religious or moral requirements. Given this intimate connection between the spiritual and the material, success in the physical world flowed directly from an individual's spiritual status. In the words of anthropologist Frederic Gleach, "Power—the ability to act rightly—was derived from the individual's connections with the various spirits."[31]

Once again, the huskanaw ritual provides significant insight into the Virginia Algonquians' world. The ritual was designed to demarcate those in society who possessed the requisite political *and* spiritual power to serve the group as priests, warriors, and leaders. It was his ability to command large amounts of spiritual and political power that made Powhatan the leader he had become. According to Gleach, Powhatan's "conquest of neighboring groups was due to the application of both military strength and moral rightness; indeed, his ability to command such military strength rested largely on his personal ties to spiritual power obtained through dreams."[32]

Within this worldview, Powhatan's rise to leadership and his success in creating the paramount chiefdom marked him as a man of considerable spiritual power, so much so that he, as well as the lesser weroances who governed the outlying districts and the chief priests, were accorded the status of *quioccosuks,* or gods on Earth. While cognizant of a godlike quality to Powhatan's bearing, the English were generally unaware of the spiritual underpinnings of his power. They therefore ascribed his authority to a kind of absolutism similar to that of their own kingships. William Strachey's writings after he encountered Powhatan demonstrate this misconception: "It is strange to see with what great fear and adoration all these people do obey this Powhatan, for at his feet they present whatsoever he commands, and at the least frown of his brow, [they inflict] the greatest punishing [upon] such as offend him." The failure to understand Powhatan cultural foundations such as this explains much of the resulting conflicts that ensued between the two groups.[33]

Since alliances represented one of the primary tools Powhatan used to maintain his chiefdom and given the considerable ethnographic literature on Algonquian spirituality discussed previously, Powhatan's strategy had to have taken on a meaning far beyond the geopolitical connotations it assumes in western cultures. In other words, Powhatan would have credited his decision to shore up his authority and territory through the use of strategic alliances not to the strategy's particular practical utility but to its adherence to the specific spiritual instructions he received through his own interactions with the supernatural world. The arrival of the Virginia colony offered Powhatan another divinely ordained opportunity, if he desired to take it, to add another ally and client to his chiefdom.

Early one morning in mid-May 1607, Captain Christopher Newport brought his flagship, the *Susan Constant,* to rest alongside the shore of the river local Algonquians referred to as the Pamunkey. He and the other leaders of the Virginia Council promptly decided to call the river the James after their sovereign back in England. A total of 104 English colonists, all of them male, disembarked and set about "erecting a great city." The men who had backed the expedition financially and who occupied most of its leadership posts expected to create what Edmund Morgan has termed "a biracial society that would remedy England's deficiencies." While the leaders of the colony may have disagreed about the particulars of how to do that, one aspect on which they concurred was the need to establish a commonwealth grounded in the proper amount of order and authority. In such a hierarchical commonwealth, all levels of society would know their proper place; if they respected that position and performed the functions associated with it, overall peace, stability, and relative prosperity would be assured.[34]

What ensued was a great disaster, the intimate details of which have been recounted by many distant and modern writers. Therefore, a minute-by-minute account of the early days of the Jamestown colony is not necessary for the purposes of this study. However, the difficulties Virginia's leaders encountered when trying to impose their vision of an orderly and stable commonwealth on both their fellow Englishmen and the Powhatans spawned both physical and intellectual conflicts that are critical for understanding Bacon's Rebellion. A few incidents from those early years of the colony provide a window through which to observe the beginning of the struggles that would wrack the colony to the dawn of the eighteenth century. The first event occurred four days after the colonists arrived, and it powerfully illustrates that the English colonists and the Powhatans understood very little about one another, yet each group assumed that its particular view of the relationship would dominate. Not long after they landed, the weroance of the Paspaheghs paid the colony an official visit. In an event strikingly similar to one that occurred in 1585 between Roanoke colonists and Algonquians at the village of Secotan, a Paspahegh Indian representative who accompanied the weroance decided that a metal hatchet constituted suitable payment for the Algonquians' promise to grant the English "as much land as we would desire to take." However, the English saw the act as simple thievery, as opposed to the necessary gift giving required of Algonquian alliances. Bloodshed seemed imminent, though in the end "the Weroance of the Paspahegh saw us take to our arms, [and] went suddenly away with all his company in great anger."[35]

Less than ten days after the incident, the Paspaheghs responded by unsuccessfully attacking the settlement. This rather hostile beginning to English-Native relations at Jamestown reveals more than an ignorance of each other's customs. It also reflects both sides' continuing desire to attempt to achieve cooperation and cordial relations with one another, but only on one-sided terms. The leaders of Jamestown expected the Native people of the Virginia mainland to assume their subordinate link in the "great chain of authority." Similar to their encounters with the Spanish Jesuits and the English at Roanoke in the late sixteenth century, Virginia's Algonquian peoples saw the English refusal to adopt Native rituals and rules for exchange as a hostile act. For both the English and the Indians of the Virginia coastal plain, these mutual violations of the other's expectations justified a violent response.[36]

The role of gender in Algonquian exchange relationships further complicates this picture. For example, the Powhatans sealed relationships such as trading agreements and alliances by creating a kinship tie between the two individuals or groups involved. They were matrilineal, so they could only form that kinship tie through a connection to a female member of the group; these spiritually imbued alliances thus also indicate much about the role of gender in Powhatan society. Specifically, the most famous instance of the female role in Powhatan alliances provides a model through which we can see both Powhatan's attempt to bring the English under his power through the strategy of alliance and the importance of women in helping him execute that strategy during this period.

In 1612 Captain John Smith penned *The General History of Virginia, New England and the Somer Isles*. This was not the first of Smith's published accounts of his travels across the Atlantic, but it has had the most lasting impact on succeeding generations of English, American, and Indian readers. In the third book of his *General*

History, Smith included more details of what transpired during his December 1607 captivity among the Powhatan Indians than he had in his previous published accounts. Captured by Powhatan's brother Opechancanough, the weroance of the Pamunkeys, Smith expected to be put to death at any moment. To his astonishment, Opechancanough and the Pamunkeys did not kill him. Instead, Opechancanough paraded Smith among the various villages of the chiefdom, all the while questioning the Englishman regarding the "nature of our ships, and sailing the seas, the earth and skies and of our God." In turn, Opechancanough divulged to Smith his knowledge of the geography and peoples of the rest of Virginia. On more than one occasion during the journey, Opechancanough's men even protected Smith from death at the hands of other Algonquians. In one instance, the father of one of the men Smith had killed during his capture attempted to break into the lodge where the Pamunkeys were quartering Smith and kill him. In another incident at a village along the Rappahannock River, Opechancanough again saved Smith. This time, the villagers sought to kill Smith because they were convinced he was the same English captain who had killed their weroance during an English reconnaissance voyage earlier in the decade. While Smith's life was in danger many times during his captivity, in each instance the Pamunkeys and their leader intervened to spare him until he reached Werowocomoco and his audience with Powhatan.[37]

According to Smith's 1608 and 1612 accounts, Powhatan received him with all the trappings and fanfare reserved for the paramount chief. After expressing much satisfaction with the knowledge of the English Smith had imparted to Opechancanough, Powhatan began to press Smith on why he and the Englishmen had come to his domain. Smith did his best (even resorting to outright falsehoods) to satisfy Powhatan's concerns without revealing that he and his fellow Englishmen planned to stay for a considerable amount of time. During the interview, Powhatan spoke at length of the Monacans and other enemies of his people who lived beyond the fall line in the western reaches of Virginia. Then, according to Smith's earliest account of his captivity, he and Powhatan entered into an agreement that, unbeknownst to Smith, could only be sealed ceremonially. After Smith and Powhatan had related to one another the particulars of their respective "kingdoms," Powhatan beseeched Smith to "live with him upon his River . . . he promised to give me Corn, Venison, or what I wanted to feed us, hatchets and copper we should make him, and none should disturb us. This request I promised to perform."[38]

Curiously, Smith chose not to include the most famous incident, his "rescue" from execution by Pocahontas, in his *True Relation of Such Occurrences and Accidents of Note as Hath Happened in Virginia,* from which the previous information comes. In fact, Smith did not include the events that have become, in many cases, the sum total of the general public's knowledge of seventeenth-century Virginia Indians

FIGURE 1.2. Powhatan. Detail from John Smith's *Map of Virginia*, Library of Congress, Geography and Map Division, Washington, DC.

prior to 1624. He did not include the story in either of the two earlier works he published on Virginia. According to historian Camilla Townsend, Smith "only told the story seventeen years later, in 1624, in the wake of an Indian rebellion, at which point Powhatan's kindred were viewed as the devil incarnate, and Pocahontas was suddenly being interpreted as exceptional among all her people."[39] In that version, after much feasting, speechmaking, and dancing, "two great stones were brought before Powhatan." The account claims that the mamanatowick then ordered the gathered multitude to grab Smith, drag him to the stones, and place his head on one of them. Smith wrote, "Being ready with their clubs to beat out his brains, Pocahontas the King's dearest daughter, when no entreaty could prevail, got his head in her arms, and laid her own upon his to save him from death." Smith went on to claim that upon witnessing Pocahontas's actions, Powhatan immediately commuted the sentence and began to treat Smith as a son.[40]

Smith's rescue by the "Indian Princess" Pocahontas (who had become a celebrity in London by the time he wrote the account) sold books and has continued to inspire feature films, but is any of it true? Despite its hold on the American imagination, the story cannot be true, at least not the sequence of events Smith described. His inclusion of the event only after the deaths of the other principal actors constitutes only the tip of the historical proof of its inaccuracy. The fact that Smith included a scene in which he was saved by a beautiful woman in many of his travel narratives, ranging from his time in Turkey to his travels in France and other parts of the European continent, also casts doubt on the Pocahontas story's validity. In including the "rescue," Smith may have simply been adhering to the literary conventions of the day. After all, Smith wrote the accounts to make money, not to provide an accurate historical record. Furthermore, Pocahontas was at most ten to twelve years old at the time of the incident in question. She was far from the buxom young maiden often depicted by Smith and later on canvas and screen.[41]

In addition, the knowledge of Algonquian cultural traditions brought to light since the mid-1980s through the use of ethnohistorical methodology likewise casts serious doubt on the validity of Smith's claims regarding the incident. The use of clubs as the method of execution does not adhere to Algonquian practice for war captives. While Algonquians used clubs as tools of execution for criminals, Smith, as a prisoner of war, would have been ritually tortured to death. Ironically, Smith himself provided the ethnographic evidence of this fact in one of his earlier works.[42]

The sequence of events described by Smith also calls his account into question. According to Townsend, "He claimed there was religious divining on the part of priests, followed by feasting, negotiating amongst the political leaders, and finally the attempted execution. Culturally speaking, this makes no sense: Algonquians might have undertaken any activity on the list but, according to all the evidence that we have, definitely not in that order."[43] Other scholars have questioned the notion that Pocahontas even encountered Smith during his captivity.[44]

By far the largest group of scholars agrees that it is highly likely that if Powhatan had wanted Smith to die, he would not have attempted to kill him in the manner

Smith described. Given the available evidence, it seems most likely that the events of his rescue by Pocahontas (or probably another female member of Powhatan's household) may actually have occurred but that they were part of an Algonquian adoption ritual. According to the available ethnographic information on the Powhatan and other similar Algonquian groups, the ritual sought to admit Smith and the English to the Powhatan physical world and to create a kin relationship between the two men. In the Algonquian worldview, such a relationship would not only assure peaceful relations between the two groups but would also commit the English, and their very powerful weapons, to join Powhatan in his wars against the many enemies that surrounded his chiefdom. In short, they would join his paramount chiefdom as a subordinate polity in the same fashion as the other villages he governed.[45]

Whether an actual ritual occurred or whether Pocahontas participated in that ritual is in many ways irrelevant to understanding the future of English-Indian relations in early Virginia. However, the apparent agreement made between Powhatan and John Smith in which Smith agreed to provide hatchets and copper in return for food constitutes the real key to understanding many of the events that followed, and the fact that a female was needed as a conduit between Powhatan and Smith is also of the utmost importance.[46] The sources also indicate that both Smith and Powhatan later referred to an agreement existing between them. At subsequent meetings between the two, Powhatan chastised Smith for failing to live up to his kinship relation to the paramount chief. Furthermore, years later in England, Pocahontas admonished Smith in the same fashion but also revealed her father's still abiding faith that Smith, as a kinsman, would reveal the truth to her and her traveling companion Uttamatomakkin, Powhatan's chosen emissaries:[47] "You did promise Powhatan what was yours should be his, and he the like to you . . . They did tell us always you were dead, and I knew no other till I came to Plymouth; yet Powhatan did command Uttamatomakkin[48] to seek you, and know the truth, because your countrymen will lie much."[49]

In light of the preponderance of evidence, John Smith seems most likely to have entered into a kinship relationship with Powhatan. Furthermore, to do so, Smith would either have had to marry an Algonquian woman (an event for which there is absolutely no evidence) or obtain the sponsorship of a Powhatan female through which he could obtain membership in the group and also a kin relationship to Powhatan. Pocahontas seems a likely candidate to have provided him with that entrée, but so were any number of Powhatan's other female kin. The identity of the female through which Powhatan hoped to establish the kin relationship is decidedly less important than the fact that such a relationship seems to have been established, regardless of whether Smith understood it.[50]

King Powhatan comands C. Smith to be slayne, his
daughter Pokahontas beggs his life, his thankfulnes
and how hee subiected 39 of their kings, reade y history.
printed by Iames Reeve

FIGURE 1.3. Pocahontas's rescue of John Smith. Detail from Smith's *Generall Historie of Virginia*, © Trustees of the British Museum.

When Smith returned to Jamestown in January 1608, Powhatan must have felt he was at the apex of his power. During the previous ten years, he had wiped out the Kecoughtans and the Chesapeakes, two of the biggest internal threats to his power, and established a diplomatic and trading relationship with the English. While the colonists were actually quite weak in terms of numbers (and getting weaker every day as a result of disease and starvation), their possession of firearms, metal, and other supplies could assure Powhatan and his people that their domination of the coastal plain would continue unabated for generations. For a people who tied all success in the physical world to the favor of beings from the spiritual world, the agreement with Smith must have represented a divine acknowledgment that a golden age was before them. John Smith and his English companions, however, would soon demonstrate a very different understanding of the Anglo-Powhatan relationship.

NOTES

1. Powhatan used the phrase "being all friends and forever Powhatans" to describe the relationship of the English and the Powhatans as one in which the English had subjected themselves to Powhatan overlordship. See Philip Barbour, ed., *The Complete Works of Captain John Smith* (Chapel Hill: University of North Carolina Press, 1986), 2:195.

2. Clifford M. Lewis and Albert J. Loomie, eds., "Letter of Luis de Quirós and Juan Baptista de Segura to Juan de Hinistrosa, September 12, 1570," in *The Spanish Jesuit Mission to Virginia, 1570–1572* (Chapel Hill: University of North Carolina Press, 1953), 89–92. See also Helen Rountree and E. Randolph Turner III, *Before and after Jamestown: Virginia's Powhatans and Their Predecessors* (Gainesville: University Press of Florida, 2002), 51–53; Martin D. Gallivan, *James River Chiefdoms: The Rise of Social Inequality in the Chesapeake* (Lincoln: University of Nebraska Press, 2003), 160–61.

3. "Letter of Luis de Quirós and Juan Baptista de Segura to Juan de Hinistrosa, September 12, 1570," in *The Spanish Jesuit Mission to Virginia*, 89–92; Rountree and Turner, *Before and after Jamestown*, 51–53; Gallivan, *James River Chiefdoms*, 160–61; "Letter of Juan Rogel to Francis Borgia, 1572," in *The Spanish Jesuit Mission to Virginia*, 107–12.

4. "Letter of Juan Rogel to Francis Borgia, 1572," in *The Spanish Jesuit Mission to Virginia*, 107–12. Seth Mallios recently argued quite convincingly that this conflict had its roots in the Jesuits' inability to understand the rules of Algonquian exchange rituals, which thus led them to respond to Algonquian trade and exchange in ways deemed punishable offenses by Don Luis's people. See Seth Mallios, *The Deadly Politics of Giving: Exchange and Violence at Ajacan, Roanoke, and Jamestown* (Tuscaloosa: University of Alabama Press, 2006).

5. For other examples of European-Indian contact in which Indians remained the more powerful of the two actors, see Juliana Barr, *Peace Came in the Form of a Woman: Indians and Spaniards in the Texas Borderlands* (Chapel Hill: University of North Carolina Press, 2007); Richard White, *The Middle Ground: Indians, Empires, and Republics in the Great Lakes Region, 1650–1815* (New York: Cambridge University Press, 1991); Pekka Hämäläinen, *The Comanche Empire* (New Haven, CT: Yale University Press, 2009).

6. Helen Rountree, *Pocahontas's People: The Powhatan Indians of Virginia through Four Centuries* (Norman: University of Oklahoma Press, 1990), 25–28; Frederic W. Gleach, *Powhatan's World and Colonial Virginia: A Conflict of Cultures* (Lincoln: University of Nebraska Press, 1997), 22–25.

7. Archaeologist Helen Rountree argues that the Powhatans were in fact the product of the melding of the original inhabitants of the area and Algonquians who later moved to the area during the first millennium CE: "As far as the excavations tell us, the Powhatan were the *in situ* result of at least fifteen hundred years of Woodland Indian adaptation to life in the Chesapeake Bay region" (Rountree, *Pocahontas's People*, 15). Others such as Stephen R. Potter, Frederic W. Gleach, and Martin Gallivan place the beginning of a discernible Algonquian presence in Virginia only as far back as AD 200. See Stephen R. Potter, *Commoners, Tribute, and Chiefs: The Development of Algonquian Culture in the Potomac Valley* (Charlottesville: University of Virginia Press, 1993); Gleach, *Powhatan's World and Colonial Virginia*; Gallivan, *James River Chiefdoms*.

8. Potter, *Commoners, Tribute, and Chiefs*, 3–4; Gleach, *Powhatan's World and Colonial Virginia*, 24–25.

9. Rountree, *Pocahontas's People*, 25–28; Gleach, *Powhatan's World and Colonial Virginia*, 22–25.

10. William Strachey, *The Historie of Travel into Virginia Britannia* (London: Hakluyt Society, 1953), 68; Helen Rountree, *The Powhatan Indians of Virginia: Their Traditional Culture* (Norman: University of Oklahoma Press, 1989), 118–19.

11. Rountree, *Powhatan Indians of Virginia*, 119; Strachey, *Historie of Travel into Virginia Britannia*, 44.

12. Rountree, *Powhatan Indians of Virginia*, 120–21, 140; Strachey, *Historie of Travel into Virginia Britannia*, 104–5 (quotation).

13. Garcilaso de la Vega, *Florida of the Inca*, ed. and trans. John Varner and Jeannette Varner (Austin: University of Texas Press, 1951), 487–89 (quotation); Jon L. Gibson, "Aboriginal Warfare in the Protohistoric Southeast: An Alternative Perspective," *American Antiquity* 39 (January 1974): 130–33. As late as the mid-twentieth century, Alfred Kroeber wrote of Indian warfare in pre-contact America in a manner strikingly similar to sixteenth-century Spaniards: "They waged war not for any ulterior or permanent fruits, but for victory; and its conduct and shaping were motivated, when not by revenge, by individual desire for personal status within one's society" (Kroeber, *Cultural and Natural Areas of Native North America* [Berkeley: University of California Press, 1953], 148). See also Lewis H. Larson, "Functional Consideration of Warfare in the Southeast during the Mississippi Period," *American Antiquity* 37 (July 1972): 383–92.

14. For more information regarding the function and patterns of pre-contact warfare among Native societies, as well as examples of wars of expansion, see Mark Q. Sutton, "Warfare and Expansion: An Ethnohistoric Perspective on the Numic Spread," *Journal of California and Great Basin Anthropology* 8, no. 1 (1986): 65–82; Douglas Bamforth, "Indigenous People, Indigenous Violence: Precontact Warfare on the North American Great Plains," *Man*, New Series 29, no. 1 (March 1994): 95–115; Hämäläinen, *Comanche Empire*; Daniel Richter, *The Ordeal of the Longhouse: The People of the Iroquois League in the Era of*

European Colonization (Chapel Hill: University of North Carolina Press, 1992); D. Bruce Dickson, "The Yanomamö of the Mississippi Valley? Some Reflections on Larson (1972), Gibson (1974) and Mississippian Warfare in the Southeastern United States," *American Antiquity* 46 (October 1981): 909–16. According to anthropologist Lewis Larson, groups in the Southeast during the late Mississippian period went to war over arable land and to ease the pressure of population growth. The authors of a 1991 study of a late prehistoric Oneota burial location in Illinois argue that warfare between Native groups in the area sprang from competition over precious natural resources and traditional hunting grounds. Others point to the desire to defend or establish trade networks as a motivation for inter-group warfare in the pre-contact era; see Larson, "Functional Considerations of Warfare," 383–92; George Milner, Eve Anderson, and Virginia G. Smith, "Warfare in Late Prehistoric West-Central Illinois," *American Antiquity* 56 (October 1991): 581–603. Seth Mallios recently argued that the inability to properly adhere to trade protocols and rituals also constituted a common rationale for warfare before and after contact (Mallios, *Deadly Politics of Giving*).

15. James Rice's work, which links environmental change in the Potomac River during and after contact, demonstrates that the advent of the Little Ice Age at the beginning of the fourteenth century placed such a strain on the resources of the Potomac watershed that groups to the south of the immediate vicinity of the Potomac River in the Virginia coastal plane began to coalesce into chiefdoms. This extended cooling period also caused the Iroquoian groups to the north of the Potomac to coalesce and engage in extended raids on the peoples of the coastal plain. This, in turn, led the small chiefdoms of the coastal plain to coalesce even further into the paramount chiefdoms of the Piscataway tayac in what is today Maryland and the Powhatan chiefdom in Virginia. See James D. Rice, *Nature and History in the Potomac Country: From Hunter-Gatherers to the Age of Jefferson* (Baltimore: Johns Hopkins University Press, 2009).

16. Samuel Purchas, *Purchas His Pilgrims* (New York: Macmillan, 1905), 954, Early English Books Online (STC (2nd ed.) / 20507); Rountree, *Powhatan Indians of Virginia*, 140.

17. Purchas, *Purchas His Pilgrims*, 952; Gleach, *Powhatan's World and Colonial Virginia*, 38–40. Rountree provides the most detailed explanation of the huskanaw ceremony itself in *Powhatan Indians of Virginia*, 80–84.

18. Barbour, *Complete Works of Captain John Smith*, 1:150; Rountree and Davidson, *Eastern Shore Indians*, 32.

19. Rountree, *Powhatan Indians of Virginia*, 141; Rountree and Davidson, *Eastern Shore Indians*, 30–43.

20. Henry Spelman, "Relation of Virginea," in *The Travels and Works of Captain John Smith,* ed. Edward Arber and A. G. Bradley (Edinburgh: John Grant, 1910), ci–cxiv.

21. Stephen R. Potter, "Early English Effects on Virginia Algonquian Exchange and Tribute in the Tidewater Potomac," in *Powhatan's Mantle: Indians in the Colonial Southeast,*

ed. Gregory Waselkov, Peter H. Wood, and Tom Hatley (Lincoln: University of Nebraska Press, 2006), 222.

22. Rountree is the primary scholar to have characterized the Potomac River Algonquians in this fashion. She writes, "The chiefdoms of the southern shore of the Potomac and of the Eastern Shore were, according to Powhatan's accounts and occasionally to their own, officially part of the empire, but in fact they were a 'fringe' on the new ethnic group that the paramount chief was trying to create" (Rountree, *Powhatan Indians of Virginia,* 4, 147–48).

23. Strachey, *Historie of Travel into Virginia Britannia,* 68–69; Rountree, *Powhatan Indians of Virginia,* 8, 122; Rountree, *Pocahontas's People,* 10.

24. Barbour, *Complete Works of Captain John Smith,* 2: 175–76; Gallivan, *James River Chiefdoms,* 11.

25. Barbour, *Complete Works of Captain John Smith,* 2: 175–76; Gallivan, *James River Chiefdoms,* 11; Helen Rountree, "Summary and Implications," in *Powhatan Foreign Relations, 1600–1722,* ed. Helen Rountree (Charlottesville: University Press of Virginia, 1993), 215; Rountree, *Pocahontas's People,* 4; Rountree, *Powhatan Indians of Virginia,* 120; John Lawson, *A New Voyage to Carolina,* ed. Hugh T. Lefler (Chapel Hill: University of North Carolina Press, 1967), 242–43; Wood, "Changing Population of the Colonial South," 44. For other examples of Powhatan warfare against non-Algonquian peoples beyond the borders of Tsenacommacah, see Alan Vance Briceland, *Westward from Virginia: The Exploration of the Virginia-Carolina Frontier, 1650–1710* (Charlottesville: University Press of Virginia, 1987); Edward Bland, Abraham Woode, Sackford Brewster, and Elias Pennant, "The Discovery of New Brittaine," in *The First Explorations of the Trans-Allegheny Region by the Virginians, 1650–1674,* ed. Clarence Alvord and Lee Bidgood (Cleveland: Arthur H. Clark, 1912). See also Nancy Shoemaker, *A Strange Likeness: Becoming Red and White in Eighteenth-Century North America* (New York: Oxford University Press, 2004), 13.

26. Rountree, *Pocahontas's People,* 25; Rountree, "The Powhatans and Other Woodland Indians as Travelers," in *Powhatan Foreign Relations,* 22 (quotation); Barbour, *Complete Works of Captain John Smith,* 1:160, 165; Strachey, *Historie of Travel into Virginia Britannia,* 104. For other examples of Powhatan warfare against non-Algonquian peoples beyond the borders of Tsenacommacah, see Briceland, *Westward from Virginia;* Bland et al., "Discovery of New Brittaine"; Shoemaker, *Strange Likeness,* 13.

27. Strachey, *Historie of Travel into Virginia Britannia,* 35, 106–7.

28. One study has gone so far as to argue that the Monacans numbered as many as 15,000 at the time of English colonization. If the Monacans alone could account for this much population, their strength when combined with the other two Siouan divisions in western Virginia would have made the Siouans the largest power in the region. See Jeffrey Hantman, "Between Powhatan and Quirank: Reconstructing Monacan Culture and History in the Context of Jamestown," *American Anthropologist,* New Series 92, no. 3 (September 1990): 676–90; Gallivan, *James River Chiefdoms,* 34–37. If these figures are correct, one wonders

what became of them. A 1669 census of Virginia Indians included the Monacans as the only western Siouan group. According to the count, only 100 to 120 individuals remained of a group that has been estimated at approximately 15,000 in 1607. Recent work by Paul Kelton suggests that their ensnarement in the growing Indian slave trade run out of Virginia doomed western Siouans because of a fatal combination of warfare and disease. See Paul Kelton, *Epidemics and Enslavement: Biological Catastrophe in the Native Southeast, 1492–1715* (Lincoln: University of Nebraska Press, 2007), 216–17.

29. Gallivan, *James River Chiefdoms,* 34–37; Hantman, "Between Powhatan and Quirank"; Jeffrey Hantman, "Monacan Archaeology of the Virginia Interior," ed. David S. Brose (Tuscaloosa: University of Alabama Press, 2006) *Societies in Eclipse: Archaeology of the Eastern Woodlands Indians, AD 1400–1700* (2006), 107–124.

30. Gleach, *Powhatan's World and Colonial Virginia,* 27–31; Rountree, "Who Were the Powhatans and Did They Have a Unified 'Foreign Policy'?" in *Powhatan Foreign Relations,* 1–20.

31. Gleach, *Powhatan's World and Colonial Virginia,* 36–37. Gleach based his analysis of Algonquian culture on other major anthropological studies of Algonquian peoples, including William S. Simmons, *Spirit of the New England Tribes: Indian History and Folklore, 1620–1984* (Hanover, NH: University Press of New England, 1984); A. Irving Hallowell, "Ojibwa Ontology, Behavior and World View," in *Contributions to Anthropology: Selected Papers of A. Irving Hallowell,* ed. Raymond D. Fogelson (Chicago: University of Chicago Press, 1976), 357–90. Even the act of engaging in battle was often as much religious ritual as it was temporal struggle, as the Powhatans made clear to John Smith in a "mock battle" they once staged for him. See Margaret Holmes Williamson, *Powhatan Lords of Life and Death: Command and Consent in Seventeenth-Century Virginia* (Lincoln: University of Nebraska Press, 2003), 143; Barbour, *Complete Works of Captain John Smith* 1:166–67.

32. Gleach, *Powhatan's World and Colonial Virginia,* 42–43.

33. Ibid., 31; Strachey, *Historie of Travel into Virginia Britannia,* 59–61.

34. Richard Hakluyt, "Virginia Richly Valued," in *The Writings and Correspondence of the Two Richard Hakluyts,* vol. 2 (London: Hakluyt Society, 1935), 503; James Horn, *Adapting to a New World: English Society in the Seventeenth-Century Chesapeake* (Chapel Hill: University of North Carolina Press, 1994), 26–28; James Horn, *A Land as God Made It: Jamestown and the Birth of America* (New York: Basic Books, 2005), 40–41. For further discussion of the desire for order among Virginia's early planners and leaders, see Andrew Fitzmaurice, *Humanism and America: An Intellectual History of English Colonization, 1500–1625* (New York: Cambridge University Press, 2003); Michael Leroy Oberg, *Dominion and Civility: English Imperialism and Native America, 1585–1685* (Ithaca, NY: Cornell University Press, 1999); Ethan A. Schmidt, "The Well-Ordered Commonwealth: Humanism, Utopian Perfectionism, and the English Colonization of the Americas," *Atlantic Studies* 7, no. 3 (September 2010): 309–28; Alexander B. Haskell, "'The Affections of the People': Ideology and

the Politics of State Building in Colonial Virginia, 1607–1754" (PhD diss., Johns Hopkins University, Baltimore, MD, 2004). For the social structure of early Virginia, see Warren Billings, Thad Tate, and John Selby, *Colonial Virginia: A History* (White Plains, NY: KTO, 1986); Warren Billings, *Sir William Berkeley and the Forging of Colonial Virginia* (Baton Rouge: Louisiana State University Press, 2004), 55–59; Bernard Bailyn, "Politics and Social Structure in Virginia," in *Seventeenth-Century America: Essays in Colonial History*, ed. James Morton Smith (Chapel Hill: University of North Carolina Press, 1959), 90–115. For another discussion of colonial social hierarchies, see Gary B. Nash, *The Urban Crucible: The Northern Seaports and the Origins of the American Revolution* (Cambridge: Harvard University Press, 1986), 6–9.

35. For the Roanoke incident, see Schmidt, "Well-Ordered Commonwealth," 316–18; James I. "Grant of Virginia unto Sir Thomas Gates, etc.," April 10, 1606, CO 5-1354, 5, British National Archives, Kew, England; "Observations by George Percy, 1607," in *Narratives of Early Virginia, 1606–1625*, ed. Lyon Gardiner Tyler (New York: Barnes and Noble, 1946), 5–13 (both quotations); John Smith, *A True Relation of Such Occurrences and Accidents of Note, as Hath Happened in Virginia since the First Planting of That Colony, Which Is Now Resident in the South Part Thereof, Till the Last Return*, in Barbour, *Complete Works of Captain John Smith*, 32–33. According to Seth Mallios, responses to the failure to comply with the cultural rituals required in an Algonquian exchange relationship ran the gamut from a simple withdrawal from the relationship by the aggrieved party to violence. So possibly, this sequence of events represents at first a response of withdrawal by the Paspahegh. However, their return ten days later seems to indicate that either they withdrew to plot a violent response to the affront or that other trade violations occurred. See Mallios, *Deadly Politics of Giving*.

36. See Schmidt, "Well-Ordered Commonwealth"; Fitzmaurice, *Humanism and America; * Richard Hakluyt, "Virginia Richly Valued," in *The Writings and Correspondence of the Two Richard Hakluyts*, vol. 2 (London: Hakluyt Society, 1935), 503; Mallios, *Deadly Politics of Giving*.

37. Barbour, *Complete Works of Captain John Smith*, 2:146–49.

38. Ibid., 1:53–57.

39. Camilla Townsend, *Pocahontas and the Powhatan Dilemma* (New York: Hill and Wang, 2004), 52.

40. Barbour, *Complete Works of Captain John Smith*, 2:151.

41. Townsend, *Pocahontas and the Powhatan Dilemma*, 52–57.

42. Rountree, *Pocahontas, Powhatan, Opechancanough*, 79; Townsend, *Pocahontas and the Powhatan Dilemma*, 55.

43. Townsend, *Pocahontas and the Powhatan Dilemma*, 55.

44. Helen Rountree, citing well-established Algonquian tradition, argues that Pocahontas would have been nowhere near Smith at the time of the event. Because the Algonquians

of Virginia were a matrilineal society, neither Pocahontas nor any of her siblings would have occupied a place of high honor because of their lack of inheritance rights to Powhatan's chiefdom. Instead, Rountree argues rather convincingly that Pocahontas would most likely have been hard at work somewhere else in the village, helping to prepare the lavish feast her father chose to bestow upon the strange visitor. In addition to Pocahontas's traditional duties of food preparation, the lack of space in the feasting room would also have precluded her attending the evening's festivities. Rountree argues: "Powhatan's heirs, who were his three brothers and two sisters, and his councillors and priests, and any visiting subject chiefs would have been entitled to be participants or observers . . . Gratuitously including an eleven-year-old prepubescent girl would not add one whit to Powhatan's mystique" (Rountree, *Pocahontas, Powhatan, Opechancanough*, 78).

45. Gleach, *Powhatan's World and Colonial Virginia*, 112–22; Williamson, *Powhatan Lords of Life and Death*, 65–72; Kathleen Brown, "In Search of Pocahontas," in *The Human Tradition in Colonial America*, ed. Ian Steel and Nancy Rhoden (Wilmington, DE: Scholarly Resources, 1999), 71–96; Karen Ordahl Kupperman, *Indians and English: Facing Off in Early America* (Ithaca, NY: Cornell University Press, 2000); Daniel Richter, *Facing East from Indian Country: A Native History of Early America* (Cambridge: Harvard University Press, 2001); Philip Barbour, *Pocahontas and Her World* (Boston: Houghton Mifflin, 1970). Rountree does not preclude the possibility that an adoption- or admittance-type ritual involving John Smith and Powhatan occurred. However, she remains adamant that the sequence of events involving his near death by clubbing and Pocahontas speaking out for his life could not have happened.

46. Camilla Townsend likewise recently argued that the idea of Powhatan establishing a kinship tie with Smith makes sense regardless of the validity of Smith's account of his supposed rescue: "Adopting Smith would have been in keeping with Algonquian culture" (Townsend, *Pocahontas and the Powhatan Dilemma*, 56).

47. Barbour, *Complete Works of Captain John Smith* 2:150–53.

48. One of the Algonquian priests who accompanied Pocahontas to London.

49. Barbour, *Complete Works of Captain John Smith* 2:260–61.

50. Both Christopher Newport's attempt to present Powhatan with a crown and scepter designed to signify his status as a vassal of King James and Powhatan's subsequent refusal to kneel upon receiving them indicate the extent to which both sides in this cultural encounter viewed the other as subservient. See ibid., 237. This same configuration of matrilineage, kin-based alliance networks, and female power has also appeared in works dealing with the Cherokee, the Indians of pre-colonial Texas and the desert Southwest. See Theda Perdue, *Cherokee Women: Gender and Culture Change, 1700–1835* (Lincoln: University of Nebraska Press, 1999); Barr, *Peace Came in the Form of a Woman*; James F. Brooks, *Captives and Cousins: Slavery, Kinship, and Community in the Southwest Borderlands* (Chapel Hill: University of North Carolina Press, 2002).

2

Hammerers and Rough Masons to Prepare Them

The First Anglo-Powhatan War, 1609–14

The events of the three Anglo-Powhatan Wars fought between 1609 and 1646 represent a key moment in the social relations of seventeenth-century Virginia. At times, the nearly forty years of intermittent warfare between Virginians and the Powhatan chiefdom interrupted much of the colony's social development, but these periodic interruptions ultimately exacerbated many of the social tensions that gave rise to Bacon's Rebellion.[1] During this period, the Native peoples of Virginia nearly destroyed the entire operation. The anxiety and hatred their resistance to English colonialism produced in the minds of English colonists became a very powerful weapon that many of Virginia's social elites wielded in an effort to both secure English control over the colony and strengthen their own grip on power. However, elite encouragement of violent retribution against Indians and the violent requisition of Indian land during the wars fostered among many Virginians the notion that unrestrained violence against Indians for land acquisition purposes by any member of white Virginia society represented the normative state of Virginia-Indian relations.

The fact that Anglo-Indian relations might fluctuate between extermination and acculturation was not altogether unexpected. As far back as the sixteenth century, such English writers and thinkers as Thomas More, John Rastell, Richard Eden, and Thomas Smith gave voice to the idea that colonized peoples, whom they and their countrymen considered inferior, ought to be given the chance to redeem themselves by committing to live as Englishmen. Furthermore, a refusal to take the

DOI: 10.5876/9781607323082.c002

English up on the offer justified a violent response by their new neighbors.[2] While these writers made reference to this idea within the broad context of Renaissance Humanism and discovery in general, one English writer penned such a prescription for dealing with Virginia Indians specifically during the earliest days of the colony. In 1609 Richard Hakluyt published "Virginia Richly Valued." The pamphlet, one of the last of Hakluyt's illustrious career as a promoter of English colonization, contained these instructions for dealing with the Indians of Virginia: "To handle them gently, while gentle courses may be found to serve, it will be without comparison the best: but if gentle polishing will not serve, then we shall not want hammerers and rough masons enough, I mean our old soldiers trained up in the Netherlands, to square and prepare them to our Preachers hands."[3] Not long after Hakluyt wrote those words, Virginians got their opportunity to "square and prepare" the Powhatans with the outbreak of the First Anglo-Powhatan War during the summer of 1609.[4]

The First Anglo-Powhatan War represents an important marker in the history of Anglo-Indian relations in Virginia and throughout the rest of England's North American colonies, for many reasons. Since it represented the first full-scale armed conflict between Native Americans and the English, the conflict became, in the words of historian J. Frederick Fausz, "an important primer for all Indian wars in British America."[5] More specific to Virginia, the First Anglo-Powhatan War created structures, conflicts, and attitudes that not only spawned two more conflicts between the Powhatans and Virginia colonists but also placed the colony on the path to the chaos of Bacon's Rebellion in 1676. Despite this reality, the conflict was not inevitable.

For the most part, an uneasy peace had existed between the Powhatan chiefdom and Jamestown ever since John Smith's capture and subsequent adoption into the chiefdom in late 1607 and early 1608. Fausz has characterized 1608 as a kind of probationary period in which both sides failed to cement a lasting peace with one another. As long as Smith and Powhatan (however much they mistrusted one another) managed to keep their respective subordinates in check, a permanent peace seemed at least within the realm of possibility. In particular, the growing trade relationship in which Powhatan and his weroances exchanged corn for English goods seemed to promise the surest avenue for continued coexistence. This trade satisfied the colony's desperate need for food and provided a basis upon which the Virginia Company could claim some success at extracting mineral wealth from the colony. In addition, from the Algonquians' perspective, such trade confirmed that they and the English had indeed entered into a reciprocal kinship relationship that would bind the English to Powhatan in the same fashion as the rest of his chiefdom.[6]

Yet by January 1609 the relationship had deteriorated to the point that Powhatan allowed Smith to visit Werowocomoco one last time so he might admonish the man he now considered a renegade weroance:

> Captaine Smith, you may understand that I having seene the death of all my people thrice, and not any one living of those three generations but my selfe; I know the difference of Peace and Warre better than any in my Country ... What will it availe you to take that by force which you may quickly have by love, or to destroy them that provide you food. What can you get by warre ... And why are you thus jealous of our loves seeing us unarmed, and both doe, and are willing still to feede you, with that you cannot get but by our labours?[7]

An occurrence from early 1608 illustrates one of the ways Smith and the Virginians contributed to the failure of this initially peaceful relationship. At that time, Smith visited Powhatan once again. On this occasion, he brought Captain Christopher Newport with him and introduced the high-ranking English mariner to Powhatan. A dispute between Smith and Newport regarding gifts to Powhatan exemplifies the complete failure by the English to understand the duties inherent in Algonquian kin relationships. Before Newport left to return to England, Powhatan gave him a gift of twenty turkeys. In the customary Algonquian fashion, Powhatan requested that Newport reciprocate by giving him twenty swords. No evidence indicates that Newport actually understood the cultural requirements of the gift, but he apparently viewed the arrangement as sensible and immediately ordered the swords delivered to Powhatan. This infuriated Smith. He seems to have believed twenty swords was too expensive a price to pay for the turkeys and determined that he would never allow such a "lopsided" exchange to take place again under his watch. However, from the Powhatan perspective, trade was not an economic exchange but a ritualized expression of one group's esteem for the other.

Smith's eventual response to Powhatan's next request for trade severely damaged the Englishman's reputation and standing as a member of Powhatan's kin network. Not long after the meeting with Newport and Smith, Powhatan sent a similar gift to Smith and requested more swords in return. Smith adamantly refused and referred to the request as insolent. When Powhatan sent warriors to Jamestown to take what he, according to Algonquian tradition, considered his, Smith responded by firing on them, taking several as prisoners, and releasing them only after obtaining a forced confession from the warriors that their original intention was to murder the entire settlement. In addition, the emergence of a black market in which individual colonists traded Virginia Company stores to Powhatan emissaries at prices well below Smith's further exacerbated the problem. His understandable ignorance of the role of exchange among the Powhatans as a means of demonstrating kin loyalty,

FIGURE 2.1. John Smith taking Opechancanough prisoner. Detail from John Smith's *Generall Historie of Virginia,* © Trustees of the British Museum.

as well as his inability to control the illicit economic activity of his fellow colonists, not only cost Smith and his English cohort their best opportunity for cementing a viable coexistence with the Algonquians of Virginia but also necessitated a violent response by the Powhatan chiefdom.[8]

Just as Smith often sought to exploit his relationship with Powhatan for his own purposes, so, too, did the paramount chief attempt to harness the power of Smith and the English for his particular ends. Powhatan's chiefdom faced many external and internal threats that predisposed him to cultivate allies whenever the opportunity presented itself. Not only did Powhatan attempt to adopt Smith and establish him as a subordinate weroance, but he also tried to hide the tenuous nature of his hold on power from the English and did his utmost to limit the English colony's access to both the more autonomous and rebellious groups in the chiefdom and his enemies without. Despite Powhatan's attempts to control their access to the rest of Virginia's Indian peoples, the English determined very shortly after Smith's return from captivity to attempt contact with the powerful Siouan-speaking Monacans to the west. They finally did so several months later, in November 1608. By the summer of 1608, Smith had also made contact with the Massawomecks, an Iroquoian-speaking group to the north whom Powhatan considered among his most intractable enemies. These encounters shattered the image of unchallenged strength Powhatan had attempted to project to the English and emboldened them to act more imperiously in their dealings with him.[9]

At this point, the relationship between the English and the Powhatan chiefdom began to spiral out of control. Smith began to train a group of men whose sole purpose was to take the fight to the Powhatans in their own territory. He also began to treat all emissaries from Powhatan as spies at best and assassins at worst. On one occasion, he gave one such messenger "twenty lashes with a rope."[10] On a visit to Powhatan's brother Opechancanough in early 1609, Smith, believing Opechancanough and his Pamunkey warriors planned to murder him, seized the powerful weroance by the hair and held him at gunpoint (see figure 2.1) until the Pamunkeys could prove to him that they would do no such thing.[11] In his writings, Smith outlined the methods he had come to rely on by mid- to late 1608 in all of his encounters with Powhatan's people: "At all times we so incountred them . . . our Captaine ever observed this order to demand their bowes and arrowes, swords, mantells and furrs, with some childe or two for hostage."[12] If there had been any doubt in Powhatan's mind that John Smith had not lived up to his responsibilities as an adopted member and weroance of the chiefdom, this behavior had to have erased it.

Powhatan responded to Smith's actions with his own calculated displays and boasts of bravado. He reportedly boasted of killing the missing English colonists who had disappeared from Roanoke twenty years before. Whether this was true may never be known, but given the Algonquians' destruction of the Spanish mission in the 1570s, it would certainly have been consistent with previous practice. Furthermore, Powhatan's recent procurement of weapons from newly arrived

Dutch colonists represented a much more immediate concern to the Jamestown colony than did the fate of Englishmen long given up for dead.[13]

For all this posturing, the First Anglo-Powhatan War may not have started in 1609 had John Smith not been fighting for his political survival as the colony's leader. In August 1609 the Third Supply of colonists and provisions sent by the Virginia Company arrived at Jamestown. Among the Third Supply were several high-ranking gentlemen who despised Smith for his disregard of the rules of deference. They carried the news that Sir Thomas Gates had been named the colony's new governor and was on the way to take up his new post. However, Gates ended up shipwrecked on Bermuda for several weeks, which gave Smith the opportunity (as acting council president in Gates's absence) to rid himself of many of his newly arrived adversaries by assigning them to establish settlements beyond Jamestown. Those settlements placed them squarely within the Powhatan chiefdom and thus in competition with the Powhatan villages in the area for the limited food and natural resources there. In this already tense atmosphere, this new example of English disregard for proper kin relationships and Powhatan sovereignty ignited a fiercely violent conflict that would rage for the next five years.[14]

In one instance, Smith dispatched Captains George Percy and John Martin to erect a settlement near the territory of the Nansemonds. When messengers Percy and Martin sent to the Nansemonds failed to return, the two became suspicious. Percy later described what they eventually learned of their emissaries' fate: "We never set eye upon our Messengers after. But understood from the Indians themselves that they were sacrificed And that their Brains were cut and scrapped out of their heads with mussell shells."[15] Percy and Martin responded to the death of their messengers with like force: "Being landed and acquainted with their treachery we Beat the Savages out of the Island burned their houses Ransaked their Temples Took down the Corpses of their dead kings from of their Tombs And carried away their pearls Copper and bracelets, wherewith they do decor their kings funerals."[16]

Percy and Martin's desecration of Powhatan temples and relics represents a deliberate strategy of attacking the religious underpinning of their enemies by the Virginians. Both the religious wars of the sixteenth century and the experience of colonizing Ireland had created in the English a belief that standard rules of warfare did not apply to people considered pagan or barbaric and that the first objective in "reducing them to civilization" was to violently break them of their heathen religious beliefs. Conversely, the strategy represented one well-known and often used by the Powhatans and, for that matter, nearly all eastern Native groups as an attempt by one people to employ their particular spiritual power in the defeat of the spiritual power of an enemy. For these reasons, Fausz has gone so far as to refer to the First Anglo-Powhatan War as a "holy war" for both combatants. Certainly, the fact that victory over the other in the First Anglo-Powhatan War took on the character of a kind of religious crusade explains much about the lingering animosity the conflict projected into the late seventeenth century.[17]

The English victory was short-lived, however, as the Nansemonds quickly regrouped and retook their leader, whom Percy and Martin had captured, as well as 1,000 bushels of corn. Percy and Martin wrote to Smith requesting thirty musketeers and then fled to Jamestown, leaving their men to face a Nansemond siege by themselves. When the requested musketeers arrived, they found that the Indians had stuffed bread in the mouths of some of the stragglers they had killed as an indication of their disdain for the constant English demands for food.[18]

Another settlement, this one established by Captain Francis West—though almost immediately moved by Smith to a more defensible location—experienced a similar fate. Though Smith had purchased (through coercion) the site of Powhatan's natal village from the local weroance, the settlers he left there under West's command proceeded to treat the local Algonquians as conquered people. According to Smith, "That disorderlie company so tormented those poore naked soules . . . that they dailie complained to Captain Smith he had brought them for protectors worse enimies than the Monocans themselves." Eventually, the local weroance ordered a series of attacks throughout the early fall of 1609 that killed almost half of the settlement, forcing West to abandon it. There was no going back. The First Anglo-Powhatan War had begun. To make matters worse, shortly after the abandonment of West's settlement in October, John Smith was badly burned in a gunpowder explosion, forcing him to return to England. While Smith was far from the faithful kin relation Powhatan had hoped to create when he adopted him nine months earlier, he was the only person who seemed to have had the ability to maintain some semblance of order among his murderous countrymen. With him went the hope of resurrecting the peace that had existed in Virginia just a few short months before.[19]

Even before Smith's injury, the Virginia Company had decided to recall him. His rigid work program for all colonists (including the gentlemen) and his refusal to maintain proper deference toward many of the gentlemen of the colony rankled his social betters. By 1609 they had managed to convince the Virginia Company in London that he was unfit to serve further. In addition, the Virginia Company concluded in 1609 that the president and council form of government, in which the company shared overall governance with the Crown, had created paralysis and dissension among the colonists. They asked the king to relinquish the Crown's interest in the colony and grant complete control of its governance to the Virginia Company. James agreed to this arrangement, and the company selected Thomas West, Third Baron De La Warr, as its first governor. De la Warr chose to delay his departure from England until the following year and sent his deputy, Sir Thomas

Gates, in his stead in 1609. Gates ended up shipwrecked on the coast of Bermuda, and nearly all of the colonists starved to death during that winter.[20]

Powhatan sensed an opportunity in Smith's departure to send a message to the English, whom he still considered recalcitrant members of his chiefdom. He quickly besieged Jamestown in November 1609. As the lack of provisions caused by the siege began to have a deadly effect, the paramount chief summoned the English to the territory of the Pamunkeys to trade with him and to discuss peace. Upon its arrival, the English delegation under the command of Captain John Sicklemore was immediately ambushed. Although he survived the initial ambush, Sicklemore was captured by Opechancanough's warriors and subsequently ritualistically tortured by women of the villages. According to George Percy's account, Sicklemore was tied to a tree and kept alive as the flesh was scraped from his body with mussel shells before his face was ultimately thrust into a fire burning nearby. This kind of action would likely have gained Opechancanough his ends if used against other Native groups. After all, it was through such calculated displays of his spiritual and temporal power over their lives and deaths that Powhatan had gained his position of leadership among his people, but against the English this display only entrenched their hatred and bloodlust.[21]

When Gates and De la Warr finally arrived in the summer of 1610, they immediately set out to accomplish two closely related goals. The first goal was to establish order among the colonists through a strict work regimen, enforced by the sword if necessary. Such a regimen would not only increase the colony's potential for profitability but would also help fashion the inhabitants into an effective fighting force to be used in the war against the Powhatan chiefdom. One of their first reports to the leaders of the Virginia Company in London spelled out their disgust at the lack of social discipline among the residents of Jamestown. They described them as "men of such distempered bodies and infected minds, whom no examples daily before their eyes either of goodness or punishment, can deter from the habitual impieties." Unlike Smith, though, those gentlemen "whose breeding," in his estimation, "never knew what a day's labor meant" were allowed to exercise their talents at government and attainment of knowledge and refinement. In short, De la Warr and Gates replaced the rough equality Smith's regimen had enforced with the well-ordered, hierarchical form of social organization they had subscribed to in England.[22]

De la Warr and Gates codified their new system of governance in *The Laws, Divine, Moral and Martial*. In this new law code, they instituted military discipline and strict punishments, including the possibility of death for such offenses as blasphemy and theft. Speaking ill of the governor or his counselors and deputies carried the prospect of either three years on a galley or execution. They also used the new code to gain direct control over all trading activities in the colony. Trading privately with any outside entity or ships carried a death sentence. From its chaotic beginnings, in which men refused to work in favor of gold panning and bowling in the streets, *The Laws, Divine, Moral and Martial* attempted to transform Virginia into a society in which people were expected to know their proper place in the social structure and stay there upon pain of destitution, humiliation, and possible death. For example, those who fled Jamestown's poor living conditions and mass starvation to live with the Indians faced punishments of "hanging, shooting, and breaking upon the wheel." A man who broke into the colony's grain stores to avert starvation was pierced through his tongue with a needle, tied to a tree, and starved to death. Gates and De la Warr aimed to restore order even if some deemed their tactics "contrary to the express letter of the King in his most gracious charter."[23]

All of this coincided with their plan to subdue the Algonquians, the second goal. De la Warr signaled his determination to bring the local Indians to heel in his first communications with his superiors. In a letter to the Virginia Company in July, he wrote, "No country yieldeth goodlier corn or more manifold increase." While acknowledging that the credit for such cultivation belonged to the Indians and not the English colonists, De la Warr nevertheless promised that he and his colonists would soon visit their wrath upon the Algonquians for their "late injuries and murthering of our men." He also promised that the English would eventually gain mastery over all the fields and lands of the area, which they would accomplish through violence. Though they still hoped to integrate Indians into their social structure, the events of the first two years of the colony had convinced them that while other Virginia Indians (most notably those on the Eastern Shore) might willingly submit to such a scheme, the mainland Algonquians would not. De la Warr and Gates immediately commenced construction of three more forts for the defense of the colony from those Indians the two men considered enemies. In addition, *The Laws, Divine, Moral and Martial* placed severe restrictions on the ability of mainland Virginia Indians to move about, trade, and interact with colonists. The Virginia Company ordered Gates to institute a program that would take Indian children away from their parents to be raised in the manner of English children. Furthermore, the company barred Gates from establishing amicable relations with the Powhatan chiefdom under any circumstances. Instead, he was to ally himself with "those that are farthest from you and enemies unto those among whom you dwell."[24]

One of Gates's first acts when he arrived in Virginia was to lead a punitive expedition against the Algonquian village of Kecoughtan. Kecoughtan was one of the villages closest to Jamestown, and animosity had been growing between the denizens of both settlements since 1607.[25] In July 1610 Gates led a force to within a short distance of Kecoughtan and ordered one of his men to play music while the rest danced about. When the Kecoughtans emerged from the village to join in the merriment, Gates unleashed his wrath. George Percy, who accompanied the expedition, described his actions, saying Gates "fell in upon them put five to the sword wounded many others . . . the rest of the savages he put to flight." Gates then returned to Jamestown and, shortly thereafter, to England.[26]

The new leadership then turned its attention to Powhatan. De la Warr sent a delegation to the Indian leader demanding that he return any guns and Englishmen he might be harboring. When Powhatan refused, Percy wrote that De la Warr became enraged and ordered a punitive expedition against the nearby Paspaheghs and Chickahominies. De la Warr put Percy in charge of the expedition, and he and his men set out in August 1610. The events that unfolded when they arrived at the Paspahegh town vividly demonstrate the tug of war between leaders such as Percy and emerging notions among the populace regarding the tactics allowable against Indians.[27]

The initial attack lasted only a few moments, and Percy described the outcome in his later writings: "Then we fell in upon them put some fifteen or sixteen to the sword and almost all the rest to flight. Whereupon I caused my drum to beat and drew all my Soldiers to the Cullers My Lieutenant bringing with him the Queen and her Children and one Indian prisoner." In keeping with his notions of acceptable punishment for inferior enemies, Percy had the male Paspahegh's head cut off and took the queen and her children as his prisoners.[28]

After burning the village and taking the crops, Percy and his men boarded their boats and returned to Jamestown. The men who made up the bulk of Percy's forces soon began to grow mutinous because Percy had spared the queen and her children. For them, the goal of the expedition was extermination, not correction. To their way of thinking, correction was a tactic reserved only for Englishmen; the Paspaheghs did not deserve the same consideration. The soldiers called a council and, disregarding Percy's authority, voted to put the prisoners to death. According to Percy, the soldiers first threw the Paspahegh children overboard and shot "out their Brains in the water yet for all this cruelty the soldiers were not well pleased and I had much to do to save the Queen's life for that time." In the end, Percy managed to prolong the queen's life only for a very short time. After he returned to Jamestown, he sought the advice of his superiors on the matter. Lord De La Warr, however, had fallen ill and taken to his bed. Not wanting to bother with the situation, he left it in the hands of Percy and Captain James Davis. Percy, sensing that the overwhelming desire of the soldiers in the settlement was to kill her, tried to obtain a more merciful and quick death for the Indian woman than the rest of her people had suffered: "I replied that having seen so much bloodshed that day now in my cold blood I desired to see no more." In the end, Davis took the prisoner from Percy, marched her to the woods, and killed her with a sword. Upon his return, he told Percy that he had been following orders from De la Warr. Percy recalled that his reaction to that statement was disbelief. "Captain Davis told me it was my Lord's direction," he remarked, "yet I am persuaded to the contrary."[29]

This incident represents the perfect moment in which to view the initial stirrings of a radically different conception of the utility of violence directed at Native Americans in Virginia. In acquiescing to the pressure, Percy unwittingly allowed a group of his subordinates the right to take Indian lives not when the colony's leadership gave them license to but whenever they, as Virginians, deemed it necessary. These Virginians, in that moment, voiced their intention to decide for themselves when to take Indian lives. Percy did not completely give in to them and did spare the queen's life for a brief moment, but neither did he attempt to punish his soldiers for their disobedience. In fact, he allowed them to burn and loot another Indian town on the way back to Jamestown. Percy's actions in both cases demonstrate the awkward position of Virginia's leaders concerning their social inferiors during the Anglo-Powhatan Wars. Victory against the Algonquians required the cooperation of common colonists who did the majority of the fighting and dying in those conflicts. However, to obtain that cooperation, leaders such as De La Warr and Percy had to stoke Indian hatred to the point that their fellow Virginians often became impossible to control.

The last days of that summer illustrate the extent to which Virginia's leadership had decided to unleash the rage of Virginia settlers on the Powhatans by recasting the conflict as a holy war akin to those they had fought against the Spanish and the Irish during the previous century. Therefore, the tactics used against the queen of the Paspaheghs and her children would become standard for the duration of the Anglo-Powhatan Wars. According to Fausz, this represents a dubious precedent in the history of Anglo-Indian relations in North America. He writes, "Specifically the use of deception, ambush, and surprise, the random slaughter of both sexes and all ages, the calculated murder of innocent captives, and the destruction of entire villages" were introduced into an American frontier conflict for the first time. However, while more dead Algonquians meant an easier path to gaining complete control of Virginia, the cost of such a strategy might mean the loss of control over the men who would carry out the campaign.[30]

Within days, Virginia forces assaulted the Chickahominies and the Warraskoyacks. Finding that both of these groups had fled, the attackers burned their villages and raided their corn supplies. In approximately one week, four different Powhatan groups had been either obliterated by the Virginians or been sentenced to a winter of starvation and disease because of a lack of food.[31] Such a ferocious and lightning-quick campaign might have driven other opponents to surrender, but just as the English viewed the conflict as a holy war, so, too, did the Powhatans.

After several skirmishes in the late fall of 1610, De la Warr resolved to take the war to the heart of Powhatan territory by launching a campaign up the James River. Despite constant raids and ambushes from either side of the river, De la Warr's forces managed to make it to the Falls of the James, where they constructed a garrison they referred to as Laware's Fort. They were quickly encircled by Powhatan warriors and spent the rest of the winter of 1611 under siege. During this time, the combatants were encamped so close to one another that they could literally carry on conversations through the works of the fort. This allowed the Powhatan warriors outside not only to boast of the many muskets they had captured from the Virginians they picked off daily but also to terrify the Virginians in the fort with their daily supplications to their deity Okeus. Such divine appeals demonstrate the extent to which, while obviously quite different from one another, Virginia settlers and their Powhatan adversaries shared a belief that supernatural forces supported their efforts against one another; thus, each felt assured of success.[32]

De la Warr eventually abandoned the fort as illness forced him to return first to Jamestown and ultimately to England. For at least a short while, the Powhatans seemed to have had the upper hand, but the arrival of the colony's new lieutenant governor, Sir Thomas Dale, in May 1611 irrevocably altered their fortunes.[33] Dale not only brought more than 300 experienced English troops but also a rage for order and obedience with which he molded the residents of the colony into a coolly effective fighting force. Dismayed at the lack of discipline that greeted him in Virginia, he set about expanding *The Laws, Divine, Moral and Martial* in such a way as to force the ragged and often insubordinate colonists he inherited into the kind of crack troops needed to successfully wage a holy war against enemies as intransigent as they were. After he had taken stock of the situation on the ground in Virginia, Dale wrote the Earl of Salisbury asking for an additional 2,000 soldiers with which to subdue the Powhatan chiefdom. While the request was never granted, Dale's description of the kind of men he needed signifies much about the kind of campaign he planned to wage. Admitting that the cost of dispatching 2,000 trained English troops to Virginia was likely more than either the Virginia Company or the English government could bear, Dale proposed another option: "If it will please his Majestie to banish hither all offenders condemned, betwixt this and then, to die, out of common Goales [Jails], and likewise so continue that grant for 3 yeres unto the Colonie . . . it would be a readie way to furnish us with men."[34]

In addition to this request for condemned convicts to use as weapons against the Algonquians of Virginia, Dale also remarked on the rough nature of the 300 men, all veterans of campaigns against the Spanish in the Netherlands, he had brought with him. Referring to them as "disordered persons, so prophane, so riotous, so full of Mutenie and treasonable Intendments," he further commented that other than their Christian names, his soldiers exhibited no outward signs of religious faith or fidelity. In other words, Dale was aware that he commanded a force made up of men he considered little better than wild beasts and, with or without 2,000 more such troops, he planned to unleash them and their wildness on the Powhatan chiefdom.[35]

In early August 1611, Dale embarked upon his first action. On this occasion, he launched a campaign against the Nansemonds at the lower end of the James River. In addition to the physical damage Dale inflicted on them, the campaign also dealt a serious spiritual blow to the Powhatans and thus helps demonstrate the religious prism through which the Powhatans viewed the war. This engagement represented the first of the war in which all of the English engaged in the battle were fully armored. The invulnerability of the armor to Powhatan arrows created an immediate spiritual emergency among the Nansemond warriors involved in the battle. George Percy described the effect of armor on the Nansemonds:

> In these Conflicts many Indians being also slain and wounded. Moreover, not being acquainted nor accustomed to encounter with men in Armor much wondered thereat especially that they did not see any of our men fall as they had done in other conflicts. Whereupon they did fall into their exorcisms conjurations and charms throwing fire up into the skies Running up and down with Rattles and making many diabolical gestures with many ungrammatical Spells and incantations Imagining thereby to cause Rain to fall from the Clouds to extinguish and put out our men's matches and to wet and spoil their powder but neither the devil whom they adore nor all their Sorceries did anything Avail them for our men Cut down their Corn Burned their houses and besides those which they had slain brought some of them prisoners to our fort.[36]

Powhatans considered success or failure in warfare directly relative to the amount of spiritual power possessed by the combatants involved in that warfare. In light of this, the sudden inability of Nansemond arrows to inflict any damage on the Virginians represented more to them than the effects of a disparity in warfare technology. Instead, the development signified the loss or failure of Powhatan spiritual power to overcome or counteract that possessed by the colonists. Therefore, the psychological effects of this development cannot be underestimated. It was more than the number of soldiers and the attitude he brought with him that allowed Dale to turn the tide of the First Anglo-Powhatan War decidedly in his favor. He had succeeded in demonstrating (regardless of whether it was his intention) that he possessed a spiritual power equal to or greater than that of the Powhatan confederacy. This was worth countless times more than 2,000 additional soldiers.

Dale quickly followed up his defeat of the Nansemonds with a campaign against the Powhatan groups living near the falls of the James River, in the heart of Powhatan's original territory. His forces were augmented in this effort by 250 additional veteran troops that had recently arrived in the colony. Establishing fortifications in what would eventually become Henrico and ultimately the city of Richmond, Dale eventually overwhelmed the Powhatans despite staunch resistance led by a war captain known as Jack of the Feather for his habit of covering himself entirely in feathers for battle. By the beginning of 1612, the war had settled into a sort of cease-fire, occasioned both by Virginia Company incompetence and the mutual need of both sides to regroup. The war would not pick up again until the second half of 1613.[37]

When the war recommenced, the Virginia leadership, particularly Sir Thomas Dale and Captain Samuel Argall, enacted a two-pronged strategy that emphasized both brute force (Dale's forte) and trade with Algonquians who would agree to abandon Powhatan and accept Virginia's terms for peace. This encouraging of the physical destruction of the Powhatans on the one hand and the inclusion of those who would submit themselves to Virginia authority on the other had to have sent mixed messages to the "wild men" Dale had set loose on the Algonquians with such fury. Despite this, the strategy worked. By the time the First Anglo-Powhatan War ended in 1614, the English had established several new settlements, destabilized Powhatan's hold on power, and taken his daughter Pocahontas captive. While most scholars consider her 1614 marriage to the Englishman John Rolfe to be the end of the First Anglo-Powhatan War, a blistering English offensive against the Powhatans immediately preceding the marriage probably had as much to do with the brief cessation of hostilities. In March 1614 Dale, bringing a company of 150 armed men, forced Pocahontas to accompany him on an expedition to her father's territory. With his small army, Dale "burned in that very place some forty houses, and of the things we found therein, made freeboot and pillage." Soon thereafter the two sides made peace, and Powhatan gave his consent to the marriage. The First Anglo-Powhatan War had come to an end. In addition to the more obvious changes it had wrought on Virginia's political and social landscape, the war had also created a template under which future conflicts with the Algonquians of Virginia would be conducted.[38]

NOTES

1. For a similar argument regarding the tendency of a common struggle to impact social relations, see Alfred F. Young, *The Shoemaker and the Tea Party: Memory and the American Revolution* (Boston: Beacon, 2000).

2. See Andrew Fitzmaurice, *Humanism and America: An Intellectual History of English Colonization, 1500–1625* (New York: Cambridge University Press, 2003); Ethan A. Schmidt, "The Well-Ordered Commonwealth: Humanism, Utopian Perfectionism, and the English Colonization of the Americas," *Atlantic Studies* 7, no. 3 (September 2010): 309–28.

3. Richard Hakluyt, "Virginia Richly Valued," in *The Writings and Correspondence of the Two Richard Hakluyts* (London: Hakluyt Society, 1935), 2:503.

4. Historians have only recently begun to refer to the deadly encounters between Virginia colonists and the Powhatan chiefdom that occurred between 1609 and 1614 as the First Anglo-Powhatan War. Not surprisingly, much debate remains as to whether it is correct to do so. However, the arguments of historian J. Frederick Fausz, one of the leading experts on this period of Virginia history, make the most convincing case for calling the events of these five years a war; therefore, this study adopts the term. See J. Frederick Fausz, "An Abundance of Blood Shed on Both Sides: England's First Indian War, 1609–1614," *Virginia Magazine of History and Biography* 98, no. 1 (January 1990): 3–56. For a contrary viewpoint, see Frederic W. Gleach, *Powhatan's World and Colonial Virginia: A Conflict of Cultures* (Lincoln: University of Nebraska Press, 1997), 129–37.

5. Fausz, "Abundance of Blood Shed on Both Sides," 4.

6. Ibid., 18.

7. Philip Barbour, *The Complete Works of Captain John Smith* (Chapel Hill: University of North Carolina Press, 1986), 2:196.

8. Ibid., 1:53–54; Fausz, "Abundance of Blood Shed on Both Sides," 18–19. My interpretation of these events draws heavily on Seth Mallios's argument concerning the role of European violations of Algonquian gift exchange norms in spawning intercultural violence. See Seth Mallios, *The Deadly Politics of Giving: Exchange and Violence at Ajacan, Roanoke, and Jamestown* (Tuscaloosa: University of Alabama Press, 2006). For more on the importance of reciprocal exchange among Algonquian peoples, see Richard White, *The Middle Ground: Indians, Empires, and Republics in the Great Lakes Region, 1650–1815* (New York: Cambridge University Press, 1991).

9. Barbour, *Complete Works of Captain John Smith*, 1:219–20, 230–31; Helen Rountree, *The Powhatan Indians of Virginia: Their Traditional Culture* (Norman: University of Oklahoma Press, 1989), 148; Fausz, "Abundance of Blood Shed on Both Sides," 19.

10. Barbour, *Complete Works of Captain John Smith*, 1:95.

11. Ibid., 2:202.

12. Ibid., 168.

13. Fausz, "Abundance of Blood Shed on Both Sides," 21; Barbour, *Complete Works of Captain John Smith*, 1:199–200.

14. Fausz, "Abundance of Blood Shed on Both Sides," 22.

15. George Percy, "A Trewe Relacyon of the Proceedings and Occurances of Moment Which Have Happened in Virginia," *Tyler's Historical Quarterly and Genealogical Magazine* 3 (1922): 263.

16. Ibid.

17. For more on the English experience in the sixteenth-century wars of religion and those in Ireland, see Ronald Dale Karr, "'Why Should You Be So Furious?': The Violence of

the Pequot War," *Journal of American History* 85, no. 3. (December 1998): 876–909; Nicholas Canny, "The Ideology of English Colonization: From Ireland to America," *William and Mary Quarterly* 30 (October 1973): 575–98. For a discussion of the defects of Indian spirituality and the English fixation on combating it, see James Axtell, *The European and the Indian: Essays in the Ethnohistory of Colonial North America* (New York: Oxford University Press, 1981), 39–86. For specifics on Virginia Algonquian ideas regarding the connection between spirituality and warfare, see Fausz, "Abundance of Blood Shed on Both Sides," 39; Rountree, *Powhatan Indians of Virginia,* 79–87, 114–25; Margaret Holmes Williamson, *Powhatan Lords of Life and Death: Command and Consent in Seventeenth-Century Virginia* (Lincoln: University of Nebraska Press, 2003), 202–9.

18. Barbour, *Complete Works of Captain John Smith*, 1:270; Helen Rountree, *Pocahontas's People: The Powhatan Indians of Virginia through Four Centuries* (Norman: University of Oklahoma Press, 1990), 52. In fact, there is no evidence that Percy and Martin knew their messengers had been killed prior to ordering the attack on the Nansemonds. Given that Algonquian peoples generally reserved the kind of ritualistic torture Percy described for war prisoners, it seems equally possible that the messengers were alive until Percy and Martin chose to attack the village and were killed sometime thereafter; Percy, "Trewe Relacyon," 262–64.

19. Barbour, *Complete Works of Captain John Smith*, 1:270–72; Percy, "Trewe Relacyon," 263–64; Fausz, "Abundance of Blood Shed on Both Sides," 24.

20. Morgan, *American Slavery, American Freedom*, 79; Barbour, *Complete Works of Captain John Smith*, 2:231–33.

21. Barbour, *Complete Works of Captain John Smith*, 1:275; Henry Spelman, "Relation of Virginea," in *The Travels and Works of Captain John Smith*, ed. Edward Arber and A. G. Bradley (Edinburgh: John Grant, 1910), ci–cxiv; Percy, "Trewe Relacyon," 265–66. See also Williamson, *Powhatan Lords of Life and Death.*

22. "Letter of the Governor and Council in Virginia to the Virginia Company of London," July 7, 1610, in Alexander Brown, *The Genesis of the United States* (Boston: Houghton Mifflin, 1890), 1: 410; Smith, "General History," 234–36.

23. "The Tragical Relation of the Virginia Assembly, 1624," in *Narratives of Early Virginia, 1606–1625*, ed. Lyon Gardiner Tyler (New York: Barnes and Noble, 1946), 422–23.

24. "Letter of the Governor and Council in Virginia to the Virginia Company of London," July 7, 1610, 409; Thomas West, Third Lord De la Warr, "The Relation of the Lord De la Warr, 1611," in *Narratives of Early Virginia*, 212; William Strachey, *For the Colony in Virginia: Lawes Divine, Morall and Martiall, etc.* (London: Walter Burre, 1612; reprinted, Cambridge: Da Capo, 1972); Susan Myra Kingsbury, ed., *Records of the Virginia Company, 1606–26*, vol. 3: *Miscellaneous Records* (Washington, DC: Government Printing Office, 1933), 12 (quotation).

25. Percy, "Trewe Relacyon," 260–82.

26. Ibid., 270.

27. Ibid., 271.

28. Ibid., 271–72. See also Karr, "Why Should You Be So Furious," 876–909.

29. Percy, "Trewe Relacyon," 272–73.

30. Fausz, "Abundance of Blood Shed on Both Sides," 33. See also Karr, "Why Should You Be So Furious," 876–909.

31. Fausz, "Abundance of Blood Shed on Both Sides," 33–34.

32. Ibid., 35; Percy, "Trewe Relacyon," 274–75; William Strachey, *The Historie of Travel into Virginia Britannia* (London: Hakluyt Society, 1953), 85–86.

33. Percy, "Trewe Relacyon," 275.

34. "Sir Thomas Dale to the Earl of Salisbury, August 17, 1611," in *Genesis of the United States,* 1:506.

35. Ibid., 507. J. Frederick Fausz seems undecided on the issue of whether the colonists who filled Dale's ranks were as wild and predisposed to unleash their rage on Native Americans as Dale described. He argues that we must at least consider the possibility that "the most haunting implication of this tragic first war is that there were probably many reluctant warriors on both sides, with more in common than three centuries of racist rhetoric permit us to appreciate, who were goaded into mutual slaughter by the same group of sadistic zealots." While it is not my intent to downplay this possibility, the evidence, such as the incident with the Paspahegh queen in 1609 and others, seems to indicate that the majority of those who made up the Virginia ground troops during the Anglo-Powhatan Wars needed little goading to engage in slaughter. Furthermore, from the Indian point of view, the spiritual and societal obligations for warfare under which they operated also indicate that Powhatan would not have needed to force them to engage the English. See Fausz, "Abundance of Blood Shed on Both Sides," 39; Rountree, *Powhatan Indians of Virginia,* 79–87, 114–25.

36. Percy, "Trewe Relacyon," 277.

37. Fausz, "Abundance of Blood Shed on Both Sides," 43–45. The Powhatan warrior Nemattanew, dubbed "Jack of the Feather" by the English for his propensity to fight while outfitted in an elaborate costume of feathers and bird wings, represents an oft-cited example of the connection between success in warfare and the favor of the spirit world. Though Fausz and Rountree disagree as to whether his adornment had any religious significance, considering the link between spiritual power and military prowess as outlined best by Frederic Gleach, it seems likely that the Powhatans attributed his extraordinary success in warfare to the power of his attendant spiritual guides. See Fausz, "The Powhatan Uprising of 1622: A Historical Study of Ethnocentrism and Cultural Conflict" (PhD diss., College of William and Mary, Williamsburg, VA, 1977), 348–49; Rountree, *Powhatan Indians of Virginia,* 76–77; Gleach, *Powhatan's World and Colonial Virginia,* 42–43.

38. Ralph Hamor, *A True Discourse of the Present State of Virginia* (Richmond: Virginia State Library, 1957), 6–11.

3

Subduing the Indians and Advancing the Interests of the Planters

The Second Anglo-Powhatan War, the Tobacco Boom, and the Rise of the Tobacco Elite, 1614–32

In late 1622, approximately six months after a devastating surprise attack by the Powhatan chiefdom, Nathaniel Butler, an Englishmen sent to report on Virginia's progress, summed up the colony's situation thus:[1] "Unless the confusions and private ends of some of the Company here . . . be redressed with speed by some divine and supreme hand that instead of a Plantation it will shortly get the name of a slaughter house and so justly become both odious to ourselves & contemptible to all the world."[2]

Despite the end of the martial law regime of the previous decade and the burgeoning tobacco economy, Virginia remained an extremely hazardous and unstable venture in which the only certainty was death. The Powhatan attack had forced the abandonment of virtually every settlement beyond Jamestown and cost the colony nearly one-quarter of its population. Within three years, the Crown would dissolve the ineffective Virginia Company and take direct control of the colony's government. By that time Virginia had been in existence for seventeen years, with very little to show for it in the way of profit or success. Yet less than twenty-five years after Butler's report, Virginia's leaders would experience the final defeat of the Powhatans, an extremely lucrative trade in tobacco, and the arrival of a nearly thirty-year "golden age" of relative peace and prosperity (for some) the likes of which the colony had never experienced.

The years between the marriage of John Rolfe and Pocahontas in 1614 and the end of the Second Anglo-Powhatan War in 1632 were critical not only to the

DOI: 10.5876/9781607323082.c003

establishment of the belief that all Virginians could utilize violence against Indians for the purpose of land acquisition but also to the creation of a society boasting a more hierarchical social order based on one's ability to control the labor power of others, engross as much land as possible, and exploit opportunities to hold multiple offices for personal gain. Specifically, during this period a small group of elite planters came to dominate the Council of State, the burgesses, and the county benches. They used the power inherent in that control to address what they saw as a lack of authority and order in the colony. While some may have done so out of a belief that therein lay the best hope of creating a society beneficial to all Virginians, many undoubtedly did so as a means of enhancing their own wealth and power. Whatever their root motivations, they responded to challenges from below with swift action and governed the colony in ways designed to enhance planter elites' control of the colony's political and social life. This, in turn, caused many of those outside that elite to view their relationship in antagonistic terms and thus contributed to a growing consciousness of class based on the divergent interests of the two groups. This class-consciousness would continue to develop until it eventually burst forth in the 1670s.[3]

Before one can analyze the effects of the Second Anglo-Powhatan War as well as the tobacco boom, the peace that followed the marriage of John Rolfe and Pocahontas also deserves attention. Specifically, it provides another excellent example of the way Virginia colonists were struggling to establish a workable state and determine their relationship to Virginia's Indian peoples while the Powhatans were engaged in a similar process. Her English acquaintances, early historians, and the general public have traditionally interpreted Pocahontas's many attempts to aid the Jamestown colony, as well as her marriage, as indications that she, unlike her reluctant father and recalcitrant uncle, eventually realized both the error of her savage ways and the benefits of adopting an English lifestyle. Both English colonists and later Americans viewed these events this way because of what Daniel Richter has referred to as their "westward-facing perspective." Given both the early colonists' extremely limited knowledge of Powhatan traditions and the preference of later generations for a romantic brand of nationalism, it is not surprising that a more nuanced interpretation based on the Algonquian culture that produced Pocahontas failed to appear.[4]

If we follow Richter's advice, however, and "face east," Pocahontas's marriage to Rolfe, her conversion to Christianity, and her fateful voyage to England take on an entirely new meaning. By the time of her marriage, her father certainly realized that his attempt to create an inviolable kinship between himself and the English through John Smith had failed. Even if Powhatan held out hope that the Englishman would one day live up to the obligations of that bond, Smith's return to England in 1609 as a result of burns suffered in a gunpowder explosion robbed the mamanatowick of the conduit through which to utilize the relationship. A new hope for such a kinship tie appeared when John Rolfe proposed to marry Pocahontas in 1614. According to Richter, both sides viewed the marriage "as an act of diplomatic alliance—vastly strengthening already existing connections." With this kinship established through the marriage, "the ceremonial, political, and economic basis for peace, as people of Tsenacommacah understood the concept, became possible." In this light, both Powhatan's willing acceptance of the match (despite the fact that it occurred while the English held his daughter captive) and his encouragement of her visit to England represent more of an attempt (of her own behest or at the direction of her father) to offer the English another opportunity to relate to the Powhatan in Algonquian terms. In Richter's words, "When Pocahontas took the name Rebecca and went to live among Europeans, she did so not to abandon her culture but to incorporate the English into her Native world, to make it possible for them to live in Indian country by Indian rules."[5]

For their part, many of the leading figures at Jamestown and in England interpreted the peace as a sign that the Powhatans had finally realized their inferiority and placed themselves under the subjugation of the English. For example, Virginia secretary Ralph Hamor felt that the peace afforded an opportunity to utilize Virginia Indians as laborers. In his estimation they would "exceed our English," whom he characterized as "no more sensible than beasts."[6] Hamor was not the only Virginia leader to express these opinions. Alexander Whitaker, assigned to convert the Powhatans to Christianity, remarked that his task would be much easier now that the English had overwhelmed them to the point that they cowered "in great fear of us." Whitaker assumed that not only would the Powhatans willingly accept Christianity but that they would now serve the colony "in our discoveries of the Country, in our buildings and plantings, and quiet provision for ourselves."[7] Therefore, the Powhatans saw the marriage and the peace agreement as a final successful attempt to create a kinship relationship between themselves and the Virginians and thus bring the settlement into the chiefdom's orbit. In contrast, the English saw it as a willing admission by the Powhatans that they were now subservient to the Virginia government. With such a doubtful footing, one marvels that the cessation of hostilities lasted as long as it did.[8]

Events intervened in Pocahontas's attempt to forge an alliance based on Algonquian notions of kinship. The peace sealed by the marriage of John Rolfe and Pocahontas barely outlasted the marriage itself. Pocahontas died while visiting England in 1617 with her husband and young son, Thomas. Her father, having relinquished titular and de facto leadership of the chiefdom to his brothers Opitchapam and Opechancanough, respectively, died in April 1618.[9] The latter, who effectively

THE WEDDING OF POCAHONTAS.
With John Rolf.

FIGURE 3.1. Wedding of Pocahontas and John Rolfe, by Geo Spohni. Library of Congress, Washington, DC.

governed the chiefdom until its dissolution in the 1640s, took a very different view of the situation than his elder brother did.

Whereas Powhatan had seen the English as potential subjects or at least allies, Opechancanough viewed them as enemies. However, Opechancanough's reasons for doubting the possibility of peace with the English were directly related to another facet of Pocahontas's mission in England as assigned to her by Powhatan. Opechancanough's rise to power coincided with the return to Virginia of Samuel Argall, now the colony's governor, and John Rolfe. In addition to the two English leaders, Uttamatomakkin, an Algonquian priest who had traveled to England as part of Pocahontas's retinue, also returned. Argall and Rolfe went back to Virginia determined to restore the colony to proper order and to ensure that the Algonquians took their place as members of the producing class. Uttamatomakkin, in contrast, arrived back in Virginia equally determined to convince Opechancanough to move against the English before it was too late. Powhatan had asked both Uttamatomakkin and Pocahontas to gather as much information about the English as possible. He had seen the vast multitudes of English citizens and realized that the English population in Virginia would soon dwarf that of the Algonquians, and

any chance of either forcing the English to leave or convincing them to live according to Algonquian wishes would be lost. We cannot say for sure what would have
happened had Pocahontas and Powhatan lived. However, it seems certain that the
failure of the English (who were still unaware of the reciprocal relationship the
Algonquians believed existed between them) to live up to their kinship obligations,
coupled with the intelligence gleaned in London, would have troubled them both
as it did Opechancanough. Within weeks, sporadic episodes of violence between
Indians and Virginians began to occur, and Opechancanough quickly indicated to
the English that his regime would be less welcoming to their settlement than his
brother's had been. Eventually, this change of attitude would result in his launching a major assault that he hoped would drive the English back across the ocean
for good.[10]

By 1622, the English occupied a seventy-mile strip from Point Comfort on the
banks of the Chesapeake Bay to the site of present-day Richmond. Despite the
recurrence of disease outbreaks that killed both Indians and Europeans, the colony
began to experience tremendous growth at the dawn of the 1620s. In the twenty
years from 1620 to 1640, Virginia's population grew nearly 900 percent, from 900
to 8,000 colonists. By 1660 the population had reached 25,000 on its way to 60,000
in 1680 and 85,000 by the dawn of the eighteenth century. Tobacco, along with
the introduction of the head-right system of land distribution, spurred this population explosion. This mixture of tobacco production and the head-right system
combined with the Second Anglo-Powhatan War to produce an emerging planter
elite who came to dominate both the social and political life of the colony during
the 1620s and 1630s.[11]

While very few actual gentlemen figured into the developing Virginia social
matrix of the seventeenth century, a group best described as a hegemonic elite
wielded considerable power, particularly after tobacco became the colony's major
staple export. They controlled access to the colony's government, as well as the
distribution of land and servants. They were the "winners" in the scramble set off
by the tobacco boom and the head-right system it spawned. They wanted Virginia
to be profitable either personally or collectively, both of which required social
stability. They also desired to limit competition from new arrivals and lesser individuals such as artisans, landless freemen, and women who challenged accepted
gender norms. In addition, though they supported and often ordered and led the
various punitive and military expeditions launched against the Algonquians of
Virginia, their goal in doing so was not to completely eradicate Virginia's Native
population (unless the Algonquians to a last man refused to submit) but instead
to force the Powhatans and their kinsmen to take their place in an ordered and
stable society.[12]

As mentioned, most of the men who made up the group of elite families who came to control Virginia throughout much of the century gained power through the tobacco boom in the 1620s. West Indian tobacco, introduced in Virginia by John Rolfe in 1612, quickly became the elusive staple export Virginians had been searching for during the first ten years of the colony's existence. Within a few years, Virginians were planting tobacco in every corner of the English-controlled portions of the colony and actively seeking to enlarge their domain so they could plant more. Tobacco reached a high price of 3 shillings per pound during the 1620s, and its cultivation so completely subsumed all other activity in Virginia that in 1619 John Pory, the secretary of the colony, remarked that "all our riches for the present doe consiste in Tobacco."[13] By 1630, Virginia was producing 400,000 pounds of tobacco each year, and production continued to climb, reaching nearly 30 million pounds per year by the 1680s. By the end of the seventeenth century, tobacco was so woven into the very fabric of Virginia society that one Virginian said "it is our meat, drink, clothes and monies."[14]

The ability to control large amounts of labor quickly became the most important element for success in tobacco-mad Virginia. Once Virginians had enough experience with tobacco to work out the best practices for planting, tending, and harvesting the crop, it was estimated that one planter could produce as much as 2,000 pounds of it per year. According to Edmund Morgan, that would have resulted in a profit of £300 per person. Therefore, if a single planter could gain control over the labor of several men and use that labor to work his personal crop, he could reap tremendous wealth. In fact, the more laborers he could accumulate, the higher his earning potential would climb. Based on these requirements for success in the tobacco trade, Virginia's demand for labor grew limitlessly. Morgan reported that "men rushed to stake out claims to men, stole them, lured them, fought over them— and bought and sold them, bidding up the prices to four, five and six times the initial cost." However, before he could even begin to think about acquiring a labor force, a would-be tobacco planter had to acquire a sufficient land base.[15]

Recent studies that have taken up the issue of the transition from white indentured servitude to African slavery provide valuable insight into the early emergence of the planter elite in Virginia and the role the Powhatan Wars played in that development. According to Anthony Parent, the first requirement for the eventual growth of a tobacco economy based on African slave labor in Virginia was the defeat of the Powhatan chiefdom. Specifically, the men who became Virginia's planter elite needed the Powhatans' land on which to plant their increasingly profitable commodity. Starting in the 1620s and 1630s they began to see land as less a symbol of one's standing in society and more as a commodity from which to build wealth through tobacco. Consequently, the defeat of the Powhatan chiefdom and the acquisition of as much of its land as possible became the primary goal of those who controlled Virginia's government and society during this period. The tobacco planters of the 1620s and 1630s were not the first Virginians to amass large land-holdings, but this repurposing of land for tobacco planting changed the relation-ship between them and those below them on the social ladder. Whereas in the past large landowners had often generated income by leasing or selling portions of their holdings to poorer settlers, they now refused to do so, instead preferring to plant their entire acreage in tobacco.[16]

The secret to satiating Virginia's land and labor hunger was found in two seem-ingly disconnected events. The first was a series of reforms instituted by the Virginia Company in 1618. To give Virginia colonists a larger personal interest in the col-ony's success or failure and therefore encourage them to exert more effort on its behalf, the company instructed Governor George Yeardley to grant anyone who had settled in Virginia prior to 1616 full title to 100 acres of land. Yeardley was fur-ther instructed to grant 50 acres to anyone who had come or paid for the transporta-tion of another after that date. This system of supplying free land to individuals in proportion to the literal number of heads they brought into the colony, known as the "head-right" system, provided a sizable portion of the means by which Virginia's hegemonic tobacco elite established dominance over the economic, social, and political life of the colony. They now had a powerful incentive to import laborers at their own expense or, even better, to find ways to claim or steal the head-rights of laborers brought over at the expense of other Virginians. Either way, the potential benefit was clear. More laborers meant individual planters could plant even more tobacco and would have an increasing supply of land on which to do so.[17]

In addition, Sir Edwin Sandys, the new treasurer of the Virginia Company, simultaneously embarked on a campaign to dramatically increase the supply of laborers willing to sail to the colony. One of the ways he sought to do this was to create a status somewhere between that of bound servants and free laborers. Sandys offered Englishmen desperate enough to want to leave England, but not so desper-ate that they would completely give up their freedom to do so, the opportunity to go to Virginia at the company's expense as "tenants." This meant that in addition to their passage to Virginia, the company would grant them land that they would cultivate as sharecroppers, turning over half of their earnings to the company for seven years. At the end of that time, they would be released from the arrangement and be granted a 50-acre head-right. Sandys then took this plan one step further. In addition to the hundreds of tenants he assigned to company-held lands in Virginia, he convinced other prominent shareholders in the company to found new settle-ments in Virginia and people them with tenants under the same terms. In return for their efforts, the founders of these settlements would receive land in proportion to their stockholdings in the settlements. This combined with Sandys's campaign to scour every English parish possible and convince them to turn over their poor and destitute to him for transportation to Virginia succeeded in bring over 3,500 new settlers to Virginia during his three-year reign as company treasurer.[18]

One other reform Sandys enacted also contributed to the development of Virginia's tobacco elite and constitutes one of the most celebrated events in American history. The Sandys regime decided to do away with the martial law that had governed the colony since shortly after the departure of Captain John Smith and replace it with the first legislative assembly in North America. This assembly would have the power to make laws for the colony subject to the ultimate approval of the company. By itself, this change might not have been integral to the growth of the elite class that came to rule Virginia. However, the company's solution to an age-old problem quickly became the vehicle with which a select few turned Virginia's government into a tool for their own aggrandizement. That problem was how to pay for the government. The Virginia Company was determined not to levy taxes on the settlers. Instead, the company decided to pay the members of the Virginia government in workers and land. The salaries of government officials would then be derived from the tobacco profits of the land and its tenants rather than taxation. According to the company, this plan would allow it to "ease all the inhabitants of Virginia forever of all taxes and public burdens as much as may be and to take away all occasion of oppression and corruption." In reality, it did just the opposite.[19]

These reforms occurred at almost the exact time the tobacco boom was beginning to gain steam in Virginia. Since the secret to success in tobacco was to control as many laborers as possible, those who were also investors in the company or members of the colony's new government had an immediate leg up in the scramble for laborers. Not only did those in positions of power receive the generous grants of tenants and land mentioned earlier (in some cases, such as that of the governor, as much as 3,000 acres and 100 tenants), their control over the levers of government afforded them the opportunity to expropriate tenants and other servants who were ostensibly the property of the company for their own personal uses.[20] Despite the many inducements in land for planters to import servants and tenants from England, the cost of doing so and the relative ease with which they could seize them from others created a mad scramble in which the larger planters, usually either those who had been in the colony from the early days or members of the government and the assembly, gobbled up laborers through any means necessary.[21]

The expansionist impulse among Virginians that resulted from these reforms represents one of the factors that led Opechancanough to attack the colony. The increase in efforts to convert Indians to Christianity is another, and the effect of European diseases on the Algonquian population constitutes a third factor. In the end, the renewal of hostilities between the Powhatan chiefdom and Virginia in the early 1620s both continued the process by which many Virginians came to see violence as the preferred policy for dealing with Native Americans and created a situation in which many small planters were forced into tenancy or servitude in an effort to flee the increasingly violent Anglo-Powhatan frontier.

In addition to his introduction of the head-right system and his efforts to import more colonists, Edwin Sandys also set about the task of bringing Indians to English civilization and Protestantism. In a project that eventually resulted in the creation of the College of William and Mary in Williamsburg, he attempted to convince Virginia Algonquians to give him their children so they could be raised in English households. According to the anonymous benefactor who funded it, the initiative's stated purpose was once again to achieve the biracial utopia envisioned by the original backers of English colonization. The program sought to bring up "the children of the Infidels: first in the knowledge of God and true religion; and next, in fit trades whereby honestly to live." When the Indians balked at the idea of sending their children away, the Virginians brokered an agreement with Opechancanough in which entire Indian families would relocate to English towns to live alongside Virginians and thus learn their ways. At roughly the same time as the Indian school project, the newly created House of Burgesses (which represented the interests of those reaping the benefits of the tobacco boom first and foremost) decreed that Indians would only be welcome on Virginia tobacco plantations if they offered themselves as laborers and refrained from contact with the white planters' family members. In Opechancanough's view, the school must have seemed little more than an attempt to steal Algonquian children and work them to death as tobacco laborers, and he encouraged his people to resist it. When the Powhatans began to refuse English requests that they relocate to English settlements to undergo this "civilizing" process, many English envoys began to apply force, and tensions mounted between the two groups.[22]

If the English expansionist and missionary efforts were not enough to convince the new Algonquian leader that the time had come for an offensive, the disastrous effect of English-borne diseases combined with the other two factors to leave him little choice. A serious outbreak struck both colonists and Indians in 1619, and epidemics continued to afflict Virginia until mid-century. One accounting, undertaken by a disgruntled investor in the early 1620s, reveals the effect of disease on the colony's white population. Of the 4,270 colonists living in Virginia at the time Sir Edwin Sandys took over leadership of the Virginia Company in 1619, only 1,240 survived in 1622. Subtracting the 347 killed in Opechancanough's 1622 attack leaves 2,683 who likely died from some combination of starvation and disease. This despite the 3,500 new colonists sent to Virginia during Sandys's tenure. The reports from the colony for the years immediately preceding the Powhatan attack actually indicate both very little scarcity in foodstuffs and few reports of starvation. We have almost no records detailing the effects of these diseases on Virginia's Indian population, except that the Algonquians suffered from large outbreaks in both 1617 and 1619. Given the latest scholarship on the effects of European diseases among indigenous communities, it is likely that while the Algonquians of Virginia probably lost a significant portion of their population because of microbes, what occurred in this period did not rise to the level of an epidemic. Nonetheless, the loss of population occasioned by disease during this period, as well as the spiritual and demographic crises resulting therefrom, must have exerted a significant effect on Opechancanough's decision making.[23]

Beyond these three underlying causes—the institution of the head-right system, the effort to increase immigration, and the attempt to convert Indians to English ideas of civilization—several other incidents served as triggers for the impending Second Anglo-Powhatan War. The Algonquians increasingly responded to English activities by raiding their settlements. In 1617 a group of Chickahominies killed several traders and took an English child captive. This group also ran afoul of both its own weroance and Opechancanough by looting a temple. Opechancanough's response provides an informative glimpse into his state of mind regarding his relationship with the English at the time. Despite promising not only to deliver the culprits to the English but also to allow the colonists to take their land, he seems never to have made good on the promise. In 1618, one of Opechancanough's top war leaders, Nemattanew, or Jack of the Feather as the English referred to him, led a raid on the English and made off with a supply of guns. As a sign of his growing discontent with the English, Opechancanough later sent the stolen guns to Jamestown with a demand that the colonists repair them for him.[24]

Over the next two years, Opechancanough brazenly tested the English on several occasions. He arranged meetings and alliances with the colonists that he did not keep and suggested insincerely that he wished to leave the chiefdom to Pocahontas's son, Thomas, who had been raised in England since his mother's death. While his erratic behavior kept the English guessing as to his true intentions, the Algonquian leader was secretly organizing a massive simultaneous attack on their settlements. According to an official Virginia Company account, Opechancanough planned to draw upon Powhatan's spiritual and symbolic power to unify the chiefdom and its neighbors into a large pan-Algonquian force with which he could drive the invading English back into the ocean. Apparently, he planned to conduct a reburial ceremony for his dead brother, an Algonquian custom reserved for leaders such as Powhatan. At that ceremony, "Great numbers of the savages were to be assembled to set upon every plantation of the colony." It seems that Opechancanough originally planned for the attack to occur in 1621, but the English caught wind of it and he had to spend several months denying his intentions and ingratiating himself to the English.[25]

The way the English learned of the plan illustrates the continuing problems the leaders of the Powhatan chiefdom encountered in trying to keep the organization together in the face of the English colonization effort. As the relationship between the Indians and the English on the western side of the Chesapeake deteriorated and eventually led to the Second Anglo-Powhatan War, the Occohannocks and Accomacs of the Eastern Shore continued to coexist peacefully with the English. At the same time Opechancanough, like his brother before him, insisted that the Eastern Shore groups swear allegiance to him as part of the paramount chiefdom. While that may have been the case twenty years earlier, the long period of peaceful relations between the Eastern Shore Algonquians and the English had seriously eroded the mamanatowick's control over the Accomacs and Occohannocks. In the summer of 1621, Opechancanough asked the Accomacs to provide him with a poisonous herb indigenous to the Eastern Shore. Instead, the Accomacs informed the English of the request and the likelihood that Opechancanough planned to use the herb against the colonists. The betrayal of his plan by the Accomacs severed the few bonds connecting the Indians on either side of the Chesapeake, ushered in a period of a peaceful yet ultimately devastating invasion of the Eastern Shore by the Virginians, and forced Opechancanough to postpone his plans for a strike against the English.[26]

Soon after the failed poisoning attempt, the English killed Nemattanew, the war leader who had been instrumental in Opechancanough's growing resistance to the English. It appears that Nemattanew had lured a colonist named Morgan to the woods with him and then returned to the English settlements wearing the man's cap. When questioned by Morgan's servants, Nemattanew replied that Morgan was dead. While the circumstantial evidence certainly points to his guilt, the response by the Englishman's servants further underscores the growing sense of autonomy among many Virginians regarding the use of violence against Indians. Without informing any colonial authorities, the men took Nemattanew prisoner. When he attempted to escape, they shot him. Even though the colony's government and the Powhatan chiefdom were officially at peace and such an incident might spark another costly war, these servants seemed confident in their unlimited right to determine the life and death of Indians as they saw fit.[27]

The death of Nemattanew placed Opechancanough in a precarious situation. Since the incident occurred shortly after the English learned of his request for the poison, he could not respond to the death of one of his most important warriors by going to war against the colony. The government had placed the entire colony in a heightened state of alert after learning of the poison request. If Opechancanough had demanded immediate vengeance for the killing, his warriors would have run headlong into a heavily armed and fortified colonial defense. Because of this, Opechancanough sent the English a message in which he not only refrained from demanding revenge for the killing but also lauded Nemattanew's death as a just punishment for his murder of Morgan. According to the Virginia Company's official records, Opechancanough referred to Nemattanew as "a man so far out of favor . . . he [Opechancanough] could be contented [if] his throat were cut." The Algonquian leader then pledged that "the death of Nemattanew being but one man should be no occasion of the breach of the peace, and that the sky should sooner fall than peace be broken." The period beginning with this letter and continuing through the spring of 1622 represents Opechancanough's most effective and skillful period as leader of the paramount chiefdom. While the English initially met his protestations with cynicism, Opechancanough's subsequent actions eventually caused many (especially among Virginia's leadership) to believe they had finally achieved a peaceful coexistence with the Algonquians. However, this was simply an elaborate illusion skillfully created by Opechancanough and the remaining chiefdom groups who continued to look to him for leadership. The differing reactions to Opechancanough's new attitude by elite and non-elite Virginians also reveal much about the growing chasm between the two groups regarding the place of Indians in Virginia society.[28]

Shortly after the Nemattanew incident, a new governor, Sir Francis Wyatt, arrived in Virginia, and it was he who received Opechancanough's message regarding Nemattanew's death. Wyatt appointed George Thorpe, the English minister who had come to Virginia to oversee the Indian school project, as his ambassador to Opechancanough. Thorpe subscribed fully to the assumptions regarding Indians characteristic of many of Virginia's leaders at the time. For Thorpe, the blame for the poor state of affairs in Anglo-Indian relations lay not with the Indians but with the colonists. In 1621 he wrote Edwin Sandys, "If there be wrong on any side it is on those who are not so charitable to them as Christians ought to be." Thorpe went on to describe the Algonquians' desire for English clothes and household items and pleaded with the Virginia Company to make a public declaration of their wish to convert the Indians to Christianity out of their love for them.

After Wyatt arrived, Thorpe set about the task of winning Opechancanough's friendship and possibly his soul. He spent considerable time in conversation with the Powhatan leader on topics including the Indian school, trade, and religion. After one of these meetings, Thorpe happily pronounced Opechancanough a friend and characterized him as having "more notions of religion in him than could be imagined." Thorpe negotiated the compromise with Opechancanough on the Indian school. He also presented him with an English house and ordered that several English mastiffs, which frightened the Algonquians, be slaughtered, over the intense objections of the dogs' English masters. Thorpe firmly believed he had finally achieved the long-awaited breakthrough in English relations with Native people. He and other Virginia leaders looked forward to the lucrative possibilities of a peaceful future with the Native peoples of Virginia, the foundation of which had been laid, but that foundation had sizable flaws from its inception. Though he worked for peace and truly believed he was acting in the Indians' best interests, Thorpe and the Virginians understood them no better than the colonists had in the sixteenth century. They still sought to impose an Anglo-centric worldview and societal structure on an unwilling people who considered themselves sovereign and their spiritual, economic, subsistence, and social structures the correct methods for successfully negotiating the Chesapeake environment.[29]

Other, less idealistic and decidedly less patrician individuals saw no value in programs aimed at bringing English civilization to Indians. Thorpe summarized the common view of Indians among many colonists: "There is scarce any man amongst us that doth so much afford them a good thought in his heart and most men with their mouths give them nothing but maledictions and bitter execrations." At about this same time, John Smith included the account of Reverend Jonah Stockham, a clergyman in Elizabeth City, in his *General History*. Stockham, unlike Thorpe, was not a member of the Virginia Council or a former member of Parliament, and his thoughts as presented by Smith certainly indicate his animosity toward Indians. He wrote that there was "no probability of bringing them to goodness . . . and till their Priests and ancients have their throats cut, there is no hope to bring them to conversion."[30]

Any doubt as to which side would win in this disagreement disappeared on March 22, 1622. That morning and the previous evening, Algonquians from several villages arrived to trade in every English settlement along both banks of the James River.[31] They brought deer, turkeys, fish, and furs and according to one account "sat down at breakfast with our people at their tables." Ever since Wyatt and Thorpe had initiated their attempts to bring the Algonquians into the English social structure, the presence of Indian people in the settlements had become commonplace. Opechancanough's manipulation of Thorpe and skillful diffusion of the Nemattanew incident had lulled the English into a false sense of security, and their desire for economic intercourse with the Indians outweighed their suspicions.

According to an account by colonist Edward Waterhouse, the colonists' houses "were generally set open to the savages, who were always friendly entertained at the tables of the English, and commonly lodged in their bedchambers." Waterhouse attributed the Algonquians' affability to their need for English shelter and defense because of their weakness in relation to the powerful English. Opechancanough recognized this English hubris and undertook to use it against them. He crafted his plan with such careful attention to detail that he made sure to send only unarmed individuals recognizable to the inhabitants of the individual towns so as not to arouse suspicion.

When Friday morning, March 22, dawned, some of the English set about their work, many chatting idly with the Indians who had arrived the night before; others welcomed new Indian visitors to their breakfast tables. At the appointed moment sometime in the midmorning, the Algonquian visitors suddenly grabbed whatever objects they could find, including hammers, axes, and other common English objects, and killed every English colonist they saw, "not sparing either age or sex, man, women, or child." The attack was so sudden in some places that many of those killed never saw the deathblow coming. When the day ended, 347 colonists, roughly one-quarter of Virginia's white population, lay dead. The survivors retreated to the original line of settlement near Jamestown. While these results demonstrate the considerable damage inflicted on the colony, the numbers could have been much higher. Opechancanough's plan called for a second wave of warriors to sweep through the rest of the colony's settlements and then attack Jamestown, but the night before the attack, several Indians who worked for white plantation owners and had established ties with them warned their masters of the plot. These planters warned the government at Jamestown and as many settlements as they could contact before dawn. Because of this break in the otherwise impenetrable veil of secrecy surrounding the plan, the devastation remained localized to the settlements in the immediate vicinity of the James River.[32]

The English reports of the event and subsequent histories based on them have made much of the fact that the attackers mutilated some of the English corpses. Waterhouse expressed horror that the attackers "fell again upon the dead . . . defacing, dragging and mangling the dead carcasses into many pieces and carrying some parts away in derision, with base and brutish triumph." Some point to the 1622 attack as the pivotal point in a transition from traditional to total warfare among the Indians of Virginia, but a more careful examination of the event reveals that neither the killing nor the mutilation was entirely indiscriminate.

The attackers did take prisoners, and they dealt with them in a manner consistent with their Algonquian culture. Male prisoners were tortured to death, and females were forced to work as laborers in the villages. The complete annihilation of an entire settlement by the Algonquians was not without precedent. The attack on the Spanish Jesuits in the 1570s and Powhatan's destruction of the Chesapeakes just before the English arrival stand as prior examples.[33] Likewise, most of the corpses mutilated were those of leading individuals whom the attackers dealt with as if they were rival weroances. For example, the Algonquian warriors sought out George Thorpe in particular and, according to Waterhouse, "not only willfully murdered him, but cruelly and felly out of devilish malice did so many barbarous despites and foul scorns after to his dead corpse as are unbefitting to be heard by any civil ear." The attackers dealt similarly with Captain Nathaniel Powell, another leading figure in the colony. In short, Opechancanough dealt with the English the way his brother had dealt with other subordinate groups who challenged his authority. He destroyed their settlements, attempted to annihilate their warrior base, took prisoners for both torture and servitude, and mutilated their leading figures as an example to the survivors of the folly of following such men. His failure to follow up on the attack also shows that the mamanatowick still perceived the Anglo-Indian relationship in Algonquian terms. Opechancanough failed to pursue the English further because he expected them to respond like Indians and withdraw their remaining inhabitants to another area. The 1622 Algonquian attack fit traditional motivations for Indian warfare, such as revenge, punishment, access to land and resources, and compliance with the demands of spiritual forces and Algonquian masculinity.[34]

While the surprise attack did not drive the English from Virginia, it nonetheless brought tremendous repercussions that fostered considerable change in both the colony's social makeup and its official policy toward the Powhatan chiefdom. The abandonment of nearly every settlement beyond Jamestown brought financial ruin to many of the adventurers who were in many cases in the early stages of establishing themselves as tobacco planters there. Faced with the loss of their lands and crops, these men were forced into tenancy. According to one contemporary source, "Every man of meaner sort, who before lived well by their labour upon their owne land," being forced to forsake their houses (which were vary farre scattered) & to joyne themselves to some great mans plantation: where . . . they are ready to perish for want of necessaries." Many of these newly destitute no doubt found themselves forced into servitude on the plantations of the emerging tobacco elite. The resumption of hostilities also ended the colony's policy of establishing towns as the preferred method of extending English control. After this, dispersed plantations constituted the norm and thus further encouraged the amassing of large tobacco-producing estates.[35]

The 1622 attack also wrought a shift in the colony's official policy toward the Powhatan chiefdom. In the wake of the attack, those who governed Virginia had concluded that they would have to force the Indians of Virginia to accept the imposition of English cultural and societal norms. The Algonquians had once again refused the supposed benefits of English civilization and Christianity when offered to them by Virginia's leaders, and, once again, these same rulers declared war on them and removed the shackles of restraint they had placed on the populace since the marriage of John Rolfe and Pocahontas. A passage from Waterhouse's account sums up the furor unleashed by the Virginians: "Victory of them may be gained many ways; by force, by surprise, by famine in burning their corn, by destroying and burning their boats, canoes and houses, by breaking their fishing weirs, by assailing them in their huntings, whereby they get the greatest part of their sustenance in winter, by pursuing and chasing them with our horses, and blood-hounds to draw after them, and mastiffs to tear them, which take this naked, tanned, deformed savages, for no other than wild beasts."[36]

In the late summer of 1622, Christopher Brooke, an English politician and poet of some renown at the time, published "A Poem on the Late Massacre in Virginia." Brooke's epic poem joined other works like that of Edward Waterhouse quoted earlier, as well as those by John Smith and others, as part of a widespread literary response to the devastating surprise attack in March of that year by the Powhatan chiefdom against the English colony in Virginia. In part of the poem, Brooke gave voice to a sentiment that pervaded nearly all of the major works dedicated to the event. Specifically, he called for the extermination of the Powhatans:

> Let me impress your hearts with my sad pen;
> And as ye are discern'd from Common men,
> So fleet not with their Stream, let these excite
> Your military Judgments to give light
> In safe securing of the residue,
> Or extirpation of that Indian crew.[37]

In another section of the poem addressed directly to the colony's governor, Sir Francis Wyatt, Brooke implored him to "inflame thy heart, take spleen," and engage in an "expiable war unto the dead" with the Algonquians of Virginia.[38]

As noted, Brooke was not the only person to espouse such a response to the Powhatan attack. John Smith, in *The General History of Virginia, New England, and the Somer Isles*, stated it much less poetically but every bit as forthrightly. In the fourth book of that work he characterized the attack as "good for the Plantation, because now we have just cause to destroy them by all meanes possible."[39] The Second Anglo-Powhatan War resurrected and broadened the processes by which many Virginians came to believe in their right to decide for themselves, without elite sanction, when lethal force might be employed against the Native Americans of Virginia.

Within weeks of the attack, former governor Sir George Yeardley and others led retaliatory expeditions against the Weyanocks in which they burned towns and fields and beheaded the few Indians they actually encountered. The English launched other attacks against the Rappahannocks, Nansemonds, and Powhatans before the year was out. An incident along the Potomac River epitomizes the free rein with which the leadership of the colony allowed all Virginians to visit violence upon the area's Algonquians. Isaac Madison, an emissary sent to the Patawomecks to trade for desperately needed corn, instead killed nearly forty of them, including women and children, whom he suspected of plotting against him. This act has even more significance than the other reprisals against the Algonquians because the Patawomecks had not participated in Opechancanough's attack and had in fact declared themselves neutral. While the government of the colony had staunchly encouraged any and all means necessary to defeat the Powhatans, there is no indication that the sanction extended beyond them. Therefore, Madison's assumption of the power to take the war to a group that had not participated in Opechancough's attack represents the way the removal of all restraint against the Powhatans had a kind of "Pandora's box"–like potential to be interpreted as blanket permission for violent campaigns against any and all Indians. Though this hatred of all Indians represented a rather uncontrollable weapon, its effectiveness could not be argued. In January 1623 the governing council wrote to the Virginia Company in London that they had killed more Indians in the last nine months of 1622 than "hath been slain since the beginning of the colony." It was only the first wave in a more than twenty-year tidal wave of bloodshed that would eventually destroy the Powhatan chiefdom as a viable political organization and transform heretofore sporadic notions of a tacit permission to use violence against Indians into a free-born and inviolable right.[40]

The failure of the English to relocate as Opechancanough had expected, coupled with the ferocious retaliatory strikes the colonists launched against the Algonquians, dealt a serious physical and psychological blow to the leaders of the chiefdom. During the spring of 1623, the Powhatan chiefdom sent a series of messages to the Virginia government that seemed to indicate that Opechancanough's hold on the chiefdom's leadership might have been slipping away as a result of his failure to drive the English from Tsenacommacah. In April, the governing council wrote the Virginia Company in London that they had received a message from the "Great King," stating "blood enough had already been shed on both sides." The message proposed a peace settlement in which the Algonquians could return and plant crops in the fields burned by the English in exchange for the release of all English prisoners taken in the March 1622 raid.

The next month the council received a message from Opitchapam, the titular leader of the chiefdom, who promised to "deliver all the rest of the captive English he had and would also deliver his brother Opechancanough who was the author of the massacre into the hands of the English either alive or dead." While the records do not state the exact identity of the "Great King" who sent the first message, the available evidence points to Opitchapam as well. Despite Opechancanough's

FIGURE 3.2. *The Indian Massacre of 1622,* by Matthaus Merian. Courtesy, Colonial Williamsburg Foundation.

day-to-day leadership of the chiefdom, Opitchapam still held the title of mamanatowick, or "great king." Furthermore, both letters proposed peace with the Virginians predicated on the release of English prisoners. The use of the phrase "all the rest of the captive English" seems to indicate a continuing dialogue on this subject. Since the second message is attributable to Opitchapam, it seems logical that he sent the first one as well. Finally, while Opechancanough may have sent the first letter in an attempt to lure the English into a trap, the exact opposite actually occurred. The English took advantage of the messages to spring a deadly surprise on the Algonquians. Therefore, the messages seem consistent with Opitchapam's outlook as opposed to that of his younger brother.[41]

Regardless of the source of the offers, the English never intended to agree to them. Instead, they seized upon the second offer to continue their quest for revenge. In March 1623 George Sandys outlined the strategy the Virginians would employ: "The Great King now sues for peace, and offers a restitution of his prisoners, for whose sakes we seem to be inclinable thereunto, and will try if we can make them as secure as we were that we may follow their example in destroying them." In a letter to Virginia Company superiors back in London, the governing council outlined in more detail its plans to lull the Algonquians into a false sense of security: "By holding them in a long hope of peace, we have come to knowledge of their places of residence." Furthermore, the Virginians had timed their plans to coincide with the ripening of the Indians' corn. This meant the Algonquians would not leave their villages until after the harvest, and thus this time the colonists would find people in the villages they attacked instead of empty dwellings. With the Algonquians thinking the conflict had ended and tied to their villages, the council considered it a perfect time to deliver "shortly a blow, that shall near or altogether ruin them."[42]

The colonists delivered that blow on May 22, 1623, near the Potomac River. On that day the English sent Captain William Tucker and a party of men to attend a peace negotiation and prisoner exchange intended to end the yearlong war. The English, however, did not intend to actually enter into a peace agreement with the Indians. Instead, Tucker brought poisoned wine that he deftly served the Indians at the conclusion of the false negotiations. According to one account, Tucker poisoned nearly 200 Indians and killed 50 more in physical combat. The party then shot the 2 Indian leaders present, whom they identified as the weroance of the Chiskiack and "the Great King Apochanzion."[43] Finally, as they left they scalped several of the now seriously ill survivors and returned to Jamestown, from whence they planned to "go upon the Warraskoyacks and Nansemonds to cut down their corn and put them to the sword." Later in the summer they moved against nearly all of the James River groups, burning every village and crop they found, but these raids netted few Indian deaths as the Algonquians generally fled their towns and dispersed into the woods as soon as the English raiding parties arrived. This successful short-term strategy only bought the James River Indians time, however. The winter of 1623–24 brought tremendous starvation and exposure to the elements as the effects of the English "scorched earth" policy took deadly effect.[44]

In 1624 the Virginia assembly added a legal front to its military campaigns against the Indians. In an effort to further stoke the fires of settler animosity, the assembly, as one of its first acts, declared March 22, the anniversary of the Powhatan attack, a colony-wide holiday. Another statute passed that year forbade all trade with Indians, while another required that all houses "be palisaded for defense against the Indians." One particular statute affords a telling glimpse into both the kind of violence encouraged against Indians and the differing interpretations of the Anglo-Powhatan War's relationship to the social structure: "That at the beginning of July next the inhabitants of every corporation shall fall upon their adjoining savages as we did the last year, those that shall be hurt upon service to be cured at the public charge; in case any be lamed to be maintained by the country according to his person and quality." While many Virginians increasingly viewed such authorizations not as authorizations but instead as acknowledgment of their freeborn right to destroy Indians, the burgesses who wrote the statute attempted to simultaneously exterminate the Indians who had heretofore resisted their right to rule and remind those they governed that rank and quality still necessitated separate statuses and rights for each respective social order.[45]

The Crown dissolved the Virginia Company in 1624 because of its failure to deliver on the promised well-ordered and profitable colony, as well as its increasing dependence on tobacco (a somewhat controversial commodity in England) for sustenance. The colony devolved to royal control, but the war against the Indians continued. That same year also saw the only pitched battle recorded between Algonquian warriors and colonial militiamen. In July the Pamunkeys and the English waged a two-day battle in which several hundred Indian bowmen engaged fewer than 100 Virginians armed with guns. The English continued their scorched earth policy by distracting the Algonquian warriors, while a small party of Englishmen sneaked behind Pamunkey lines and burned their cornfields. When they saw their burning fields, the Pamunkeys halted their offensive and the English withdrew, satisfied that the coming winter would bring more privation to a people whose numbers had already dwindled considerably since they nearly annihilated the entire colony in 1622.[46]

The next two years witnessed only small skirmishes, with neither side gaining a clear advantage. The combined effect of multiple years of burned crops and their defeat in the July 1624 battle severely hampered Virginia Algonquians' ability to feed their families, let alone support major attacks. For their part, the Virginians had nearly exhausted their entire store of gunpowder in their earlier reprisals against the Algonquians. According to one account, powder was in such short supply that the colonists could barely "defend our houses, much less to persecute our revenge upon the savages." Despite these appeals to royal officials in England, the Virginians had to wait until 1627 to continue their extermination campaign against the Powhatan chiefdom. In the summer of that year, they attacked the remnants of the Chickahominies, Appamattucks, Powhatans, Warraskoyacks, Weyanocks, and Nansemonds along the James River and prepared for an assault on the York River groups. These assaults, however, produced little in the way of results. The Second Anglo-Powhatan War seemed to have settled into a kind of stalemate punctuated by periodic but indecisive raids.[47]

While neither side scored a decisive military victory in 1627, the year brought one development that further supports the argument that many in Virginia had come to believe in their right to engage in violence against Native Americans. In January the English decided to occupy a former Chiskiack village near the York River. The former inhabitants of the village had moved away to avoid English attacks. While the decision to occupy the village means little in and of itself, the eventual decision to entice settlers with free land represents a pivotal moment in the social history of seventeenth-century Virginia. By communally distributing Indian land acquired through the extermination campaigns of the 1620s to any Virginians who would settle there, Virginia's leadership unwittingly created a potentially dangerous expectation on the part of many Virginians. Specifically, the program signaled that not only did their leaders agree with them that extermination represented the most effective policy of dealing with Indians but also that all colonists would have unfettered access to all lands gained from such a policy.[48]

However, the remaining years of the war seem to indicate a desire among Virginians who controlled the colony's Council of State to rein in these ideas of unmitigated warfare against all Indians. As discussed in greater detail later, this coincided with a period in which those who had gained the most from the tobacco boom and who likewise held a stranglehold on the highest offices in the colony used their power to pursue their own private interests "with little interference from the traditional restraints imposed on a responsible ruling class."[49]

The distribution of the lands acquired during this round of attacks also provides a glimpse into the intentions of elite Virginians regarding who should benefit from a Virginian victory. Members of the tobacco elite usually commanded the forces that attacked Algonquian villages during the Anglo-Powhatan Wars, but the makeup of the forces they led was decidedly less elite. This pattern held true in the late 1620s and early 1630s. For example, William Claiborne, a prominent Virginia official since the early 1620s, led the force that demolished the Algonquian town of Cantauncack during this period. After the war, the government rewarded him by granting him the entire tract of land on which the village had been located.[50]

Despite the signing of a peace treaty in September 1632, sporadic eruptions of individual violence persisted. The available evidence indicates that these acts were often perpetrated by Virginians outside the inner circle of government who often lived in the frontier areas closest to the Powhatan chiefdom. During this period, Virginia's population kept growing, and the colonists continued to push their settlements deeper into Algonquian territory. As had been the case in the past, those with the least to lose served as the trailbreakers and shock troops for these new settlements. As a result of these circumstances, the government endeavored to keep whites and Indians from coming into contact with one another. At the same time as the signing of the peace treaty in 1632, the Virginia General Assembly codified this desire for the separation of frontier settlers and Indians:

IT is ordered, That no person or persons shall dare to speak or parley with the Indians either in the woods or in any plantation if it can possibly be avoided by any means. But if any Indian shall voluntarily press upon any in the woods, or into any plantation, as soon as can be, they shall bring them to the commander, or give the commander notice thereof, upon penalty of a month's service for any freeman offending, and twenty stripes for any servant. But for the planters of the Easterne Shore, the commanders are required to observe all good terms of amity, and that they cause the planters nevertheless to stand upon their guard, and not to suffer the Indians to . . . abode in their houses, and if any English without leave resort unto their towns, the commanders are to bind them over to the next quarter court.[51]

In addition, the 1632 assembly took the power to make decisions regarding military action against Indians out of the hands of the populace and placed it under the purview of government-appointed commanders. These developments reflect the beginnings of a shift in elite thinking about the role of Native people in Virginia's future. Even in the days immediately following the 1622 attack, the surviving members of the Council of State—most notably men such as George Sandys, Francis West, Francis Wyatt, and George Yeardley—rejected the oft-proposed solution of completely exterminating the Powhatans. In fact, during the course of the Second Anglo-Powhatan War, the survival of the Powhatans as a cohesive people was tantamount to these men's plans for the colony. Instead of engaging in large-scale campaigns designed to destroy the entire chiefdom, the members of the Council of State, each with his own private army made up mostly of men made landless by Opechancanough's attack, opted for a strategy of small-scale raiding. This strategy represents yet another result of the nearly simultaneous occurrence of the beginning of the tobacco boom and the Second Anglo-Powhatan War. Such a strategy allowed the "chieftains," as the men of the council came to be called in reference to their leadership of private armies, to weaken the Powhatans and thus drive them further from colonial settlement, as well as to take their corn. Taking the Powhatans' corn during raids then allowed them to devote all of their land and servants to the production of tobacco, which in turn fed a tremendous increase in the amount of tobacco produced during the decade.

According to J. Frederick Fausz, "With captured Powhatan corn keeping them alive, and fear of Powhatan attacks keeping them in line, English laborers cultivated record amounts of tobacco for the Council oligarchs throughout the 1620s, ever increasing the power and profits of the Lords of those Lands."[52] Now that the war was over, Virginia's leaders realized that melding poor Englishmen and Indians into one laboring class was impossible. These men had also begun to enter into various trade relationships with Indian groups both inside and outside the Powhatan chiefdom. Finally, they knew that peace would ease the fear of Indian attacks that Fausz credits with keeping their servants and tenants docile during the 1620s. Servants, tenants, and other non-elites might now be much more willing to challenge the chieftains' authority. Eventually, Virginia's leaders hit on a solution to all of these issues, which required the separation of frontier whites and Indians and the passage of new laws designed to circumscribe the autonomy of lesser individuals.[53]

Over the next twelve years, the assembly continued to take steps aimed at curtailing lower-class autonomy and reinforcing a hierarchical social structure. In 1633 the assembly members completely banned "mechanics" from planting tobacco. It seems they intended that such activity should remain the prerogative of the elite; allowing the rougher sort to participate would dilute elite ranks with pretenders to status. The 1630s also witnessed the prohibition of nearly all trade with Indians (except that expressly permitted by the governor). The result of these two enactments was to effectively straightjacket many Virginians without the land base with which to engage in tobacco production into a life of manual labor, with no hope of advancement. Trade with Indians and tobacco planting represented the first- and second-best routes, respectively, to wealth and status in Virginia. Thus, elite Virginians attempted to monopolize them.[54]

This program fit a broader pattern throughout the 1620s and early 1630s in which Virginia's planter leaders attempted to consolidate their hold over the colony. The same 1632 assembly instituted a one-month jail term for any workmen who failed to finish the job they had contracted for and punished drunkenness by fining the offender 5 shillings. The assembly set the penalty for swearing at 1 shilling. In addition to these prohibitions on common plebeian behavior, the assembly members granted tremendous privileges to themselves. One small enactment from that session granted that "all the old planters that were here before or came in at the last coming of Sir Thomas Gates shall be exempted from their personal service to the wars and any public charges." The assembly took further advantage of the opportunity the newly minted peace afforded them by decreeing that the market determine the price of corn, that all fields be enclosed, and that no Virginian "presume to be disobedient to the present government, nor servants to their private officers, masters and overseers, at their uttermost peril." As mentioned, these 1632 enactments represent the culmination of a pattern of aggrandizement among a very wealthy clique who had used the tobacco boom, the war with the Powhatans, and the dissolution of the Virginia Company to establish their dominance over Virginia's social, economic, and political affairs. While many of the original councilors who had prosecuted the war against the Powhatans from the start were dead or gone from the colony, a group of Virginians who had served as some of the chieftains' best lieutenants, such as William Tucker, Samuel Matthews, and William Claiborne, now took prominent parts in the governing of the colony and the continuing pattern of merging "public service with private gain, [which] established the prototype for the seventeenth-century Virginia Council."[55]

As early as the mid-1620s, it had become obvious to observers from various backgrounds, both within and beyond the colony, that Virginia's leaders were fast transforming it into their own fiefdom at the expense of company profits, traditional English rights, and the opportunities for advancement promised the lesser individuals who made up the majority of the colony's population. In 1624 a colonist named William Tyler was brought before the Governor's Council for, among other things, publicly stating his belief "that poor men could hardly get any right, and that the great men would hold all together." Tyler had also been reported to say that had he been important enough to sit on the council, he would not have done so, as he questioned whether he could live with himself if he engaged in the same kind of corruption he felt the council was party to.[56]

It is not just from those outside the official levers of power that we find evidence of the bacchanal of self-interest a small group of elite Virginians carried out in the early days of the tobacco boom. In April 1623 Edwin Sandys's brother George, who was serving as treasurer of the colony, wrote to John Ferrar regarding business Sandys had conducted in Virginia on Ferrar's behalf. Among other things, Sandys noted that those tenants still under the control of the company, as opposed to private planters, were in the worst shape of any because they were assigned to the lands private planters had worn out through successive years of tobacco planting. Hence the tenants who were supposed to produce wealth for the company were placed on lands that were completely unable to do so. All of this, of course, was designed to maximize the private gain of individual planters at the expense of the company and the colony in general.[57]

This fixation on the accumulation of laborers eventually led Virginians to view a servant as "a machine to make tobacco for somebody else," in a "labor system that treated men as things."[58] Outsiders also noticed the dehumanization of labor under way in Virginia during the tobacco boom. According to one Dutch ship captain, Virginia tobacco planters even used servants as the stakes in card games.[59] Whereas the climate and disease environment had combined to make Virginia a death trap in its earliest days, the lure of tobacco profit was doing the same by the 1620s.

Despite the ocean that separated them, the Privy Council also began to express concerns that Virginia's government was being used solely as an instrument to further the tobacco interests of those who controlled it rather than advancing the will of the company or the good of the colony. In a series of instructions to the Virginia Company on July 2, 1623, the Privy Council, among other things, decreed that the government of Virginia should cut the number of men engaged in tobacco cultivation by as much as two-thirds and redirect much of that labor to the erection of public works and expeditions designed to find a water passage to Asia. However, the Privy Council further commanded, "Provisions necessary for food [should] be cared for before matters of profit."[60] In other words, not only were far fewer workers to be used for tobacco production, but they were also to be employed in the production of food first. The Privy Council would likely not have taken the extraordinary step of issuing such specific directives to the Virginia Company were it not quite concerned about the activities of the colony's government.

Even before these orders were issued, the leadership of the Virginia colony was aware that the Privy Council was fast running out of patience. In an effort to place themselves back in their superiors' good graces, the council members sought to blame others in the colony for Virginia's condition. Specifically, the councilors complained of "diverse contracts made wholly without our consents . . . by avaricious and unconscionable men intending their own private lucre and gain."[61]

The councilors neglected to mention their own role in the mad dash for land and servants that created the conditions about which Butler complained. In 1625, two years after Butler had "unmasked" their greed, fifteen Virginians owned ten or more laborers. During the 1620s, eight of these fifteen men rotated on and off the Governor's Council, while three of them took turns in the Governor's chair.[62]

From these positions of power, they found it easy to manipulate both the labor supply and the colony's legal system to their own ends. The fate of 50 tenants shipped to Virginia aboard the *Bona Nova* provides a striking example of these men's brazen appropriation of workers intended to labor for the Virginia Company. When the ship arrived in November 1619, it carried 100 tenants, all of whom were intended to labor for the common good of the plantation on company-held lands. However, upon their arrival the leaders of the colony quickly parceled out the 50 they considered the hardiest and set them to work on their private plantations. The Privy Council soon began receiving reports about the way these tenants had been "unmercifully used" by their new "masters." The Virginia Council showed little inclination to rectify the situation.[63]

In addition to engrossing as many servants as possible, Abraham Peirsey, Captain William Tucker, and Edward Blaney—all of whom served multiple terms on the Governor's Council—found opportunities to gouge their fellow Virginians as well as the Virginia Company through their merchant activities. Peirsey had originally come to Virginia as the company's cape merchant. In that position he controlled the colony's magazine, a sort of general store set up by the Virginia Company to provide goods and supplies to the colonists at as low a cost as possible while still deriving a profit for the company. During Peirsey's tenure, he seems to have disregarded both requirements of the job, selling the items at exorbitant prices yet reporting a loss and never paying Virginia Company investors back for the purchase of the goods. Yet in the 1625 census, he and former governor George Yeardley were tied atop the list with thirty-nine laborers each. In 1623, at a meeting in London convened by the Earl of Southampton for the purpose of inquiring into the condition of the colony, one member of the company noted that though Peirsey had arrived in Virginia with very little, he had fast "become exceeding rich" and that Peirsey's means of gaining such wealth bore further investigation. If that investigation ever occurred, it appears that nothing of consequence came of it. Despite Peirsey's supposed "failure" to produce a profit for the company during his time as cape merchant, he died in 1626 with what one Virginian described as "the best Estate that was ever yet known in Virginia."[64]

Edward Blaney, who became cape merchant in 1620, quickly proved that he had learned much from his predecessor. Like Peirsey, he also died in 1626, having never paid for the goods he sold from the magazine. He also successfully claimed the estate of a man he was not related to but who bore the same last name as his wife's first husband. Blaney, while less successful than Peirsey, controlled the labor of seventeen men when he died.[65]

William Tucker, who first came to the colony as a ship captain, eventually contracted with John Ferrar, a member of the Virginia Company, to sell goods on the latter's behalf in Virginia. By 1622 Ferrar was suing Tucker for his failure to provide either the profits from the sale of the goods or the goods themselves. Ten years later, Tucker was still up to his old tricks. In a 1632 petition to the Privy Council, the House of Burgesses complained that it had "long groaned under the cruel dealings [of] unconscionable merchants who . . . have engaged the inhabitants in debts of tobacco, to the value of almost their entire crop." The burgesses added that "among [those] whom we have good cause to complain of [is] Captain Tucker, who hath far exceeded all other merchants."[66]

One of the men Sir George Sandys (illegally) controlled provided this evaluation of the relationship between powerful planters like Sandys and those who toiled under them: "He maketh us serve him whether wee will or no and how to help it we do not know for he beareth all the sway."[67] According to the available records, the man who offered this assessment of life under George Sandys's supervision was a freeman whom Sandys forced into servitude. In addition, Sandys counted among his thirty-seven servants in 1625 at least sixteen company tenants he had simply appropriated for his personal use. Though he cited the allotment due him as treasurer of the colony as the basis for pilfering these laborers, he refused to relinquish them when he left that office.[68]

One of his contemporaries once described three-time governor Sir George Yeardley as a "right worthy statesman, for his own profit."[69] Were it not for the nefarious means with which he accomplished the feat, Yeardley might be regarded as one of America's first rags-to-riches stories. Having arrived in Virginia with next to nothing, Yeardley was the first governor to enjoy the 3,000 acres of land and 100 tenants the Virginia Company decided to assign governors in lieu of a salary derived from taxes. When he left the governor's office (and moved seamlessly into a seat on the Governor's Council) in 1621, he refused to return more than half of the tenants. When pressed by the Virginia Company to force Yeardley to return them, the council responded that "as for the rest of the tenants Sir George Yeardley denyeth to make them good. And sayeth that having made no strong agreement with you at any time he holdeth not himself tied unto it . . . Now seeing Sir George Yeardley denyeth that there was any agreement made between you and him for the making good of the 100 tenants upon the governor's land, we have forborne to compel him thereunto."[70] Yeardley served as governor again in 1627 and died in office, but not without first engendering a host of complaints regarding his constant attempts to seize other planters' servants.[71]

Perhaps no example better represents the machinations of Virginia's elite planters to fulfill their own private interests and their elite brethren's penchant for looking the other way than the case of former governor Dr. John Pott and his successor, John Harvey. Harvey, the first governor not to be drawn from the ranks of the now entrenched planter elite, succeeded Pott in 1630 and faced an uphill battle from the start. Upon his arrival, he was bombarded with numerous complaints regarding Pott's management of the colony during the previous year. Pott was accused of allowing a convicted murderer to go free because it profited him to do so. He was also charged with "cutting out the marks of other men's neat cattle and marking them for himself with his own hands, whereby he hath gotten into a great stock of cattle."[72] In addition, Harvey discovered that Pott had prevented William Capps, the king's agent in the colony, from returning to England because Pott and the rest of the council feared that Capps would expose their many acts of self-indulgence and fraud.[73]

By this point, even King Charles had come to suspect that the members of Virginia's tobacco elite were transforming the colony into their personal domain subject to no rule of law save their own personal desires. In his instructions to the newly appointed governor, he ordered Harvey first and foremost to investigate Capps's failure to provide the reports on Virginia's condition that the king had commanded him to submit in 1627. The king provided Harvey with specific instructions if it turned out that any member of the council was responsible for hindering Capps in his duties or perpetuating any other acts of oppression against the general populace of the colony: "And if any of his Majesties' Council fall out to be the offenders to proceed the more roundly against them, their offenses being of the worst example, and if any shall have given just cause for it, to sequester or remove them from the Council as he shall think fittest."[74]

After conducting an investigation into Pott's activities, Harvey removed him from the council, placed him under house arrest, and ordered him to repay all the government monies he had taken for himself.[75] Of course, by prosecuting Pott, Harvey aligned himself in direct opposition to the interests of the planters who dominated his government. After all, if he were to punish Pott for his illicit activities, what would stop him from coming after the rest of them? In addition, before his arrival in Virginia, Harvey had been a vocal member of the parliamentary faction that had brought about the end of the Virginia Company and openly called into question all grants of land made during the company's tenure. His outsider status, his alignment with forces already identified as openly opposed to the interests of the planter elite, and his actions concerning the Pott case assured that his tenure as governor would not go smoothly. The relationship between Harvey and the planter elite continued to decline over the next five years as he tried to diversify the colony's economy by decreasing its dependence on tobacco. In 1635 the members of the council rose up against Harvey and imprisoned him. The musketeers who surrounded his house the night of his imprisonment were commanded by John Pott.[76] Harvey returned to England, cleared his name, and forced his accusers to likewise return to England and defend themselves. When they did so, they managed to damage Harvey's reputation so drastically that he left public life in disgrace.[77]

Virginia's emerging tobacco elite dealt with challenges to their power from below with a similar ferocity. In response to his criticism of the governor in 1624, the council ordered that one man "be disarmed, and have his arms broken and his tongue bored though with an awl." After they deemed this punishment not sufficient, the man was then forced to run a gauntlet of forty soldiers before finally being banished from the settlement.[78] Similarly, in 1630, "for scandalous speeches against Governor and Councell," Daniel Cugley was sentenced to be pilloried.[79]

When insulted by a man named John Heny, Captain William Tucker convinced his fellow council members to sentence the man to sixty lashes and a fine of 100 pounds of tobacco, payable to Tucker, of course. During the same council session a man was sentenced to a day in the pillory, a year's servitude, and the amputation of his ears for words he uttered against the leadership while on a boat off the coast of Canada.[80]

By the mid-1630s, the group of men who had benefited most from the now decade-old tobacco boom had largely succeeded in consolidating their power. They held the majority of the colony's land and servants and controlled the levers of power through their monopoly over the Governor's Council and their control of the judicial apparatuses. This allowed them to dominate the colony's agenda during the following decades in such a way that historian Bernard Bailyn has characterized the major public issues that arose in at least the thirty years after the dissolution of the Virginia Company as stemming from the pursuit of the tobacco elite's private interests.[81] In the words of Richard Crocker, these men governed the colony solely by dealing "upon nothing but extortion," for which assessment he was imprisoned, pilloried with nails driven through his ears, and fined 300 pounds of tobacco.[82]

While Nathaniel Butler's 1622 report on conditions in Virginia had contributed to the downfall of the Virginia Company, it seems that the iniquities it highlighted regarding the "private ends" of the Virginia leadership had only increased by the mid-1630s.[83] During the second two decades of the Virginia colony, the elite tobacco planters had capitalized on the displacements of the Powhatan surprise attack in 1622, the rise of tobacco as a staple crop, the fall of the Virginia Company, the lack of Crown oversight that followed, and the steady decline of the Powhatan chiefdom to make for themselves a virtual kingdom that existed seemingly for their personal enrichment. However, from the beginning of the venture, many Virginians of lesser means, be they servants, tenants, or smaller landholders, arrived in the colony with a very different vision of Virginia's future and their role in it.

NOTES

1. I paraphrase in the chapter title from the commission granted by Charles I to William Berkeley naming him governor of Virginia. While these phrases for the most part represent the standardized language used in such royal commissions and are taken from a commission issued a decade later, they nonetheless provide a rather accurate summation of the years under investigation here. See Warren Billings, ed., *The Papers of Sir William Berkeley, 1605–1677* (Richmond: Library of Virginia, 2007), 25.

2. Susan Myra Kingsbury, ed., *The Records of the Virginia Company of London* (Washington, DC: Government Printing Office, 1935), 2:374–76.

3. Nicholas Spencer to Lord Culpeper, August 6, 1676, CO 1/49, 107; Richard Hakluyt, *A Discourse of Western Planting* (London: Hakluyt Society, 1993), 212; Robert Johnson, "Nova Britannia" (London: Samuel Macham, 1609; reprint, Cambridge: Da Capo, 1969), 19; Robert Rich, "News from Virginia," in *A Good Speed to Virginia,* ed. Wesley Frank Craven (New York: Scholars Facsimiles and Reprints, 1937), 5; Robert Johnson, *The New Life of Virginia: Declaring the Former Successes and Present Estate of That Plantation, Being the Second Part of Nova Britannia* (London: Feliz Kyngston, 1612; reprint, Cambridge: Da Capo, 1971), 10; Peter Linebaugh and Marcus Rediker, *The Many-Headed Hydra: Sailors, Slaves, Commoners, and the Hidden History of the Revolutionary Atlantic* (Boston: Beacon, 2000), 13–16; "John Beaulieu to William Trumbull, November 30, 1609; December 7, 1609" and "Pedro de Zuniga to Philip III, December 31, 1609," both in *The Jamestown Voyages under the First Charter,* ed.

Philip Barbour (New York: Cambridge University Press, 1969), 2:287–89. See also Philip Levy, "A New Look at an Old Wall: Indians, Englishmen, Landscape and the 1634 Palisade at Middle Plantation," *Virginia Magazine of History and Biography* 112, no. 3 (2004): 226–65. Levy provides an excellent analysis of the way the 1634 palisade at Middle Plantation existed as a symbolic marker of the emerging planter elite's success at driving the Powhatan chiefdom out of the area and therefore opening up Middle Plantation for lucrative tobacco cultivation. I contend that such symbols of elite success only strengthened the desire of Virginia's less fortunate to emulate the tobacco elite's formula of Indian dispossession and tobacco cultivation if the opportunity presented itself. For an argument that cites a desire to establish the proper authority in Virginia as a means of winning popular support for the colony's government, see Alexander B. Haskell, " 'The Affections of the People': Ideology and the Politics of State Building in Colonial Virginia, 1607–1754" (PhD diss., Johns Hopkins University, Baltimore, MD, 2004). I, however, see the personal interests of Virginia's leaders during this period coinciding with this goal of state building; see Introduction, note 24. See also Warren Billings, Thad Tate, and John Selby, *Colonial Virginia: A History* (White Plains, NY: KTO, 1986), 5; Anthony Parent, *Foul Means: The Formation of a Slave Society in Virginia, 1660–1740* (Chapel Hill: University of North Carolina Press, 2003), 32–40. As discussed earlier, Parent places the rise of this planter elite much later in the century, whereas I see the initial stirrings of planter elite class-consciousness as early as the 1620s. Perhaps the explanation for this difference between us lies in our particular definitions of class and class-consciousness. Parent sees class and class-consciousness in a more classic Marxist formulation, as "determined by the relations of production, [in which] a group's status, cultural attributes, and interests flow from economic conditions. The chief classes in a society are the owners of the means of production and the actual producers" (ibid., 3). The definition I am employing here flows more from the work of E. P. Thompson, which both relies more on human agency and allows for the existence of a class-consciousness in which factors other than relationship to the ownership of the means of production are determinative. In Thompson's words, "Class happens when some men, as a result of common experience (inherited or shared) feel and articulate the identity of their interests as between themselves, and as against other men whose interests are different from (and usually opposed to) theirs." While productive relations may largely determine those interests, other factors such as political power, gender, religion, geography, ethnicity, and race, to name just a few, can also govern them. See E. P. Thompson, *The Making of the English Working Class* (New York: Vintage, 1966), 9. For more on the particular definition of class and class-consciousness at play here, see Introduction, note 11, as well as Gary Nash, *The Urban Crucible: The Northern Seaports and the Origins of the American Revolution* (Cambridge: Harvard University Press, 1986), xii; E. P. Thompson, "Eighteenth-Century English Society: Class Struggle without Class?" *Social History* 3 (1978): 149.

4. Daniel Richter, *Facing East from Indian Country: A Native History of Early America* (Cambridge: Harvard University Press, 2001), 76–77.

5. Ibid., 78.

6. Ralph Hamor, *A True Discourse of the Present State of Virginia* (Richmond: Virginia State Library, 1957), 2, 11. For a fuller discussion of how such an assumption squares with sixteenth-century elite English assumptions regarding the place of Native Americans in their future colonies, see Ethan A. Schmidt, "The Well-Ordered Commonwealth: Humanism, Utopian Perfectionism and the English Colonization of the Americas," *Atlantic Studies* 7, no. 3 (September 2010): 309–28; Andrew Fitzmaurice, *Humanism and America: An Intellectual History of English Colonization, 1500–1625* (New York: Cambridge University Press, 2003).

7. Alexander Whitaker, *Good Newes from Virginia* (London: Felix Kyngston and William Welby, 1613), 40.

8. Samuel Purchas, *Purchas His Pilgrims* (New York: Macmillan, 1905), 19:117–22; Helen Rountree, *Pocahontas's People: The Powhatan Indians of Virginia through Four Centuries* (Norman: University of Oklahoma Press, 1990), 64.

9. While Opitchapam was the next brother in the matrilineage and therefore acceded to the title of mamanatowick, he was regarded as too old and mentally unstable to lead the chiefdom. Opechancanough seems to have made nearly all major decisions for his older brother until Opitchapam's death sometime in the 1630s. At that time, Opechancanough exercised both titular and practical leadership of the chiefdom. See Rountree, *Pocahontas's People,* 66, 81.

10. Purchas, *Purchas His Pilgrims,* 19:117–22; Rountree, *Pocahontas's People,* 64, 69; Helen Rountree, *The Powhatan Indians of Virginia: Their Traditional Culture* (Norman: University of Oklahoma Press, 1989), 118.

11. James Horn, *Adapting to a New World: English Society in the Seventeenth-Century Chesapeake* (Chapel Hill: University of North Carolina Press, 1994), 136; Bernard Bailyn, "Politics and Social Structure in Virginia," in *Seventeenth-Century America: Essays in Colonial History,* ed. James Morton Smith (Chapel Hill: University of North Carolina Press, 1959), 90–115.

12. The historical literature centering on what exactly motivated the English colonization of Virginia and beyond is varied, but for the most part it tends to agree that what those who planned and led the Virginia enterprise wanted most was stability and order. Whether they prized that order for military reasons, as argued by Stephen Saunders Webb in *The Governor's General: The English Army and the Definition of the Empire, 1569–1681* (Chapel Hill: University of North Carolina Press, 1979), for intellectual reasons, as espoused by Andrew Fitzmaurice in *Humanism and America,* or possibly for a combination of both, as I have previously argued in Ethan A. Schmidt, "The Well-Ordered Commonwealth: Humanism, Utopian Perfectionism, and the English Colonization of the Americas," *Atlantic Studies* 7, no. 3 (September 2010): 309–28, the end result is the same. That is, they prized a stable and ordered society above all else. Michael Leroy Oberg's *Dominion and Civility: English Imperialism and Native America, 1585–1685* (Ithaca, NY: Cornell University Press, 1999) argues

along similar lines that English colonial planners were most concerned with creating stability on their frontiers for the purposes of expanding commerce, striking a blow against their European foes, and bringing Christianity to Native people. Unlike the other works cited, he stresses the division between English metropolitans and colonial frontier residents as the definitive relationship in this formulation. At its most basic root, however, I favor the notion that individual economic gain and the need to provide profits to investors and the government represented the underlying reasons for this need for order in Virginia.

13. Edmund S. Morgan, *American Slavery, American Freedom: The Ordeal of Colonial Virginia* (New York, W. W. Norton, 1975), 108; "John Pory, Secretary of Virginia, to Sir Dudley Carleton, 1619," in *Narratives of Early Virginia, 1606–1625,* ed. Lyon Gardiner Tyler (New York: Barnes and Noble, 1946), 284.

14. Horn, *Adapting to a New World,* 142; Hugh Jones, "Part of a Letter from the Reverend Mr. Hugh Jones to the Reverend Dr. Benjamin Woodroofe, F. R. S. Concerning Several Observables in Maryland," *Philosophical Transactions (1683–1775)* 21 (1699): 439.

15. Morgan, *American Slavery, American Freedom,* 114–15. See also Kingsbury, *Records of the Virginia Company,* 4:235.

16. Parent, *Foul Means.*

17. Morgan, *American Slavery, American Freedom,* 94–98.

18. Ibid., 98; Kingsbury, *Records of the Virginia Company,* 1:304–7, 411–12, 479–80, 489.

19. Morgan, *American Slavery, American Freedom,* 97, 123–26; Kingsbury, *Records of the Virginia Company,* 3:99. See also Lorena S. Walsh, *Motives of Honor, Pleasure and Profit: Plantation Management in the Colonial Chesapeake, 1607–1763* (Chapel Hill: University of North Carolina Press, 2010), 89; Bailyn, "Politics and Social Structure in Virginia," 90–98; Warren Billings, *A Little Parliament: The Virginia General Assembly in the Seventeenth Century* (Richmond: Library of Virginia, 2007), 87–113.

20. Kingsbury, *Records of the Virginia Company,* 1:256, 268.

21. According to records in the British National Archives, in 1623 the cost of transporting just six such laborers to Virginia amounted to nearly £115. In addition to the cost of transportation, one could not guarantee that they would survive the voyage or the "seasoning" period in which new immigrants to Virginia either adjusted to the climate and disease environment or died. It was much better to get one's hands on servants and tenants already in Virginia if at all possible; "A Proportion of the Charge to Furnish and Transport Six Men to Virginia, 1632," Public Record Office CO 1/2 Colonial Office, British National Archives, Kew, England, 210.

22. Purchas, *Purchas His Pilgrims* 19:128, 134–35; His Majesty's Council for Virginia, *A Declaration of the State of the Colony and Affairs in Virginia* (London: T.S., 1620; reprint, Cambridge: Da Capo, 1973), 12; Rountree, *Pocahontas's People,* 70; Morgan, *American Slavery, American Freedom,* 97–98.

23. Mr. Wroth, "Notes from Lists Showing the Total Number of Emigrants to Virginia, 1622," in *Records of the Virginia Company,* 3:536–37; Sir Nathaniel Rich, "Notes of

Letters from Virginia, May-June, 1623," in *Records of the Virginia Company*, 4:158–59; Morgan, *American Slavery, American Freedom*, 101; Purchas, *Purchas His Pilgrims*, 19:122–25; Rountree, *Pocahontas's People*, 66–69; J. Frederick Fausz, "The Powhatan Uprising of 1622: A Historical Study of Ethnocentrism and Cultural Conflict" (PhD diss., College of William and Mary, Williamsburg, VA, 1977), 1:311. Paul Kelton recently argued quite convincingly that the preconditions for large-scale disease epidemics were not present in the Southeast (including Virginia) until the advent of the Native slave trade during the last half of the sixteenth century. However, his argument does not mean the localized impacts of European diseases could not still have been catastrophic. See Paul Kelton, *Epidemics and Enslavement: Biological Catastrophe in the Native Southeast, 1492–1715* (Lincoln: University of Nebraska Press, 2007).

24. Rountree, *Pocahontas's People*, 68–69; H. R. McIlwaine, ed., *Minutes of the Council and General Court of Virginia, 1622–1632, 1670–1676* (Richmond: Virginia State Library, 1979), 27–29.

25. Rountree describes such a ceremony in *Powhatan Indians of Virginia*, 113: "Powhatan rulers were distinguished from lesser folk in death as in life. Whereas 'common people' were buried in the ground, either individually or in groups, a ruler's body eventually came to rest in a temple. The body was first disemboweled and then placed on a scaffold for decomposing . . . The dry bones were either made into a disarticulated bundle or else laid out properly articulated; they were then 'hung' with jewelry and wrapped in skins and mats before being placed on a platform in the chiefdom's main temple. Whenever the temple was abandoned, in a migration of the people, the building and the bone bundles in it were left to disappear in the course of time." See also Rountree, *Pocahontas's People*, 70–71; Council in Virginia, "Letter to the Virginia Company of London, 20 January 1622," in *Records of the Virginia Company*, 4:10 (quotation).

26. Rountree, *Pocahontas's People*, 71; Helen Rountree and Thomas E. Davidson, *Eastern Shore Indians of Virginia and Maryland* (Charlottesville: University Press of Virginia, 1997), 50–51; Barbour, *Complete Works of Captain John Smith*, 2:288–91.

27. Barbour, *Complete Works of Captain John Smith*, 2:293; Rountree, *Pocahontas's People*, 71; Fausz, "Powhatan Uprising of 1622," 2:353–55.

28. Council in Virginia, "Letter to the Virginia Company of London, 20 January 1622," 10–11; Rountree, *Pocahontas's People*, 71.

29. George Thorpe and John Pory, "A Letter to Sir Edwin Sandys, 15&16 May 1621," in *Records of the Virginia Company*, 3:446–47; Council in Virginia, "Letter to the Virginia Company of London, January 1621," in *Records of the Virginia Company*, 3:584. For more on the growing disagreement over what approach to use with the Powhatans in the years after the First Anglo-Powhatan War, see Haskell, "Affections of the People," 135–36.

30. Thorpe and Pory, "Letter to Sir Edwin Sandys, 15&16 May 1621," 446; Barbour, *Complete Works of Captain John Smith*, 2:285–86.

31. Opechancanough's group of warriors may actually have been larger than the one Powhatan had commanded during the First Anglo-Powhatan War. Since taking over leadership of the chiefdom, Opechancanough had set about concentrating his settlements in the York and Pamunkey River areas. During that same time, English settlement had become more widespread and dispersed. Furthermore, the Chickahominies and the Nansemonds, groups that had resisted Powhatan's rule, had now sworn loyalty to Opechancanough. It would seem, therefore, that despite the losses of the previous war, increased English immigration, and death as a result of disease, the Algonquians began the Second Anglo-Powhatan War in a stronger position than they had been in when they began the first. See Fausz, "Powhatan Uprising," 2:361–62.

32. Edward Waterhouse, "A Declaration of the State of the Colony and a Relation of the Barbarous Massacre," in *The Records of the Virginia Company of London, 1606–1626*, 3:550–51 (quotations); Fausz, "Powhatan Uprising of 1622," 362–69; Rountree, *Pocahontas's People*, 74; Barbour, *Complete Works of Captain John Smith*, 2:293–94.

33. Waterhouse, "Declaration of the State of the Colony," 556–57. See also Seth Mallios, *The Deadly Politics of Giving: Exchange and Violence at Ajacan, Roanoke, and Jamestown* (Tuscaloosa: University of Alabama Press, 2006).

34. Waterhouse, "Declaration of the State of the Colony," 551–53; Barbour, *Complete Works of Captain John Smith*, 2:294–95; Rountree, *Pocahontas's People*, 75; Fausz, "Powhatan Uprising of 1622," 2:369.

35. Robert C. Johnson and Joseph Mead, "The Indian Massacre of 1622: Some Correspondence of the Reverend Joseph Mead," *Virginia Magazine of History and Biography* 71, no. 4 (October 1963): 410. Both Lorena Walsh and J. Frederick Fausz also argue that the 1622 Powhatan attack exacerbated the gulf between the planter elite and those of lesser means. See Walsh, *Motives of Honor*, 84, 120–21; Fausz, "Powhatan Uprising of 1622."

36. Waterhouse, "Declaration of the State of the Colony," 557–58.

37. Christopher Brooke, "A Poem on the Late Massacre in Virginia," *Virginia Magazine of History and Biography* 72, no. 3 (July 1964): 285. See also Waterhouse, "Declaration of the State of the Colony," 3:541–79; Barbour, *Complete Works of Captain John Smith*, 2:293–305.

38. Brooke, "Poem on the Late Massacre," 286.

39. Barbour, *Complete Works of Captain John Smith*, 2:298.

40. Ibid., 310–15; Rountree, *Pocahontas's People*, 76–77; "Council in Virginia to the Virginia Company of London, 20 January 1623," in *Records of the Virginia Company of London*, 4:10.

41. "Council in Virginia to the Virginia Company of London, 4 April 1623," in *Records of the Virginia Company of London*, 4:98; "A Preparative Court Held on Monday in the Afternoon the 17th of November 1623," in *Records of the Virginia Company of London*, 2:483. Both Rountree and Fausz attribute the first offer of peace to Opechancanough, but I find that neither offers a convincing argument as to why they do so. As stated above, I feel the

evidence leans toward Opitchapam as the most likely originator of the first message, but, as with much of colonial American ethnohistory, the sources do not exist for us to say definitively. They probably never will, but for the reasons heretofore stated, I consider Opitchapam the most likely source. See Rountree, *Pocahontas's People,* 77; Fausz, "Powhatan Uprising of 1622," 2:495.

42. "George Sandys to Sir Samuel Sandys, 30 March 1623," in *Records of the Virginia Company of London,* 4:75; "Council in Virginia to the Virginia Company of London, Sometime after 4 April 1623," in *Records of the Virginia Company of London,* 4:102.

43. Rountree, Fausz, and Frederic Gleach all believe that Opechancanough attended this meeting and was one of the two "Kings" the English saw fall. However, the records refer to the "Great King Apochanzion." Even accounting for the wide variety of English spellings of Opechancanough and his later name, Mangopeesomon, this hardly represents solid proof of his presence at the meeting. In addition, his lack of interest in pursuing peace both before and after this incident, the lack of any subterfuge on the part of the Algonquians, and Opechancanough's obvious survival of the poison and gunshot lead me to conclude that he was indeed not present. While I am open to the possibility of his attendance, little evidence exists to convince me of it. See Rountree, *Pocahontas's People,* 77; Fausz, "Powhatan Uprising of 1622," 2:497–99; Frederic W. Gleach, *Powhatan's World and Colonial Virginia: A Conflict of Cultures* (Lincoln: University of Nebraska Press, 1997), 102.

44. "Robert Bennett to Edward Bennett, 9 June 1623," in *Records of the Virginia Company of London,* 4:222; Rountree, *Pocahontas's People,* 78.

45. William Waller Hening, *The Statutes at Large: Being a Collection of All the Laws of Virginia from the First Session of the Legislature in the Year 1619* (New York: R&W&G Bartow, 1823), 2:110.

46. "Council in Virginia to the Earl of Southampton and the Council and Company of Virginia, 2 December 1624," in *Records of the Virginia Company of London,* 4:507–8.

47. "Council in Virginia to the Commissioners for the Affairs of Virginia, 15 June 1625," in *Records of the Virginia Company of London,* 4:566; Rountree, *Pocahontas's People,* 80. In addition to the lack of powder, Fausz cites a decline in Virginians' willingness to fight as a primary cause of the "noticeable de-escalation of combat after 1625." While this seems plausible in the case of elite Virginians, I think it is unlikely that non-elite colonists had tired of the campaigns against the Algonquians. Fausz cites only records of the burgesses and the governor and council for this conclusion. Non-elite voices may have told a different story. See Fausz, "Powhatan Uprising of 1622," 2:513.

48. Rountree, *Pocahontas's People,* 79; Nell Marion Nugent, *Cavaliers and Pioneers: Abstracts of Virginia Land Patents and Grants, 1632–1800* (Richmond, VA: Dietz, 1934), 1:44.

49. Bailyn, "Politics and Social Structure in Virginia," 96 (quotation). See also Parent, *Foul Means,* 25; Robert Brenner, *Merchants and Revolution: Commercial Change, Political Conflict, and London's Overseas Traders, 1550–1653* (Princeton, NJ: Princeton University

Press, 1993), 141–48; Aubrey C. Land, "Economic Behavior in a Planting Society: The Eighteenth-Century Chesapeake," *Journal of Southern History* 33, no. 4 (November 1967): 469–85.

50. McIlwaine, *Minutes of the Council and General Court,* 482; Conway Robinson, "Notes from the Council and General Court Records, 1641–1659," *Virginia Magazine of History and Biography* 13 (1905–6): 389–401; Rountree, *Pocahontas's People,* 81.

51. Hening, *Statutes at Large,* 1:192–93.

52. J. Frederick Fausz, "Merging and Emerging Worlds: Anglo-Indian Interest Groups and the Development of the Seventeenth-Century Chesapeake," in *Colonial Chesapeake Society,* ed. Lois Green Carr, Philip Morgan, and Jean B. Russo (Chapel Hill: University of North Carolina Press, 1989), 54–55.

53. Hening, *Statutes at Large,* 1:193; Fausz, "Merging and Emerging Worlds," 56–57. The desire to inculcate order and authority as argued by Alexander Haskell more than likely figured into these enactments as well. See also Haskell, "Affections of the People."

54. Hening, *Statutes at Large,* 1:208, 219.

55. Ibid., 193–99; Fausz, "Merging and Emerging Worlds," 53–59 (quotation on 53). See also Parent, *Foul Means,* 25.

56. McIlwaine, *Minutes of the Council and General Court,* 19–20.

57. "George Sandys to John Ferrar, April 8, 1623," Colonial Papers General Series (hereafter CO) 1/2, 147–48, National Archive, United Kingdom.

58. Morgan, *American Slavery, American Freedom,* 129.

59. Ibid., 128. See also New York Historical Society, *Collections,* 2nd series, 3, 1857, 36.

60. Privy Council, "Rules for Bettering the Government of Virginia, July 2, 1623," CO 1/2, 166.

61. Virginia Council, "Letter to Henry Viscount Mandeville, March 30, 1623," CO 1/2, 126.

62. In the 1625 census, tenants and servants were reported together in the same number. See Morgan, *American Slavery, American Freedom,* 119.

63. Kingsbury, *Records of the Virginia Company,* 3:226, 246, 479, 489.

64. Ibid., 1:333, 2:219; McIlwaine, *Minutes of the Council and General Court,* 118; "Virginia in 1638–1639," *Virginia Magazine of History and Biography* 11, no. 11 (October 1903): 181 (quotation).

65. Kingsbury, *Records of the Virginia Company,* 3:449, 502–5, 4:263–65; "George Sandys to John Ferrar, April 8, 1623," CO 1/2, 147–48; McIlwaine, *Minutes of the Council and General Court,* 93, 121; Morgan, *American Slavery, American Freedom,* 120.

66. McIlwaine, *Journals of the House of Burgesses of Virginia, 1619–1658/59,* 1–3:55–56; CO 1/4, 111; Virginia State Historical Society, "Governor West and the Council to the Privy Council, March 4, 1628," *Virginia Magazine of History and Biography* 7, no. 3 (January 1900): 259–60.

67. J. H. Lefroy, *Memorials of the Discovery and Early Settlement of the Bermudas* (London: Bermuda Historical Society, 1981), 264.

68. "Governor West and the Council to the Privy Council, March 4, 1628," 259–60. See also Richard Beale Davis, *George Sandys, Poet-Adventurer: A Study in Anglo-American Culture in the Seventeenth Century* (London: The Bodley, 1955). For a discussion of the changing role of tenants in the Virginia labor system, see Walsh, *Motives of Honor,* 106–9.

69. Kingsbury, *Records of the Virginia Company,* 4:37.

70. Ibid., 3:583–84.

71. Ibid., 2:113, 119; 4:510–14.

72. Virginia State Historical Society, "Virginia in 1629 and 1630," *Virginia Magazine of History and Biography* 7, no. 4 (April 1900): 381.

73. Massachusetts Historical Society, *Collections,* 4th Series, 9 (Boston: Massachusetts Historical Society, 1871), 142n–143n.

74. Virginia State Historical Society, "Virginia in 1629 and 1630," 372.

75. Virginia (Colony), Colonial Papers, Letter of Governor John Harvey, May 31, 1630, Box 141, Folder 1, Accession 36138, State Government Records Collection, Library of Virginia, Richmond; Virginia State Historical Society, "Virginia in 1629 and 1630," 378.

76. J. Mills Thornton, "The Thrusting Out of Governor Harvey," *Virginia Magazine of History and Biography* 76, no. 1 (January 1968): 12.

77. Bailyn, "Politics and Social Structure in Virginia," 96–97; Morgan, *American Slavery, American Freedom,* 145. For more information and differing interpretations of John Harvey's tenure as governor, see Thomas Jefferson Wertenbaker, *Virginia under the Stuarts, 1607–1688* (New York: Russell and Russell, 1959); Wilcomb Washburn, *Virginia under Charles I and Cromwell, 1625–1660* (Williamsburg: Virginia 350th Anniversary Celebration Corporation, 1957).

78. McIlwaine, *Minutes of the Council and General Court,* 14.

79. Hening, *Statutes at Large,* 1:146.

80. McIlwaine, *Minutes of the Council and General Court,* 85.

81. Bailyn, "Politics and Social Structure," 96. See also Walsh, *Motives of Honor,* 89–90.

82. McIlwaine, *Minutes of the Council and General Court,* 135–36.

83. Kingsbury, *Records of the Virginia Company,* 2:374.

4

If You Did but See Me You Would Weep

Expectation versus Reality in the Lives of Virginia Immigrants, 1609–40

In 1620 the Virginia Council issued "A Declaration of the State of the Colony and Affairs in Virginia." The pamphlet painted an image of Virginia as a sort of new promised land flowing with milk, honey, and opportunity for all:

> The Country is rich, spacious, and well watered; temperate as for the Climate; very healthful after men are a little accustomed to it; abounding with all Gods natural blessings: The Land replenished with the goodliest Woods in the world, and those full of Deer, and other Beasts of sustenance: The Seas and Rivers . . . full of excellent Fish, and of all sorts desirable; both Water and Land yielding Fowl in very great store and variety: In Sum, a Country, too good for ill people; and we hope reserved by the providence of God, for such as shall apply themselves faithfully to his service, and be a strength and honor to our King and Nation.[1]

Three years later an indentured servant named Richard Frethorne, one of those drawn to Virginia in search of the bounty promised by this and other, similar descriptions of the colony, wrote his family regarding his life there. He found Virginia a far cry from the bounteous land of opportunity described by the Virginia Council. Instead of having found a "very healthful" and "temperate climate," Frethorne described himself as "in a most heavy case by reason of the country, [which] is such that it causeth much sickness, [such] as the scurvy and the bloody flux and diverse other diseases, which maketh the body very poor and weak." He revealed that he had eaten nothing but peas and water gruel since his arrival, adding "as for deer or

DOI: 10.5876/9781607323082.c004

venison I never saw any since I came into this land. There is indeed some fowl, but we are not allowed to go and get it." Frethorne went on to describe many of his fellow indentured servants as in such a miserable condition that they would literally give their arms and legs to return to England and live as beggars. He pleaded with his parents to send whatever scraps of food they could, even old cheese. Finally, he spoke directly to his father: "Good father, do not forget me, but have mercy and pity my miserable case. I know if you did but see me you would weep to see me."[2]

Richard Frethorne's experience, while unique in some aspects, embodies the general disappointment many immigrants to Virginia experienced. Many of those who were not able to capitalize on the burgeoning tobacco economy to the extent of the few planters who dominated Virginia's politics found their situation in Virginia at best no different than what they had experienced in England and at worst a complete disaster that had shattering and often deadly consequences. These various people included many artisans, tenants, and indentured servants, as well as freemen, whether former indentured servants or small landholders. Despite their differences, these groups shared one basic commonality: they came to Virginia expecting opportunity. They were promised it in the promotional literature in general and specifically by those who either paid their way or recruited them to undertake the journey. In response to these recruiting efforts, members of the English laboring classes who immigrated to Virginia saw the colony as a place in which to re-engineer the social matrix that underlay English society. Their vision of the future of Virginia was one in which they expected to enjoy more economic success and political power than they had in England. According to historian James Horn, "Whatever their backgrounds or reasons for leaving England, whether impoverished and desperate or seeking a new life 'beyond the seas,' all embarked for Virginia in the hope of making their fortune or at least finding a comfortable sufficiency."[3] Instead, they found their pursuit of happiness blocked by economic, social, and political barriers and themselves exploited by powerful planters looking to capitalize on the tobacco boom. This tremendous gap between the immigrants' expectations and the realities of life in Virginia represents one of the key components of dissatisfaction that factored into the events of Bacon's Rebellion.[4]

The desire of poorer immigrants to create an entirely new life and social system in Virginia specifically and the colonies in general is evident as early as 1609. In late July of that year, a little more than a week out from the coast of Virginia, the *Sea Venture,* part of a nine-vessel convoy bound for the colony, became separated from the other ships in the group during a storm. Sir Thomas Gates, one of the leaders of the supply expedition, later recounted to William Strachey the horror experienced by the individuals aboard the ship:[5] "For four and twenty hours the storm in a restless tumult, had blown so exceedingly, as we could not apprehend in our imaginations any possibility of greater violence, yet did we still find it, not only more terrible, but more constant, fury added to fury, and one storm urging a second more outrageous than the former."[6]

The situation only got worse when the passengers and crew of the *Sea Venture* realized that the boat had sprung a sizable leak during the initial moments of the storm. After days of attempting to bail enough water out of the ship to keep it afloat, the exhausted Englishmen aboard the vessel spotted what Gates referred to as "the Devil's Islands"—so called, according to Gates, because they were "terrible to all that ever touched on them, and such tempests, thunders, and other fearful objects are seen and heard about them." As the boat drew nearer to the island (later known as Bermuda), where the men aboard hoped at least to land and repair their vessel, the crew realized that the water near the island was too shallow to allow them to anchor. However, anchoring the boat in deeper water would do nothing to stop the constant influx of water into the hull. In the end, the expedition leaders made the decision to "run her ashore, as near the land as we could . . . by the mercy of God unto us, making out our Boats, we had ere night brought all our men, women, and children, about the number of one hundred and fifty, safe into the Island."[7]

While there, a curious social experiment unfolded. A dispute arose along class lines in which those who had been destined for a life of labor in Virginia revolted against the leaders of the shipwrecked party. The prospect of creating the world anew on Bermuda represented a more attractive opportunity for many than what was ahead in Virginia. During the forty-two days in which the party lay shipwrecked on Bermuda, no fewer than five conspiracies arose. Each plot aimed to derail the building of a new vessel in which to continue the voyage to Virginia. "So willing were the major part of the common sort," complained Gates, "to settle a foundation of ever inhabiting there . . . some dangerous and secret discontents nourished amongst us, had like to have been the parents of bloody issues and mischiefs."[8]

Who were these "discontents"? According to historians Peter Linebaugh and Marcus Rediker, we cannot know their individual identities, but we can safely assume that "a number of dispossessed were among them." Considerable historical evidence supports Linebaugh and Rediker's assumption. On the eve of Bacon's Rebellion in 1676, one Englishman referred to Virginia as "a sink to drain England of her filth and scum." The author of that sentiment should not have been surprised by the reality it described. That "sink" had been draining the so-called scum of England since the very beginning. In 1584 Richard Hakluyt argued that colonization would rid England of "numbers of idle men." In the same year as the shipwreck, the Virginia Company offered similar sentiments in its "Nova Britannia," a pamphlet aimed at convincing the English that the colonization of Virginia had not been a failure. Among other things, the pamphlet's author, Robert Johnson, argued that Virginia existed "to rid our multitudes of such as lie at home, pestering the land with pestilence and penury, and infecting one another with vice and villainy, worse than the plague itself."

Also in 1609, the Virginia Company came up with a scheme to increase its number by asking the city of London to allow the company "to ease the city and suburbs of a swarm of unnecessary inmates" and transport them to Virginia. Finally, Robert Rich and Thomas Gates, two of the leaders of the expedition stranded on Bermuda, referred to their fellow castaways as "vagrants" and "wicked Imps not knowing otherwise how to live in England," respectively. Eventually, Captain Christopher Newport, Sir Thomas Gates, and Sir George Somers managed to regain control, but only after dispensing "two of the earliest capital punishments in English America, hanging one man and executing another by firing squad to quell the resistance and carry on with the task of colonization." While Newport, Gates, and Somers did finally reestablish authority, the incident suggests that even as early as 1609 the laboring classes who made up the bulk of the emigrants to Virginia went there with the expectation that their economic and social well-being would be significantly improved. In addition, the events on Bermuda in 1609 suggest the lengths to which at least some Virginians would go to achieve their dream of economic and social success in their new life.[9]

As mentioned, these ideas did not simply develop in a vacuum but instead were fostered by a combination of poor economic conditions in England and the outpouring of promotional literature from Virginia's backers aimed at convincing their fellow countrymen to emigrate. It seems no coincidence that one of the best examples of this promotional literature appeared the same year as the wreck of the *Sea Venture*. "Nova Britannia," published anonymously but since attributed to Robert Johnson, represents one of the earliest and most famous examples of the publicity campaign undertaken by the Virginia Company. While the 1620 pamphlet quoted earlier subtly invited readers to draw parallels between Virginia and the biblical promised land of Canaan, "Nova Britannia" represented a much more overt attempt to connect the two. Johnson began the section of the pamphlet in which he described Virginia's climate and natural resources thus: "And now in describing the natural seat and disposition of the country itself: if I should say no more but with Caleb and Joshua, The land which we have searched out is a very good land, if the Lord love us, he will bring our people to it, and will give it [to] us for a possession."[10] Of course, the Caleb and Joshua referred to in this section were the two lone Israelite spies who faithfully reported the bounties of the promised land to Moses and counseled that, with God's help, they could defeat the Gentile kingdoms there and take possession of Canaan for themselves. Johnson's message was obvious: just as God gave Canaan to his chosen people for their benefit, so, too, did he provide

Virginia for the benefit of all English. With such divine sanction, it is not surprising that the immigrants believed so fervently in the colony's potential to provide for their every need and improve their condition.

In addition to biblical parallels, Johnson provided more specific descriptions of Virginia that also helped lure Englishmen desperate for opportunity. Unfortunately for most of those immigrants, his portrayals were grossly inaccurate. He described the voyage as not long or tedious. While it is true that this voyage was shorter than those to Asia or the eastern coast of Africa, the difference was relative. The miseries of those aboard the *Sea Venture* stand as testament that the voyage to Virginia was often not a pleasure cruise. Johnson extolled the "infinite store" of game, fruits, fish, minerals, and other resources, as well as Virginia's "sweet and wholesome" climate, as reasons to emigrate. Surely such a place could not have produced the conditions described by Richard Frethorne in 1623.[11]

Finally, "Nova Britannia" also represents one of the first manifestations of a strategy for mobilizing the populace that would come to play a prominent role in spawning Bacon's Rebellion. Specifically, Johnson once again employed biblical references to argue that the settlement of Virginia provided an opportunity to enlarge the glory of England in the same fashion as the Jewish kingdoms of the Old Testament. When he wrote that "certainly the state of the Jews was far more glorious, by the conquests of David, and under the ample reign of Solomon, then [*sic*] ever before or after," Johnson seems to have been holding out the possibility of military conquest against England's European competitors and the Native groups of Virginia as an enticement for emigration. Whether he intended it this way or not, Johnson provided the initial encouragement for many Virginians to view the violent conquest of Native land in Virginia as sanctioned by the architects of the colony and necessary for the creation of the society they hoped to create there. The events of the Powhatan Wars in the years 1609–46 only solidified this interpretation.[12]

Johnson's pamphlet represents only the leading edge of the avalanche of promotional literature that sought to entice down-on-their-luck Englishmen to make their way to Virginia on either theirs or someone else's dime. Just one year after publication of "Nova Britannia," the Virginia Council published *A True Declaration of the Estate of the Colony in Virginia*. In it, the council did nothing to rectify any of the misinformation contained in "Nova Brittania" and even added to the mix of inaccurate information. In the tradition of Johnson, *A True Declaration* greatly exaggerated the excellence of Virginia's climate, as well as the abundance of food and natural resources.[13] Beyond that, the council added more erroneous information in its descriptions of the Powhatan Indians. In regard to their population, the council claimed, "there is roome sufficient in the land . . . for them, and us: the extent of an hundred miles, being scarce peopled with 2000 inhabitants."[14] In reality,

Powhatan exercised leadership over as many as 15,000 people, and the Monacans to the west counted at least that many, if not more.[15] *A True Declaration* made a point to highlight Christopher Newport's presentation of the trappings of English vassalage to Powhatan without mentioning that the Algonquian leader refused them. To English readers of the pamphlet, these half-truths were meant to assuage their fears of the deadly effects of Virginia's climate and the danger of conflict with the Powhatans. By dismissing them in this manner, the council hoped to clear away two of the largest impediments to increased immigration to Virginia.

Not to be outdone, Robert Johnson returned to the struggle once again in 1612 with the publication of his sequel to "Nova Britannia" titled *The New Life of Virginia*. Once again, Johnson hammered on the familiar themes of Virginia as the New Canaan, the abundance of food and natural resources supposedly to be found there, and the appeal of military conquest as a means of proving England's glory in the eyes of heaven.[16] Therefore, within three years of the commencement of the publicity campaign, Englishmen had been bombarded with comparisons of Virginia to the biblical promised land, as well as descriptions of it as a virtual paradise with an abundance of food, wealth-producing resources, plentiful land for all, and a mild climate. Furthermore, the local Indian groups were described as small and inconsequential, but despite that, the conquest of said groups was encouraged. The promotional literature argued that the conquest would provide a visible sign of England's place as one of Earth's favored nations. One could not blame Virginia immigrants for arriving there with the belief that a much better life awaited them than they had in England and that they were expected to violently subdue Indians to attain that life. There was more to come, as the next seven years saw the production of more promotional literature that only reinforced these erroneous characterizations of life in Virginia.

The Reverend Alexander Whitaker's *Good Newes from Virginia,* published in 1613, added yet another facet to the already extremely distorted picture of Virginia foisted on English readers. While the main body of *Good Newes from Virginia* represents a Christian appeal to wealthy Englishmen, exhorting them to give of their wealth to alleviate the "poor estate of the ignorant Inhabitants of Virginia," the introduction by William Crashaw provides the most interesting addition to the misinformation campaign about the colony. In responding to the growing chorus of bad news from the colony and accusations of mismanagement by the company's leaders, Crashaw employed some rather specious logic. Specifically, he argued that since many who were destitute in England had left for Virginia and not returned in large numbers, that must be evidence that Virginia had greater capacity to supply their needs than England had. Therefore, those who left England in search of more opportunities must be finding them in the colony. What Crashaw failed to mention was that many immigrants could not afford a return trip to England and that many ended up dead before they could begin to consider a return. Therefore, whatever was keeping poor Virginia immigrants from returning to England, it most likely was not contentment.[17]

Ralph Hamor's *A True Discourse of the Present Estate of Virginia,* published in 1614, continued many of the trends discussed heretofore. In addition to his exaggerated estimation of the food and natural resources found there, Hamor also sought to cast Virginia as a good country for the poor. In a section that mirrored Crashaw's arguments, Hamor described Virginia as a place where poor immigrants would find "a handsome house of some four rooms or more, if he have a family, to repose himself in rent free, and twelve English Acres of ground, adjoining thereunto." Hamor further regaled his readers with promises of free tools and livestock. Finally, he summed up that section of his discourse by predicting that the poor Englishman who went to Virginia would live happily, "as do many there, who I am sure will never return."[18]

The Virginia Council's *A Declaration of the State of the Colony and Affairs in Virginia* represents the culmination of over ten years of promotional literature designed to entice the English (particularly those of the laboring classes who found themselves down on their luck) to venture across the Atlantic in hopes of finding comfort and increased economic opportunity. Despite plenty of contradictory firsthand evidence, the Virginia Company, its backers, and its council in the colony had waged a furious battle of words with those they saw as motivated by nothing more than the destruction of the company to paint a picture of Virginia characterized by easy access to land, water, and game, as well as the opportunity to add to the glory of England by violently displacing Native Americans. Those who argued that actual conditions in Virginia failed to live up to these less than ideal scenarios were labeled defamers, "of a corrupt mind and ill purpose."[19]

This analysis is not meant to divorce these pieces of promotional literature from their proper context. The individuals and organizations that published these writings had specific goals in mind that often had more to do with either their own political conflicts or the fate of their investments than with providing for fellow Englishmen an accurate picture of conditions in the colony. Instead, the inclusion of these promotional materials is meant to demonstrate that over the years a picture developed in the minds of many Virginia immigrants of a colony that represented the solution to all their ills. Whether these writings were meant for purposes other than providing an accurate description for potential immigrants is largely immaterial. The fact is that many immigrants based their decision to travel to Virginia, at least in part, on these descriptions and were therefore bound to be disappointed when they arrived.

Of course, historians have long since established that the reality of life in Virginia during this time was far from that portrayed in the promotional literature. According to Edmund Morgan, between the years 1625 and 1640, approximately 15,000 immigrants crossed the Atlantic from England to Virginia, yet at the end of this period the total population of the colony had only increased by 7,000. What happened to the other 8,000? While it is possible that some returned to England, Morgan does not think this can account for much of the discrepancy. Since most arrived as indentured servants, bound to a master for a certain term of years and with few resources of their own, a return voyage was likely out of the question for all but a few of the immigrants to Virginia during this period. Therefore, only one probable explanation exists: the majority of the approximately 8,000 missing immigrants likely died. Again according to Morgan, "No matter how one reads the figures, they show that Virginians had to cope year after year with a death rate comparable only to that of severe epidemic years in England." Virginia was a death trap, and it remained so well after the initial years of settlement.[20] In fact, in 1638 the House of Burgesses responded to a request by King Charles to limit the amount of tobacco produced in the colony by claiming it could not calculate the amount of tobacco to limit each person to because it had no way of knowing the colony's population from year to year. Specifically, wildly fluctuating population numbers as a result of heavy immigration coupled with high mortality had produced a situation in which the burgesses were "not at any time certain of the number of our Inhabitants."[21] This same reality also made it impossible to arrive at an exact calculation of the amount of debt owed by Virginia's planters as, according to the House of Burgesses, a full third of that debt was held by men who had recently died.[22]

It comes as no surprise that servants made up the majority of the immigrants who died. While little or no concrete data exist on which to base servant life expectancies in Virginia during the early seventeenth century, an analysis of Maryland during the second half of that century provides a useful point from which to speculate. Lorena Walsh and Russell Menard found that in Maryland, also a colony heavily dependent on staple tobacco production and therefore on indentured servants, the average life expectancy for all immigrants (69% of which in their survey arrived as indentured servants) was between 20.3 and 24.2 additional years for a male immigrant who arrived in Maryland in his early twenties.[23] By contrast, a man who reached age 20 in Plymouth Colony during the seventeenth century could expect to live an additional 48.2 years. A man in Leicestershire, England, during the seventeenth century could expect to live 43 years beyond age 20.[24]

Additional evidence indicates that the death rate for immigrant servants to Virginia during the first half of the seventeenth century was probably worse than these numbers suggest. Given the fact that epidemic diseases took their worst toll on the first waves of Virginia immigrants and that the numbers cited here for Maryland are from the second half of the century rather than the first, we can assume a higher death rate for earlier immigrants to the Chesapeake. Furthermore, the data produced by Walsh and Menard do not include those who died during the so-called seasoning period. According to Walsh and Menard, if one assumes a seasoning rate of 5 percent (that is, 5 percent of immigrants died within the first year), the average life expectancy for a 22-year-old Maryland man between the years 1652 and 1699 is reduced to 21.6 additional years. A seasoning rate of 20 percent yields a drop in life expectancy at age 22 to 18.3 years. So, while we cannot pinpoint the exact life expectancy of servants in Virginia during the years of the tobacco boom, the available data suggest a death rate considerably higher than those in both New England and England during the period.[25]

Those who survived the so-called seasoning period, in which they either died or grew accustomed to Virginia's disease environment and climate, faced still other dangers. Tenants faced the ever-present threat that unscrupulous planters would summarily downgrade their status to that of a servant. Servants, as Richard Frethorne's letter vividly illustrates, often experienced malnutrition, the worst of already poor sanitary conditions, and little of the necessary clothing or shelter to protect themselves from the elements. In many ways, Frethorne's letter only scratches the surface. Laborers (both free and indentured), tenants, and artisans faced a legal and social system designed to exploit them to the maximum amount possible to accrue the greatest possible monetary and social benefits for the few elites who had gained control of the tobacco boom. Specifically, economic disappointment, barriers to social advancement, a legal system tilted in favor of elites, as well as sexual regulation and sexual violence combined with the disease environment and brutal work regimes to create a shattering experience for many Virginia immigrants enticed there by either the inflated claims of the promotional materials of the 1610s or the lure of quick but often elusive tobacco profits.[26]

The nature of both work and life in Virginia contrasted starkly with what laboring Virginians had experienced back in England and what the literature promoting the Virginia settlement had promised them. Farm labor in England was often seasonal and even sporadic. Periods of intense work and long hours were often interspersed with other periods of relative leisure. Furthermore, agricultural labor in England, while not wholly subsistence in nature, was not driven by profit the way tobacco cultivation in Virginia revolved solely around selling the crop at a market. The need to extract as much profit as possible from the soil, rather than the need to derive only sustenance, combined with the ability to trade for other necessities caused Virginia masters to treat servants differently than did their English counterparts. They drove their servants harder, punished them more often and more severely, and ultimately came to conceive of other human beings as nothing more than inputs in a vast machine designed to profit those who could exercise the most control over those human inputs.[27]

The lofty expectations of Virginia immigrant laborers smashed into the rock that was the reality of life and work in Virginia with the force of a thousand ship- wrecks. As early as 1619, John Rolfe, the man who had touched off the tobacco boom, remarked that many back in England considered "this buying and selling of men and boys . . . a thing most intolerable."[28] In 1625 one English sea captain went so far as to refuse to transport servants to Virginia, citing the fact that "servants were sold here up and down like horses."[29]

The difference in the servant-master dynamic between England and Virginia was not lost on the servants. In 1623 Thomas Best complained bitterly that his mas- ter "hath sold me for a £150 sterling like a damned slave."[30] In 1640 Anne Belson reported that her master, Theodore Moyses, had, in addition to pledging to provide her with a certain amount of livestock, promised her when she entered into her indentures "that he would use her more like his child than his servant and that he would teach her to read and instruct her in the rudiments of religion and have a paternal care over her." Apparently, in the seven years since that promise, he had not only failed to provide her with the promised livestock but also abused her physi- cally and subjected her to "grievous and tyrannical usage," to such a degree that she was granted immediate freedom.[31]

Moyses's failure to deliver on his promises to better Belson's financial and social outlook was not an isolated incident. Such complaints by servants against mas- ters appear fairly often in the records of the seventeenth century. Fourteen years before Belson's case, Richard Townsend, a servant of the notorious Dr. John Pott, sued his master because Pott had promised to teach him the necessary skills to become an apothecary upon his release from servitude. In five years, Pott had taught him nothing.[32]

As one might expect, these distressed conditions among indentured servants led many to resort to theft and other illegal activities to meet their basic needs and supplement their financial situation. These activities, when discovered, were vigor- ously punished. For example, in Accomack County in the 1630s, both milking other people's cows and stealing pigs were punishable by at least thirty lashes.[33]

The plight of servants whose masters died intestate also underscores the extent to which servants had come to be seen less as people and more as objects to be bought, exploited, and sold. Servants whose masters died without a will and therefore with no legal declaration as to what was to be done with those servants were forced to choose new masters despite the fact that no man had an actual legal claim to their services.[34] What had started out for many servants and tenants as a chance for a new

beginning in a new land, with seemingly endless opportunities for their advancement, had turned into at best an extreme disappointment and at worst a nightmare
for many Virginia laborers.

In addition to the poor working conditions and the deterioration of the master-
servant relationship, immigrant laborers in Virginia also found specific legal,
economic, and social roadblocks to their advancement, erected purposely by the
wealthy planters who ruled society. It has been well established that immigration
to the Chesapeake could provide a female servant with the opportunity (once she
had served her contracted time) to increase her social standing through marriage.[35]
Furthermore, the available evidence from Virginia suggests that this phenomenon
may have existed more by design than happenstance. The first meeting of the assembly in 1619 expressly forbade any "maid or woman servant" from marrying without
the consent of her parents (who were more than likely not there) or her master.[36]
According to historian Kathleen Brown, there were two reasons behind this restric-
tion. The first was the assembly's desire to protect its investments in female servants
by restricting young unmarried men's access to them. The second was to preserve
rank: "Acknowledging the power of marriage to undermine social distinctions, the
Assembly tried to control ordinary men's use of this route to upward mobility." So
at least in Virginia, the sexual imbalance does not in itself explain the many opportunities for servant women to marry above their rank. Instead, this situation may
have had as much to do with elite fears that laboring men would marry either free
or servant women above their station and thus gain some of the labor needed to
compete with larger planters, as well as acquire instant social advancement.[37]

Leaders of the Virginia Company in London were torn as to whether to support
these limitations. Ultimately, they went along with them, saying "though we are
desirous that marriage be free according to the law of nature . . . yet would we not
have these maids deceived and married to servants, but only to freemen or tenants
as have means to maintain them."[38]

Furthermore, the cost of importing women to Virginia was six times that of
importing a male servant. Therefore, masters had a definite financial interest in
keeping their female servants away from men looking to engage them in romantic
entanglements. Smaller planters, as well as newly freed servants, could not dream of
importing a potential wife to Virginia themselves because of the up-front expense
required. To underscore the extent to which elite planters sought to control access
to women in Virginia based on their own self-interests, they often ignored the
Virginia Company's initial regulations stipulating that all women imported into
Virginia be brought there to be married to a planter rather than used as servants.
Finally, planters sidestepped their own prohibitions against female servants marrying other servants if doing so served their purposes.[39] For example, in 1639 Elizabeth

Starkey's master allowed her to marry another servant, but only on the condition that she agree to serve three years beyond the end of her indenture.[40]

Facing deadly environmental conditions, strict work regimes, and the debasement of their social status compared to their compatriots in England, as well as barriers to social advancement once their indentures ended, immigrant laborers in Virginia (particularly, but not always, women) also experienced a high degree of sexual regulation and abuse. Specifically, the regulation of sexual activity among servants seems to have been motivated not by strict moral codes (as one might expect to find in Puritan New England) but instead by the intense labor demands of the tobacco economy. The simple act of consensual sex could earn servants punishments as harsh as those for thievery, as it did for Ellen Muce, a servant of Philip Taylor of Accomack County, in 1632. According to court records, she engaged in sex with one John Littell. Littell, as far as the records indicate, was not a servant but a freeman. For having sex with Muce, Littell was ordered to pay a fine and to lie with "neck and heels close for three hours." Muce was whipped. However, she was not punished simply for having engaged in sexual activity (although she likely would have received some form of punishment for that) but instead for lying to the court about Littell having raped her. The fact that Littell was punished despite Muce's admission that she had lied about the rape supports Kathleen Brown's argument regarding the desire of masters to prevent their servants from engaging in any sexual contact that could deprive their masters of their services for an extended period. Littell's punishment was therefore intended as a deterrent to other men who might be interested in developing liaisons with female servants.[41]

As much as their freedom to engage in sexual activity was closely regulated by their masters, servants also faced the possibility of sexual abuse by those same masters. For female servants, prevailing beliefs about the rapacity of female sexuality made it virtually impossible to successfully accuse a man of rape at this time. Again, according to Brown, "motivated to protect the property of masters and predisposed to believe women were lusty creatures, barely capable of controlling their own bodily urges, the courts were little inclined to view servant women as the victims of coercion."[42] A 1638 case from Norfolk County provides a template on which nearly every other accusation of sexual abuse involving a female servant against her master seems to have been based. In that year, Deborah Hancock accused Captain John Silbey of impregnating his maidservant. Despite her testimony, Silbey was not punished, but Hancock received 100 lashes for making a false accusation.[43] Similar cases with identical results were found in Norfolk County nearly fifty years later when the county court dismissed three cases in 1684 alone by acquitting the accused and punishing the accuser. In a 1670 case from Accomack County, two female servants who accused their master of raping them not only lost their case but were ordered to serve him longer. As Brown notes, "During the seventeenth century, although several white women accused white men of rape, none succeeded in bringing her case to the General Court."[44] The possibility of sexual abuse by their masters, as well as the certainty that the legal system would be of no use to them, had to have added to the disillusionment of female servants who had come to Virginia in hopes of attaining the prosperity and happiness promised them by the colony's promoters.

Perhaps no other court case better epitomizes the hegemonic relationship of masters, the sexual peril servants found themselves subject to, and the extent to which the governmental and judicial entities of seventeenth-century Virginia dispensed justice based not on exact legal standards but instead on what served their interests than the case of a servant named William Couse. In 1624 Couse was a servant of Captain Cornish aboard the ship *Ambrose*. One day in August of that year, Cornish instructed Couse to change the linens in his bedchamber, which Couse did. Cornish then attempted to force Couse to have sex with him. According to Couse's testimony, Cornish "made him go into the bed . . . and there lay upon him and kissed him and hugged him." Despite Couse's protests, Cornish proceeded to force himself on Couse. In the days and weeks that followed, he continued to fondle Couse and demand that he perform various sexual acts with him. When Couse refused, Cornish called Couse before the entire ship's crew, decreed that henceforth Couse would cook for the entire ship, and banned any of the crew from eating with the servant.[45]

Couse eventually reported the assault and Cornish was brought before the council, where he was found guilty and sentenced to death. Since Cornish had died without a will, no man had a legal claim to Couse's labor; despite this, the council ordered Couse to choose a new master and continue as a servant. Since he had come to Virginia, Couse had more than likely experienced disease, as well as the privations and strict work routines of the typical servant; he had also been sexually assaulted by his master and was now forced to continue in that life of servitude because of the council's need to meet the voracious labor demands of staple tobacco production. In fact, not only was Couse ordered to pick a new master, but his choice was limited to two of the most powerful men in the colony: Captain Nathaniel West, brother of Lord De La Warr, or council member Ralph Hamor. Despite the relatively strong legal case for doing so, there is no record that Couse challenged his continued servitude. Those who did challenge the system through the courts or other variants of the public arena often suffered harsh consequences.[46]

Servants, both male and female, suffered non-sexual physical abuse as well. The records of the early seventeenth century abound with instances of brutal disciplinary actions and purposeless acts of violence against servants. In a rare court victory, Jane Winlee won her 1633 suit against James Knott for "misusage of her son Pharaoh who is an apprentice unto the said James."[47] Many servants were not as lucky as Pharaoh, who was released back to his mother. A 1635 Accomack County case alleged that one Mrs. Stonne "kept servants and starved them to death."[48] Two years later, also in Accomack County Court, Elizabeth Starkey complained of "rigourous abuse offered her by Alex Mountney, she being his servant."[49]

However rigorous the abuse Starkey suffered, it likely did not reach the level of brutality Elizabeth Abbott and Elias Hinton endured. Abbot and Hinton, servants of John and Elizabeth Proctor, died within approximately thirteen months of one another, ostensibly as a result of severe beatings by the Proctors or other servants acting at their behest. In July 1623 John Proctor, for an unspecified offense, "did strike him [Hinton] with a rake some three or four blows." Later that day, Hinton confided to an acquaintance his fear that Proctor had injured him seriously, possibly fatally. That acquaintance, Thomas Cross, later testified that the conversation was the last he ever had with Hinton, who was found dead shortly thereafter.[50]

In August 1624 the Proctors ordered one of their servants to deliver 500 lashes to Elizabeth Abbott. Thomas Gates, a neighbor to whom Abbott appealed for help after the whipping, confronted John Proctor, telling him that he may as well have killed the girl. Proctor responded that he did not care whether the girl lived or died. Another witness described Abbott's flesh as raw and "very black and blue." This same witness, a servant on a neighboring plantation, also testified that the whip used to beat Abbott had fishhooks attached to it. With the exception of Thomas Gates's attempt to confront Proctor (and even Gates never tried to remove the girl from the situation), none of the individuals to whom Abbott pleaded for help did anything but return her to the Proctors and ask them to forgive her. Finding no help from her neighbors, Abbott ran away from the Proctor household to the nearby woods where two weeks later Gates, attempting to check on her condition, found her lifeless body.[51] Despite sworn statements from their other servants, as well as other neighbors, of the brutal treatment they visited upon Elias Hinton and Elizabeth Abbott, the Proctors were never punished. Hinton and Abbott became just another two laborers fed to the voracious machine that was the Virginia tobacco boom.[52]

As mentioned, attempts at resistance—whether legal, physical, or even symbolic—often made things worse for laborers who undertook them. For those who had reached the boiling point, physical or rhetorical violence usually ended with severe punishment. For example, Anne Fowler of Norfolk County earned twenty lashes simply by telling one of the county's leading citizens to "kiss her arse."[53] If verbal retorts resulted in the perpetrator receiving a moderate to severe whipping, one can imagine what more serious offenses brought. It was because of the fear of punishment that very few of those who dreamed of running away actually made it to freedom, as did John Neale, who ran away from his master's plantation in Accomack County in 1638. Two of his fellow servants, William Abraham and Thomas Powell, who had conspired with him in the escape plot, could not go through with it for fear of the punishment they would receive if they got caught. While the sources do not indicate the penalty Abraham and Powell incurred for plotting to run away and concealing Neale's plans to do so, other, similar cases provide ample evidence as to what they could have expected.[54] A group of servants who plotted to run away to the Dutch colony of New Netherland in 1640 were branded with an "R" on their cheeks, given thirty lashes, and forced to serve as much as seven years beyond the expiration of their current indentures. For every John Neale who made it to the relative safety of New Netherland, countless others either died along the way or were apprehended and subjected to punishments such as these.[55] The conditions that led servants to attempt to run away seem to have changed little as the century wore on, as even during the post–Bacon's Rebellion era we find court records pertaining to the punishment of runaway indentured servants.[56]

Similar to cases in which female servants accused their masters of rape, servants who sought legal redress against their masters faced a decidedly uphill battle. As servants William Berry and Anthony Hewett found out, the penalty for failing to prove accusations against prominent members of the community, in this case Captain Adam Thoroughgood and Captain John Silbey, could be stiff. For failing to prove the allegations they made against the two men, both of whom sat on the court that passed judgment on them, Berry and Hewett were sentenced to "50 stripes across their bare shoulders."[57] The hammer fell even harder on those who sought to create solidarity among their fellow servants for the purpose of collective protest of their condition.

By the 1640s, the promises of the promotional literature used to lure so many poor Englishmen to Virginia must have seemed like a cruel joke to those who labored there. Denied opportunities for economic and social advancement and exposed to the deadly spiral effect of a hostile disease environment, poor sanitary conditions, and a labor-intensive work regimen, as well as sexual and physical abuse by capricious masters buttressed by a legal and political system that provided them with little or no redress, many Virginia laborers were no doubt profoundly disenchanted with life in the colony. It had not proven to be even remotely close to what they had been promised or led to expect. They had come to seize on an opportunity for a brighter future for themselves and their children; instead, they were nothing but an input to be used in the production of tobacco that could be discarded as their masters and other elites saw fit. This disappointment among many who ranked below the planter elite in seventeenth-century Virginia, coupled with the planter elite's overwhelming desire to inculcate sufficient authority and order in the colony, led to increasing friction between the planter elite and those at the bottom of Virginia society.

Despite all of the reasons for doing so, why did servants, tenants, artisans, and landless freemen and the rest of Virginia's laboring classes not rise up against this system in any meaningful way during the first half of the century? The ability of the planter elite during this period, as well as for the first three decades after the end of the Anglo-Powhatan Wars, to maintain the loyalty of middling and small planters represents to the key to Virginia's relative social stability during the first three-quarters of the seventeenth century. As we have seen, both the fear of and the desire to defeat the Powhatan chiefdom created a nominal amount of stability in Virginia's social structure during the war years 1622–32. In addition, the fact that not every immigrant to Virginia ended up like Richard Frethorne explains much about that lack of social unrest during the colony's first seventy-five years. A growing class of small and middling planters achieved enough success to bind them to the planter elite for most of the period. Lorena Walsh has referred to the period 1640–80 as the age of the small planter in Virginia. During this time frame, she asserts, "Thousands of men and women were not deterred from pursuing the opportunities they continued to believe the Chesapeake offered." Furthermore, these immigrants affected a "steady rise in the quantities of tobacco pouring into England." In addition, those who ran Virginia during the forty-five years between 1630 and 1675 came to believe that as long as they held the majority of property holders (the yeomanry and the gentry) in their corner, their rule was safe from challenge. As such, they became very astute at cultivating the support of small and middling planters by always endeavoring to be seen as looking out for their interests. Finally, the era of peace, prosperity, and stability that characterized the early years of Sir William Berkeley's two tenures as governor also contributed to the absence of open social conflict.[58]

To once again refer to E. P. Thompson's field of force analogy, the elite pole still possessed enough attraction for middling and small planters to deter them from joining the chorus of discontent rising from below them, but that would change by 1676.[59] More servants were beginning to outlive their indentures by this period, and those who did held out hope that, given the opportunity to obtain their own small piece of ground, they might make something lasting and permanent for themselves and their families. Many of them hoped the final victory over the Powhatan chiefdom in 1646 would open up large swathes of land in the West that would guarantee them the opportunities they had heretofore been denied. When the government refused to grant them these opportunities, their discontent boiled over into an uproar. The ultimate failure of many of Berkeley's ambitious and extremely expensive state-building plans, combined with his increasingly irascible behavior and threats from Indians beyond Virginia as well as the Dutch, eventually led a considerable number of middling and small planters to lend their support to the calls of those who saw the destruction of all Indians in Virginia as their only hope for social advancement.

NOTES

1. His Majesty's Council for Virginia, *A Declaration of the State of the Colony and Affairs in Virginia* (London: T.S., 1620; reprint, Cambridge: Da Capo, 1973), 2–3.

2. Susan Myra Kingsbury, ed., *The Records of the Virginia Company of London* (Washington, DC: Government Printing Office, 1935), 4:58–60.

3. James Horn, "Leaving England: The Social Background of Indentured Servants in the Seventeenth Century," *Virtual Jamestown* (n.d.), at http://www.virtualjamestown.org /essays/horn_essay.html.

4. For a discussion of the conditions in England that drove many immigrants to Virginia during the seventeenth century, see James Horn, *Adapting to a New World: English Society in the Seventeenth-Century Chesapeake* (Chapel Hill: University of North Carolina Press, 1994), chapters 1 and 2; A. L. Beier, *Masterless Men: The Vagrancy Problem in England, 1560–1640* (New York: Methuen, 1985); David Galenson, *White Servitude in Colonial America: An Economic Analysis* (New York: Cambridge University Press, 1981).

5. "Grant of Virginia to Sir Thomas Gates and others, April 10, 1606," Public Record Office, CO 5/1354, Colonial Office, Board of Trade, America and the West Indies, British National Archives, Kew, England (hereafter CO), 31.

6. Strachey quoted in Samuel Purchas, *Hakluytas Posthumous or Purchas His Pilgrimes* (Glasgow: James Maclehose, 1905), 19:5–7.

7. Ibid., 8–13.

8. Ibid., 28–41.

9. Peter Linebaugh and Marcus Rediker, *The Many-Headed Hydra: Sailors, Slaves, Commoners, and the Hidden History of the Revolutionary Atlantic* (Boston: Beacon, 2000), 13–16 (capital punishment quotation); "Nicholas Spencer to Lord Culpeper, Aug. 6, 1676," CO 1/49, 107; Richard Hakluyt, *A Discourse of Western Planting* (London: Hakluyt Society, 1993), 2:2; Robert Johnson, "Nova Britannia" (London: Samuel Macham, 1609; reprint, Cambridge: Da Capo, 1969), 19; Robert Rich, "News from Virginia," in *A Good Speed to Virginia*, ed. Wesley Frank Craven (New York: Scholars Facsimiles and Reprints, 1937); Gates cited in Johnson, *The New Life of Virginia: Declaring the Former Successes and Present Estate of That Plantation, Being the Second Part of Nova Britannia* (London: Feliz Kyngston, 1612; reprint, Cambridge: Da Capo, 1971), 1:10; "John Beaulieu to William Trumbull, November 30, 1609; December 7, 1609," and "Pedro de Zuniga to Philip III, December 31, 1609," in *The Jamestown Voyages under the First Charter: Documents Relating to the Foundation of*

Jamestown and the History of the Jamestown Colony up to the Departure of John Smith, Last President of the Council in Virginia under the First Charter, Early in October 1609, 2 vols., ed. Philip Barbour (New York: Cambridge University Press, 1969), 2:287–89.

10. Robert Johnson, "Nova Britannia" (London: Samuel Macham, 1609; reprint, Cambridge: Da Capo, 1969), 8.

11. Ibid., 8–10.

12. Ibid., 10–13.

13. The Council for Virginia, *A True Declaration of the Estate of the Colony in Virginia* (London: William Barret, 1610), 12–14.

14. Ibid., 6.

15. For Powhatan strength at the time of contact, see Helen Rountree, *The Powhatan Indians of Virginia: Their Traditional Culture* (Norman: University of Oklahoma Press, 1989), 120–21, 140; William Strachey, *The Historie of Travel into Virginia Britannia* (London: Hakluyt Society, 1953), 104–5. For information on the Monacan population, see Jeffrey Hantman, "Between Powhatan and Quirank: Reconstructing Monacan Culture and History in the Context of Jamestown, *American Anthropologist,* New Series 92, no. 3 (September 1990): 676–90.

16. Johnson, *New Life of Virginia.*

17. Alexander Whitaker, *Good Newes from Virginia* (London: Felix Kyngston and William Webb, 1613).

18. Hamor, *True Discourse of the Present Estate of Virginia*, 19–20.

19. His Majesty's Council for Virginia, *Declaration of the State of the Colony and Affairs in Virginia*, 5.

20. Morgan, *American Slavery, American Freedom*, 159–60.

21. H. R. McIlwaine, ed., *Journals of the House of Burgesses of Virginia 1619–1658/59* (Richmond: Virginia State Library, 1915), 59–61.

22. Ibid.

23. Lorena S. Walsh and Russell R. Menard, "Death in the Chesapeake: Two Life Tables for Men in Early Colonial Maryland," *Maryland Historical Magazine* 69 (1974): 215.

24. Robert V. Wells, "The Population of England's Colonies in America: Old English or New Americans?" *Population Studies* 46, no. 1 (March 1992): 94.

25. Walsh and Menard, "Death in the Chesapeake," 215–16.

26. John Ruston Pagan's *Anne Orthwood's Bastard: Sex and Law in Early Virginia* (New York: Oxford University Press, 2003) provides the best example of the kinds of sexual regulation Virginia servants faced. In addition, Pagan masterfully illuminates the way self-interested elites often ended up making legal decisions that personally involved them or their family/associates to the detriment of those less political and socially powerful.

27. Morgan, *American Slavery, American Freedom*, 126–27.

28. Rolfe quoted in Barbour, *Complete Works of Captain John Smith*, 2:268.

29. McIlwaine, *Minutes of the Council and General Court,* 82.

30. Kingsbury, *Records of the Virginia Company,* 4:235.

31. McIlwaine, *Minutes of the Council and General Court,* 465.

32. Ibid., 117.

33. Beverley Fleet, *Virginia Colonial Abstracts* (Baltimore: Genealogical Publishing, 1988), 1:21, 25.

34. McIlwaine, *Minutes of the Council and General Court,* 137.

35. Lois Green Carr and Lorena S. Walsh, "The Planter's Wife: The Experience of White Women in Seventeenth-Century Maryland," *William and Mary Quarterly* 34 (October 1977): 542–71. Specifically, Carr and Walsh argue that so many women came to the Chesapeake as servants, combined with the fact that there was a dearth of women to begin with, that the majority of elite planters married former servant women, thus instantly boosting their brides' social standing.

36. Lyon Gardiner Tyler, *Narratives of Early Virginia, 1606–1625* (New York: Barnes and Noble, 1946), 273.

37. Kathleen Brown, *Good Wives, Nasty Wenches, and Anxious Patriarchs: Gender, Race, and Power in Colonial Virginia* (Chapel Hill: University of North Carolina Press, 1996), 81.

38. Ibid., 81–82.

39. Ibid.

40. Fleet, *Virginia Colonial Abstracts,* 1:88.

41. Ibid., 11; see also Pagan, *Anne Orthwood's Bastard.*

42. Brown, *Good Wives,* 192–93.

43. Norfolk County Minute Book, 1637–46, April 2, 1638, Norfolk County Microfilm Reel 1a, Library of Virginia, Richmond, 14–15.

44. Brown, *Good Wives,* 208–9.

45. McIlwaine, *Minutes of the Council and General Court,* 34.

46. Ibid., 47.

47. Fleet, *Virginia Colonial Abstracts,* 1:4.

48. Ibid., 26.

49. Ibid., 39.

50. McIlwaine, *Minutes of the Council and General Court,* 23.

51. Ibid., 22–24.

52. Morgan, *American Slavery, American Freedom,* 127.

53. Norfolk County Minute Book, 1637–46, 1–2.

54. Fleet, *Virginia Colonial Abstracts,* 1:71.

55. McIlwaine, *Minutes of the Council and General Court,* 466.

56. Warren Billings, ed., *The Old Dominion in the Seventeenth Century: A Documentary History of Virginia, 1606–1689* (Chapel Hill: University of North Carolina Press, 1975), 143.

57. Ibid., 16–17.

58. See Walsh, *Motives of Honor,* 122–93, quotations on 131; Haskell, "Affections of the People," 179; Warren Billings, *Sir William Berkeley and the Forging of Colonial Virginia* (Baton Rouge: Louisiana State University Press, 2004).

59. See E. P. Thompson, "Eighteenth-Century English Society: Class Struggle without Class?" *Social History* 3 (1978): 149.

5

The Best of Times, the Worst of Times

The Rise and Decline of Sir William Berkeley's Golden Age, 1642–74

In March 1642 Sir William Berkeley, a playwright, favorite courtier of Charles I, and staunch supporter of the king in his growing dispute with Parliament, arrived in Virginia with a commission appointing him the colony's governor and captain general. The situation he entered was in many ways unlike that any of his predecessors faced. First, unlike Sir George Yeardley or Sir John Harvey, who had been elevated to the gentry during their lifetimes, Sir William hailed from an ancient aristocratic family with ties to the royal court of Elizabeth I, among others.[1] Having served as a Gentleman of the Privy Chamber to Charles I, Berkeley brought to Virginia both an air of aristocracy and political acumen the likes of which the colony had never seen: "Will Berkeley had daily seen Charles I in person, had conversed with him, and acted as the king's personal emissary. No Virginian ever approached that degree of proximity, so he projected an aura of might that exalted him more highly than anyone among them. His time at court imparted lessons in the intrigues and arts of politics. He recognized in stagecraft an essential ingredient of statecraft. Observing how Charles mixed the two, he learned when and where to draw the line between them."[2]

In addition to the issue of how his elevated social status might affect his relationship with those he was to govern, Berkeley's avid support of Charles I's government had the potential to cause him difficulty in governing Virginia. As the events surrounding Harvey's removal less than ten years before demonstrate, Sir William had been made the governor of a colony that boasted a cadre of local

DOI: 10.5876/9781607323082.c005

magnates who were used to doing things their way. Berkeley would need all the political skill he could muster to walk the fine line between adhering to his instructions (providing for a better defense, diversifying the colony's economic base, and instilling the proper respect for authority in the colony's populace) and not running afoul of those who ran the council, such as William Claiborne and Samuel Matthews. In addition, he arrived in Virginia at almost the same time as the notice of his appointment, so he would not only have had to deal with a population that was entirely unprepared for him but also with former governor Sir Francis Wyatt. Wyatt was being removed from his second stint as royal governor not primarily because of something he had or had not done but simply because Berkeley, who had considerable influence at court, wanted the job.[3] Despite a large body of scholarship over the years that has applied the failures of his final years in office to the rest of his tenure, Sir William Berkeley met nearly every one of these challenges so skillfully that by the mid-1660s he and his closes advisers were convinced that they had finally succeeded in instilling in Virginia the proper relationship between liberty and authority. Unfortunately, the failures of his final years in office, particularly his policies regarding Indians, alienated small and middling planters as well as younger members of the planter elite whose plantations were some distance from Jamestown, to the point that many rose up against him. To focus too much on the disasters of his last years as governor, though, is to obscure the considerable achievements of his early years in office.[4]

Almost from the instant he set foot onshore, Berkeley began to demonstrate how masterful a politician he was when in his prime. Well aware of the influence many members of the Council of State were used to wielding yet determined to obey his orders from Charles to rein them in, Berkeley sought to co-opt them from the start. In matters that were either trivial from his standpoint or on which he probably already agreed with them, he allowed the council members to make decisions that would traditionally have been his prerogative. He also took the unprecedented step of allowing them to see his private instructions from the king. Each of these calculated moves quickly diffused what could have been a very adversarial relationship and bound some members of the council to Berkeley with a loyalty that remained steadfast for at least thirty years and in some cases until his death.[5]

Likewise, Berkeley's handling of William Claiborne, one of the few councilors who remained his adversary throughout the 1640s, also displays the depth of his political skills. Claiborne was one of the most successful of the warlords who emerged from the Second Anglo-Powhatan War, but over the years he made the bulk of his fortune not in the tobacco he planted but in his establishment during the 1630s of a beaver trading network in which he, as middleman, linked the Susquehannock Indians north of the Potomac River to Puritan merchants in

FIGURE 5.1. Portrait of Sir William Berkeley. Courtesy, Berkeley Charitable Trust, Berkeley Castle, Berkeley, Gloucestershire, England.

London eager to profit from the trade in beaver fur. However, as the events of the English Civil War began to unfold during the 1640s, because of his financial connections to the Puritan faction, he consistently found himself in opposition to Berkeley, the devoted royalist. Ultimately, Berkeley defeated Claiborne by appealing directly to the Virginia populace. In doing so, he painted Claiborne as a political elitist and an opportunist who supported Puritanism only because it was economically profitable for him to do so. In addition, by 1646 Berkeley had performed the impressive political feat of convincing a majority of colonists that Claiborne (who had been in Virginia since 1621) was an outsider who represented the interests of merchants in London as opposed to the good of the colony. Had it not been for the victory of the Puritan forces in England in 1651, Claiborne's defeat would have been final.[6]

These successes notwithstanding, Berkeley wisely realized that they would gain him only so much in his relationship with the council. Its members had been allowed to dominate the colony's legislative, executive, and judicial functions for too long to give them all up because of a few relatively minor gestures on his part. Sir William realized that the key to bring the government under his control was to gain the loyalty of the House of Burgesses. In his first meeting with the members, he informed them that a faction back in England made up of supporters of the old Virginia Company was endeavoring to reconstitute the company and convince the Crown to turn the colony back over to its control. Knowing that the burgesses had come to value the autonomy nearly twenty years of minimal Crown oversight had engendered, Berkeley informed them of the development as a means of providing an instant issue around which he and they could bond. In addition, he did not dissolve the previous assembly that had been under way when he arrived, though it would have been customary for him to do so. By not dissolving the assembly, he allowed reforms his predecessor, Sir Francis Wyatt, had proposed to work their way through, thus avoiding a situation in which the burgesses might feel their time had been wasted and going a long way toward smoothing over any ill feelings Wyatt might have harbored at being replaced.[7]

While these moves certainly helped establish Berkeley on good terms with the House of Burgesses, two other decisions he made during his early days in Virginia brought the burgesses firmly into his camp and secured his position as the colony's ultimate political authority. During the 1642–43 session, Berkeley made the assembly truly bicameral. Up until this point, the Council of State and the House of Burgesses had met jointly, which often allowed the very powerful members of the council to exert tremendous influence over the burgesses, thus rendering them rather ineffective as a check on the council's power. Berkeley, realizing that a truly independent House of Burgesses could be a useful ally in his bid to bring the council under his full control, changed this situation for good. In addition, during that same session he allowed the burgesses to choose their own leadership. According to Berkeley's biographer Warren Billings, his giving up his power to appoint the burgess's leaders represented a tremendous abdication of power on his part but ultimately proved well worth the sacrifice:

Yet there was an underlying political logic to what he [Berkeley] did, especially in the context of his own situation in the spring of 1643. He still lacked more than a nucleus of support. His concession was in keeping with his already assiduous court- ing of the burgesses in search of allies. Besides, it did not cost him all that much. He could charm the House, or he could bring it around with other means at his disposal. More important, his chief concern remained the mastering of the council, which, to his way of thinking, still posed the greatest hazard to the success of his administra- tion. Inviting the burgesses to found a house of their own lessened that risk on two accounts. Physically separating the councillors from the burgesses curtailed conciliar sway over them. Institutionally, the House itself counterbalanced the council, which would enable him to play the two against each other.[8]

In addition to these actions, Berkeley encouraged the exploration and trad- ing activities of many of the most prominent men in the colony, such as Francis Yeardley, Abraham Wood, John West, and even Claiborne and Mathews, both in an official and unofficial capacity. These trading alliances not only resulted in the flourishing beaver trade in which Claiborne became so prominent but ultimately led to Virginia's entry into the lucrative Indian slave trade in the second half of the seventeenth century. Such associations profited Berkeley economically as well as politically.[9]

Sir William also augmented his support among those at the local level by increas- ing both the jurisdiction of the county courts and the standing of local justices of the peace. Once again, according to Billings, this advanced Berkeley's overall divide and conquer strategy by fostering more of a separation of authority between the county and the colony governments. This, in turn, provided him with a less unified opposition to his plans for the future of the colony. Ultimately, though, it was the elderly Opechancanough who provided Berkeley with his best opportunity to win the colony's allegiance.[10]

On April 18, 1644, Opechancanough, now the titular and de facto leader of the Powhatan chiefdom, launched another surprise attack against the English. Despite his advanced age and the dwindling population of his chiefdom, Opechancanough demonstrated his talent for striking at the optimum time to inflict the greatest pos- sible physical and psychological damage. With Berkeley still settling in as gover- nor and the Civil War raging in England, the Indian leader surmised correctly that Virginia's defenses might be neglected to the point that he and his warriors could inflict fatal damage on the colony. In addition, well aware of both the possibility that a religious holiday could lead the Virginians to drop their guard even more and the psychological potential of an attack on such a day, Opechancanough chose Maundy Thursday as the day for the assault. Unlike the 1622 attack, however, very few records have survived from which we can construct a narrative of the actual events. The few pieces of evidence that remain place the number of English settlers killed in the attack at somewhere between 400 and 500. Even the high end of that range, although as many as 200 more than were killed in the 1622 attack, represents a mere 6 percent of the colony's estimated population. The 1622 raid, in contrast, killed almost 30 percent of the English inhabitants of Virginia.

Berkeley saw in his response to the attack an opportunity to once again secure the allegiance of the Virginia populace. He therefore called an emergency session of the Virginia General Assembly to seek its counsel and support for his plans to respond. He received both. However, it became very clear that Virginia was in no shape to mount a significant campaign against the Powhatan chiefdom. Nearly fifteen years of relative peace had resulted in a severe shortage of arms, ammunition, and other essential materiel of warfare. Therefore, Berkeley soon thereafter boarded a ship for England to request the needed supplies with which to defeat the Powhatans once and for all. When he returned in the summer of 1644, Berkeley led his troops on what the Virginians referred to as the "Pamunkey and Chickahominy march." The campaign resulted in the abandonment of the Chickahominy village of Oraniock and the destruction of Opechancanough's capital village of Menmend. Later that summer, the English attacked the Nansemonds, Weyanocks, Powhatans, and Appamatucks. In 1646 they constructed forts along their border with Algonquians to aid in their harassment of the chiefdom's remaining groups. In March 1646 Berkeley himself marched against the Algonquians, ostensibly to negotiate peace with Opechancanough. When the mamanatowick refused his offers of negotiation, Berkeley took "that bloody monster, upon 100 years old," to Jamestown as his prisoner.

By October of that year, the Third Anglo-Powhatan War was over, and the paramount chiefdom of Powhatan, Opitchapam, and Opechancanough had been destroyed. A treaty signed by Berkeley and representatives of the remaining chiefdom groups placed the Indians in a subordinate position to the Virginians. Whereas lesser groups had once paid Powhatan tribute, the remains of his chiefdom were now required to present an annual tribute of twenty beaver skins to the governor of Virginia. Believing that the surest way to keep the peace was to keep Virginians and Indians as far apart from one another as possible, the treaty forbade Indians from entering the main area of English settlement between the James and York Rivers unless they wore a special striped coat indicative of their status as messengers to the governor.[11] In addition, the treaty reserved the territory north of the York River for Indians and forbade English settlement there without express permission from the governor and his council. Not only did the treaty forbid Englishmen to settle north of the York, but it also classified violation of the ban as a felony.[12]

During the legislative session immediately following acceptance of the treaty, the assembly also repealed all previous acts sanctioning violence against Indians, placing the decision of who could and who could not have contact with Indians in the hands of the governor. Regardless of whether this was Berkeley's intention, it effectively allowed him and his associates to monopolize trade with Indians. Another provision that made it a capital offense to kill Indians carrying badges denoting their status as trade messengers on their way to see the governor further underscores this point. Finally, blocking their access to Indian land would prevent non-elites from attaining a sufficient land base with which to challenge the authority of the more established planters.[13]

William Bullock's 1649 tract *Virginia Impartially Examined* echoed the need to cultivate trade with Virginia Indians as a means to bring them fully under English control. For Bullock, it was critical that Virginia make overt attempts to integrate Algonquians into the trans-Atlantic market economy so completely that they would come to resemble Englishmen in their desire for commodities and, through those desires, succumb to dependence on the Virginians: "Wherefore if ever they be reclaimed it must be. First, by making them sensible of their nakednesse. Secondly, By taking them off from their confidence upon nature, whereby they may take care for the future. Thirdly, that they may desire comerce. Fourthly, that they may be brought to depend [on Virginians]."[14] Hence, keeping the remnants of the Powhatan chiefdom and Virginia settlers separate from one another represented an essential element of the postwar program of Sir William Berkeley and many of the colony's other leaders.

However, from the beginning, Berkeley was in many ways powerless to prevent the blurring of the boundary between whites and Indians. While he managed to prevent full-scale warfare between Virginia and the Indians for over thirty years, he could do little about the small-scale outbursts of interpersonal violence that flared rather steadily during that period. In addition, he exempted the men (most of whom served on his council) involved in the Indian trade from the restrictions designed to keep Virginians and Indians apart. By doing so, he created a system that many less fortunate Virginians would come to resent in which well-connected and wealthy men enjoyed the fruits of trade with Indians, to the exclusion of everyone else.[15]

A description of a 1648 meeting with Opechancanough's successor as leader of the Pamunkeys (one of the most, if not *the* most, powerful remnants of the Powhatan chiefdom) illustrates crucial factors about the new relationship between Virginia Algonquians and the Virginia government that eventually came to figure into the grievances surrounding Bacon's Rebellion. The account, taken from John Ferrar's 1649 publication "A Perfect Description of Virginia," describes the first visit of Necotowance, the newly recognized leader of the former Powhatan chiefdom groups, to Jamestown. Ferrar's summation of the encounter is exceedingly brief but highly suggestive. According to the account, Necotowance and five other Indian leaders under his authority arrived at Jamestown to present the governor with the twenty beaver skin tribute required by the 1646 treaty. After he presented the gift, the Indian leader expressed his hopes for the future of the Virginia-Algonquian relationship. According to Ferrar: "He concluded with this Protestation; That the Sun and Moon should first lose their glorious lights and shining, before He, or his People should evermore hereafter wrong the English in any kind, but they would ever hold love and friendship together: And to give the English better assurance of their Faith, He had Decreed, That if any Indian be seen to come within the limits of the English Colony, (except they come with some message from him, with such and such tokens) that it shall be lawfull to kill them presently." Necotowance then informed the Virginians of the world beyond his people's borders: "And the *Indians* have of late acquainted our Governour, that within five days journey to the Westward and by South, there is a great high mountain, and at foot thereof, great Rivers that run into a great Sea; and that there are men that come hither in ships, (but not the same as ours be) they wear apparel and have reed Caps on their heads, and ride on Beasts like our Horses, but have much longer ears and other circumstances they declare for the certainty of these things."[16]

This incident reveals three key issues about the future of the Virginia-Indian relationship that ultimately contributed to Bacon's Rebellion. The first is that, by submitting themselves so fully to Virginia authority (or at least presenting themselves as fully submissive), the Algonquians of Virginia opened a new era with the Virginia government in which trade rather than warfare dominated their relationship. Second, by declaring that whites could legally kill any Indian who ventured into their territory, Necotowance unwittingly played into notions that violence against Indians by any member of Virginia society was a justifiable and normative response, with or without government permission. Finally, his description of the lands beyond his realm touched off an era of aggressive English expansion that ultimately opened very lucrative trading networks organized and controlled by elites in which tributary Indians, such as the Pamunkeys and others, would play key roles as middlemen.

These three factors—exclusive elite trade with loyal and peaceful tributary Indians, the belief that unchecked violence against Indians remained their prerogative, and the opening of another trade with Indians to the west from which many Virginians were largely excluded—combined to drive a significant wedge between the few who benefited from this new relationship and the many Virginians barred from profiting from it. During the thirty years between the end of the Powhatan Wars and the beginning of Bacon's Rebellion, Virginia Algonquians skillfully played the meager hand they had been dealt to their best advantage in an effort to survive. By doing so, they created powerful reasons for some to protect tributary Indian land rights and lives from those who came to view those lands as a sort of birthright and their relationship as middlemen in the trade with western Indians as a hindrance to the economic aspirations of many former servants and smaller planters. Despite Berkeley's belief that the separation of Indians and Virginians was the best way to maintain peace and stability, this situation eventually led to a belief among many that the government favored the rights of Indians over those of poorer Virginians. For former indentured servants, landless poor tenants, and small as well as western planters who had come to see the violent acquisition of land from Virginia's Indian population as both a sort of birthright and their only hope for economic success, Berkeley's Indian policies further inflamed their growing resentment of the elite classes. This resentment would play a critical role in driving younger planters who lived near the tributary Indians, as well as middling and poor Virginians, into the union with one another that developed in 1676.

For the majority of the planter elite, as well as those who had enriched themselves in the Indian trade, there was no longer a need for further animosity toward what was left of the Powhatans. In fact, the Powhatans quickly became important both as middlemen in the trade with western groups beyond the mountains and as a military buffer for the colony. However, many other Virginians who had not achieved the success they desired in tobacco or who looked to the lands of these now tributary Indians as the key to their political and social advancement had different ideas. The fate of Opechancanough after his capture provides a telling glimpse of many Virginians' persistent hatred toward Indians and their belief in a right to vent that hatred through unsanctioned violence. According to Robert Beverley's *History of the Present State of Virginia,* Opechancanough languished in English captivity while Berkeley made plans to take him to England to stand trial, but the aged Algonquian leader never boarded a ship for England. In 1646, soon after Berkeley brought him to Jamestown in shackles, one of his jailors took matters into his own hands and fatally shot him. The sources remain silent as to whether the colony punished Opechancanough's assassin. Whether the man was punished in many ways matters little, as the act of dispensing his own brand of justice, despite knowing that Berkeley planned to have the Indian leader tried, speaks volumes. Whereas Sir William felt Opechancanough deserved the same process afforded to any Englishman accused of a crime, Opechancanough's assassin expressed in no uncertain terms his belief that as an Indian he had no rights. At the time, this difference of opinion caused little in the way of social disruption. In 1676, it would threaten the entire colony.[17]

Opechancanough's capture and death and the signing of the peace treaty in 1646 ended the third and final Anglo-Powhatan War. It also made Sir William Berkeley a hero and ushered in a nearly thirty-year period of relative peace and stability, unprecedented in Virginia. Berkeley capitalized on his new renown among the colonists by remaking Jamestown from the ramshackle hamlet he found on his arrival to a more permanent and stately (at least for this side of the Atlantic) capital city. He also set about establishing free trade agreements with the Dutch in an effort to avoid having to deal with the Puritan merchants in London who backed William Claiborne's faction and to enrich the colony in general.[18]

Unfortunately for Berkeley, the diminishing fortunes of his sovereign during the second half of the 1640s forced him to postpone many of the tasks he had set for himself when he arrived in the colony. In addition, though Virginia had largely been spared the religious strife between Puritans and Anglicans that had rent their motherland asunder, by late in the decade those same disputes had begun to encroach upon the colony's shores. Though Berkeley personally felt it was unwise to force others to accept one's own religious beliefs, as a loyal supporter of Charles I he could not show open disobedience or hostility to the church. When he banished a clergyman for refusing to use the Book of Common Prayer, he made powerful enemies in the Puritan-controlled Parliament. In 1651, when parliamentary forces defeated those of the royalists, Berkeley's days as royal governor were numbered. Though he held out as long as possible, in the fall of 1651 the Cromwellian government in England appointed many members of the Council of State (all of whom had commercial ties to Puritan merchants in London) as commissioners tasked with "the reducing of Virginia to the obedience of this Commonwealth." By January 1652 they were in Virginia demanding Berkeley's surrender. After a brief but rather anxious impasse, in which it looked as though Berkeley and his supporters might resist the imposition of parliamentary control with violence, an agreement was struck that allowed Berkeley and his political allies to remain in Virginia and go free as long as they left public life. He retired to his plantation, Green Spring, shortly thereafter to live the rest of his days, ostensibly as a private citizen.[19]

Much like their royal predecessors, the officials of the Cromwellian protectorate were often too preoccupied with events in Europe to pay much attention to Virginia. However, one particular difference between the rule of Sir William Berkeley and that of the general assembly contributed significantly to the idea that unrestrained violence against Indians in the quest of land was permissible for all Virginians. During the eight years of Cromwellian control in Virginia, the colony engaged in an explosive period of expansion at the expense of the remnants of the Powhatan chiefdom. The lack of a powerful royal governor meant there was no check whatsoever on the rapaciousness of Virginia's budding tobacco planters in their search for acreage on which to either start their plantations or enhance the size of their crops. According to one history of the 1650s, "The government could not effectively restrain the Englishman nor protect the Indian." So campaigns of intimidation and outright extermination against Indians became the norm during this period. With each new campaign, the inclination of frontiersmen to believe that not only was government powerless to stop them but that it also lacked the legal power to do so grew considerably. In 1650 Virginia consisted of nine counties. By 1660 that number had nearly doubled, to seventeen. More than half of the new counties were formed from lands of the tributary remnants of the Powhatan chiefdom.[20]

Beyond this rather significant difference, much about the interregnum Virginia government remained the same as it was under Sir William Berkeley. In fact, a majority of the speakers of the House of Burgesses during the eight years between 1652 and 1660 were known royalists. Royalists also figured prominently in the membership of the council. Many of these councilors had been close associates of Berkeley, so, with the exception of the aggressive land acquisition policies, much remained the same. This carryover among the leadership of the Virginia government from Sir William's time also allowed him to keep well apprised of the inner workings of the colony's politics in anticipation of an opportunity to return to the post. Such an opportunity arose with the abdication of Richard Cromwell as lord protector in 1659 and the sudden death of Samuel Matthews, Virginia's Cromwellian governor.[21]

Invited by the general assembly to return to the governorship on an interim basis after Mathews died in January 1660 and officially confirmed in the position on a permanent basis by the newly restored Charles II in September of that year, Berkeley first set about getting the assembly to officially repudiate most of the acts passed during the interregnum. He then turned his attention to a grand scheme to overhaul the colony's constitution and its economy. Despite having just returned to the position, Berkeley seems to have interpreted the unanimous vote of the Council of State and the burgesses to invite him back as a sign that the efforts he had undertaken during his first term as governor had won the undying allegiance of at least those who held property in the colony. He and his closest advisers interpreted this to mean that they, unlike their predecessors, had finally achieved the perfect combination of liberty and authority long sought by Virginia's leaders. With this confidence in the people's approbation of his leadership, he embarked on what historian Alexander Haskell has termed a "sudden surge of ambitious state-building legislation," including the construction of new towns, the establishment of a college, and the implementation of a program to wean the colony off of its dependence on tobacco. Such a grand design for the future of the colony carried a high price tag that would have to be borne by the colonists in the form of increased taxation. However, Berkeley was confident that not only would the rewards justify the costs but also that, given the high esteem in which property holders held him, they would willingly agree to the levies.[22]

Before he could commence this program, however, events were set in motion across the Atlantic that would eventually hamper his ability to realize his dreams for Virginia and seriously damage his credibility with those he governed. Not long after returning to office, Berkeley received word that yet another attempt to revive the Virginia Company was afoot in England. Even more disturbing was news that Parliament, at the urging of Charles II, had recently passed the Navigation Act of 1660, effectively cutting the Dutch out of trade with the English colonies completely. As they had during his previous stint as governor, profits from a robust trade with the Netherlands and its colonies figured prominently in Berkeley's economic policies for the colony. Without this revenue, he would be hard-pressed to successfully transform Virginia according to his plans. Convincing the assembly members of the dire nature of this intelligence, Berkeley encouraged them to send him to London to lobby the Crown against the reimposition of the Virginia Company and for the repeal of the Navigation Act.[23]

The trip produced mixed results. Personally, Berkeley fell upon an opportunity to become a proprietor of Carolina, one of England's newest colonial ventures planned for development just south of his Virginia. As far as his official business went, the scheme to revive the Virginia Company failed, but Charles II denied Berkeley's pleas to allow Virginia to engage in free trade. The newly restored king, his brother James, Duke of York, and their advisers had returned to power determined to transform England into a trans-Atlantic trading empire greater than that of the Dutch. Therefore, the idea of allowing their colonies to trade with their economic rival was a non-starter. However, while lobbying the king for repeal of the Navigation Act, Berkeley had argued that such a repeal would allow him to diversify the colony's economy to the extent that it would surpass Barbados, the most profitable of England's colonies, in its economic output. Though Charles could not agree to repeal of the Navigation Act, he did respond favorably to Berkeley's plans for economic diversification and gave them his blessing (but no money). While in England, Berkeley had also argued for a stint in tobacco production under the premise that it would help him achieve his plans for diversification. Many saw the stint as an attempt by the planter elite on his council to drive the price of tobacco higher. Challenged by Lord Baltimore, the proprietor of Maryland, and facing a Crown concerned about what such a stint in tobacco production would mean to the royal coffers, his proposal ultimately failed, but he had won both the king's blessings for the diversification scheme and a promise that the Crown would refrain from intruding in the colony's internal affairs. To Berkeley's way of thinking, these successes outweighed his failures. Now he had to convince the Virginia property holders to see things this way as well. Unbeknownst to Sir William, however, another obstacle was developing that would seriously hamper his ability to carry his plans to fruition.[24]

Not long after his father was beheaded, Charles II had granted all of the lands between the Potomac and Rappahannock Rivers in Virginia (known as the Northern Neck) to a group of seven proprietors. One of these was Sir William's older brother, the Baron Berkeley. Because of the Civil War and Charles's subsequent exile, the grant had lain dormant since nearly the moment it was concluded. In 1662 the proprietors renewed their claims to the area, but in the years between the original grant and their attempts to renew the proprietorship, Virginians had begun to settle the area in increasing numbers. The issue of how to get the proprietors to renounce their claim to the Northern Neck bedeviled Berkeley throughout the 1660s and early 1670s, ultimately costing the colony's taxpayers a considerable amount of money and sparking much of the dissatisfaction preceding Bacon's Rebellion.[25]

When he arrived back in Virginia in November 1662, Berkeley could not have foreseen the difficulties the Northern Neck and his diversification program would eventually cause him. Instead, he set about putting his plans in motion. Not long after his arrival he pushed through an export duty on tobacco, which he had been instructed to do by the king. He also succeeded in getting the general assembly to pass an act creating a town-building program, which would be paid for by a head tax of thirty pounds of tobacco per person throughout the entire colony. While much new building did occur over the next two years, the town-building program was interrupted by the outbreak of the Second Anglo-Dutch War in 1665, as well as by incursions by Indians from Maryland and an aborted servant rebellion—all of which occurred during the years 1663–67. Though it was restarted modestly after the end of the war, the town-building program never fully lived up to its billing or, in the minds of many Virginians, its cost.[26]

Furthermore, Sir William Berkeley and many of his closest advisers believed the key to securing the future of the colony lay in their ability to place their government on as permanent a footing as possible. The way to do this, they felt, was to convince the overwhelming majority of property-holding Virginians that the government was looking out for their interests. Therefore, Sir William and his government made a calculated decision to address the issues most important to the landed members of Virginia society, regardless of the effect of those decisions on the landless. In doing so, they created animosities among the servant, landless, and tenant populations, as well as smaller property holders. In a situation similar to the one historian Gary Nash found in the cities of pre-Revolutionary America, members of the groups outside the planter elite began to "struggle in relation to these conflicting interests."[27]

The responses of the colony's leadership to these challenges from those below them accelerated the burgeoning class-consciousness developing among the lower ranks of Virginia society.

Harking back to the efforts of their predecessors in the 1620s and 1630s, the colony's leaders sought to reinforce the hierarchical social order they viewed as crucial to theirs and the colony's future. As had been the case during the reign of John Pott, Abraham Peirsey, William Tucker, and their comrades, control of the court system constituted one of their most effective weapons. For example, the simple act of expressing displeasure with elite leadership drew a harsh response, as demonstrated by the case of Mary Calvert. Having confessed in 1653 to stating in private that the men who ran Virginia were "Rogues Traytors and Rebells," Calvert received thirty lashes on her bare shoulders for her speech.[28] Five years later, Ben Cartwright also received lashes for "opprobrious language uttered against the sheriff in contempt of his office."[29]

Perhaps no other case represents the way the county and colony elite used their monopoly over the court system to enforce their hegemony than that of *William Presly v. Ann Smith* in Northumberland County. According to the surviving court records, Presly brought a complaint against Smith in November 1652, claiming "she hath spoken scandalous words and speeches" against him.[30] One other fact makes this case so noteworthy. William Presly was no ordinary citizen of Northumberland County. He had served as the county's first burgess and, at the time of his suit, was a sitting member of the Northumberland County Court. For this offense, Presly and the other members of the court sentenced Smith to ten lashes on her bare shoulders and forced her to beg his forgiveness in open court. Once she had acknowledged her fault in court, Presly waived his right to have her whipped.[31] At first glance, his actions seem magnanimous, which is exactly how he meant them to be seen. In keeping with English traditions of punishment and clemency, by sparing Smith from the physical punishment, Presly reinforced his status as an elite member of society. By demonstrating his power to punish or spare Smith from physical pain, he affirmed one of the key purposes of punishment in the early modern world. The sovereign and those authorized to act on his behalf, in this case the Northumberland County Court, held complete power over the lives and deaths of the king's subjects.[32] However, Presly's decision not to have Smith whipped carried out a social function as well because William Presly occupied a dual role in this situation. While on the one hand he represented the neutral and impassive state that punished individuals for the sake of maintaining state authority, on the other, as the person bringing suit for a breech of norms designed to enforce his societal hegemony, his actions demonstrated the extent to which the court system in Virginia had been co-opted for the purpose of enforcing that hegemony.

In addition to their use of the courts as a means to enforce their authority, members of the postwar tobacco elite also sought to retain as many servants as they could for as long as possible. According to Edmund Morgan, the end of the Anglo-Powhatan Wars coincided with a considerable increase in the number of servants who lived out their indentures and thus earned their freedom. This situation threatened elite tobacco profits; therefore, what to do about these newly freed former servants ranked high on the Virginia elite's list of priorities. According to Morgan, between 1658 and 1666 "the assembly, as always a collection of masters, revised the terms to give themselves and other masters a longer hold on their imported labor."[33]

In many ways, this process began even before the end of the Anglo-Powhatan Wars. A 1642 law required every freedman to obtain a certificate from his former master verifying his freedom to hire himself to someone else.[34] Increasing penalties for various crimes constituted another of the ways the Virginia planter elite accomplished this. Servants who ran away, engaged in forbidden sexual activity, or pilfered livestock to supplement their meager fare received as much as six additional years of service as punishment for their transgressions.[35]

In addition to laws aimed at enforcing hierarchy and those designed to ensure a sufficient labor force for their needs, the 1646 House of Burgesses made it even harder for newly freed servants or newly arrived immigrants to work their way up the colony's economic and political hierarchy. New statutes required that planters register new land claims and enclose those lands within five years, according to specific guidelines drawn up by the government. These requirements presented little or no hardship for established planters, but the cost of registration and enclosure, added to the cost of simply establishing the claim, almost certainly prevented many would-be planters from legally instituting their patents. Furthermore, the assembly also levied new taxes to pay for the years of warfare against the Powhatans and lifted all previous tax exemptions for residents of newly seated areas. Thus, the tax burden fell heaviest on those least able to pay it. A newly arrived settler or newly freed indentured servant first had to encumber the costs of obtaining the land, which he would likely have to buy from an elite speculator at an exorbitant rate. Then he would have to enclose it and pay high land taxes before he could consider his claim legitimate. In addition, the fact that in 1660 only thirty men held 100,000 acres of the land most readily suited to future tobacco planting illustrates the way masters kept the economic ambitions of lesser Virginians in check. With so much land in the hands of a few wealthy planters, many newly freed Virginians were left with little choice but to become tenants of their former masters or one of his peers. Thus, by the 1660s this situation had, in effect, created yet another layer of stratification in Virginia society. The members of this new strata were "the part of the population that had begun to grow most rapidly: the freedmen who had finished their term of service. They were entitled to set up households of their own, but they were finding it harder to do than [had] the men who became free in the preceding decade."[36] In other words, while large numbers of indentured servants were managing to escape the ravages of disease and malnutrition so prevalent in the early days of the colony, the colony's leaders had erected significant barriers to the prosperity they had been promised when they signed their indentures.

An analysis of tithable lists from the third quarter of the seventeenth century illustrates this reality. Morgan compiled statistics for four counties (many of the records for other counties during this period were later damaged or destroyed) between 1653 and 1679. By cross-checking the lists of tithables (the number of men over age fifteen in any one household) with the lists of men who were either granted freedom or who, according to the dates on which they signed their indentures, legally deserved freedom, he found that in Lancaster County, for example, slightly less than 10 percent of freedmen had managed to become householders by 1679. Between 1664 and 1677, the numbers were higher in Northampton County on the Eastern Shore, but less than 30 percent of former indentured servants were able to set themselves up as householders, and eighty-eight of them later dropped back into the ranks of landless freedmen. When those eighty-eight are factored in, the percentage of freedmen in Northampton County who managed to set themselves up as householders and maintain that status drops to approximately 18 percent. In addition, Morgan's analysis revealed that counties bordering the lands of the tributary remnants of the Powhatan chiefdom, such as New Kent, Surry, Henrico, and Isle of Wight, boasted the largest numbers of both landless freedmen and small landholders.[37] Those counties were the most restive during the 1660s and 1670s and ultimately served as the cradle of Bacon's Rebellion.

Beyond attempts to prevent current servants from gaining their freedom and to block all routes to prosperity open to freedmen, elite planters in the postwar years also endeavored to gain control of as many new laborers as possible using whatever means necessary, fair or foul. The claiming of orphans as wards represented one often-used strategy for gaining a leg up in the continuing scramble for servants. While ostensibly a planter was granted charge of an orphan out of charitable motives (and no doubt that did motivate many), in several cases the orphan was treated as an additional servant. In others, the guardian absconded with the orphan's inheritance and left the child "without necessary provision to stay even starke naked." In most of these cases, the guardianship agreement stipulated that the guardian put aside a certain amount of livestock the child would inherit when he or she reached maturity, but often when that time arose many guardians were either unable or unwilling to produce said livestock.[38]

In addition, a statute passed in 1646 created two flax houses to be worked by the children of destitute planters. Not surprisingly, many parents refused to part with their children. The assembly referred to such sentiments as motivated by either "fond indulgence or perverse obstinacy." Workhouse programs had become more prevalent by the 1670s. With the supply of immigrants willing to indenture themselves beginning to dry up as a result of improving economic conditions in England, elites in Virginia seemed to have set their sights at least in part on the children of their less fortunate brethren.[39] Enactments such as this added to a growing sentiment among many that Virginia had fallen into the hands of those who sought to use the colony only for their own aggrandizement.

When colonists registered concern that the governor or the council had overstepped their bounds, the ruling elites responded with indignation. In 1648 many Virginians complained that the governor and council had no authority to impress men into the militia for the purpose of defending the colony against the Dutch without the approval of the assembly. The colonists who complained reasoned that such an act constituted a violation of their liberties as Englishmen. The assembly sided with the governor and council, declaring that those who felt their liberties were infringed upon were "mistaken" and further that the king's commissions to the governor and council made clear their power to make all decisions regarding peace and war. Finally, the assembly scolded the objectors, remarking that true servants of the king "ought humbly to acknowledge his Majesties royal care of his subjects in establishing such a power wherein are naturally placed so many concernments to the peace and safety of all good subjects."[40]

The curtailment of political and legal rights represents another area in which the interests of elites dictated policy and trumped the aspirations of Virginia's less fortunate. Act XX of the 1647 session unleashed a two-headed monster designed to devour what little political autonomy those outside the tobacco elite enjoyed. The act required that all freemen vote in the election of burgesses. Failure to appear at an election would cost the individual 100 pounds of tobacco. The idea that a seventeenth-century government would go to such lengths to encourage more political participation seems liberal for the time, but the assembly further decreed that all elections of "Burgess or Burgesses [be] but by plurality of voices, and that no hand writing shall be admitted." The inclusion of this clause seems to signify that some locales had been selecting burgesses through a secret or semi-secret ballot. Furthermore, the relatively small number of servants who outlived their indentures to gain freedom meant that they posed little threat as either a coordinated voting bloc or a violent mob. These two provisions considered in tandem represent a move by the Virginia government to keep closer tabs on the political activities and preferences of the populous. After 1646, citizens could no longer oppose a social superior in the political arena anonymously. The government unleashed the requirement of deference on the political process in a move undoubtedly intended to create political submission.[41]

In 1658 the assembly further eroded the legal options of small planters and freemen by removing cases for sums under 1,000 pounds of tobacco from the jurisdiction of the county courts. Henceforth, one county commissioner was empowered to decide cases involving less than 350 pounds of tobacco, while two commissioners were deemed sufficient to adjudicate cases ranging from 350 pounds to 1,000 pounds. Clearly, membership in the elite classes had privileges.[42]

In 1670 the House of Burgesses reversed the course set in 1646 and stripped landless freemen of all their suffrage rights. The preamble to the act described those recently freed from indentured servitude as "having little interest in the country." The burgesses complained that freemen often created "tumults at the election to the disturbance of his majesty's peace." While these charges may have been reason enough to deny freemen the right to vote, the burgesses also cited their fear that the ever-growing freemen voting bloc might gain so much influence that it could turn the entire economic, social, and political structure of Virginia in its favor. This represented the harshest blow yet to the hopes of non-elites that they might share in the political, economic, and social fruits gained by the subjugation of the Powhatan chiefdom and the introduction of tobacco agriculture.[43]

In addition to the failure of Berkeley's town-building and diversification schemes, as well as the growing perception that his government favored the planter elite, the Second Anglo-Dutch War also contributed to a precipitous decline in his standing among Virginians. Despite his best efforts, the defenses Berkeley had spent most of his time directing since the outbreak of the war failed to prevent a devastating Dutch attack in 1667. To be fair, Berkeley preferred a different strategy than the one foisted on him (and changed subsequently on numerous occasions) by Whitehall. In a daring surprise attack, a Dutch squadron sailed up the James in June 1667, burned several tobacco ships, bottled up the rest of Virginia's tobacco fleet, and threatened to attack Jamestown as well. Berkeley attempted to launch a counterattack but had difficulty convincing the captains of the merchant ships he commandeered to go through with it. The Dutch took advantage of this hesitation and escaped. To add insult to injury, a hurricane ravaged much of Virginia's coast just two months after the Dutch attack.

The combination of the loss of free trade, his failure to defend the colony from Indian and Dutch attacks, the high cost of reforms that had never been fully accomplished, and Berkeley's advancing age and seeming lack of concern for the opinions and plight of many of Virginia's newer planters had mostly eroded the goodwill he enjoyed among property holders in Virginia that, just a few years before, he had been certain would sustain him for many years to come.[44] By the mid-1670s his authority was being challenged more openly and more often. At a meeting of the General Court in late September 1674, council members bemoaned the fact that several county sheriffs had refused to post the orders with which they disagreed. This refusal demonstrates the extent to which nearly thirty years of policies designed to keep the peace between whites and Indians, yet to instill hierarchy and authority while advancing the interests of property holders, had frustrated the desires of many Virginians in the lower orders of the colony's social hierarchy. In addition, this response by those whose position in county leadership marked them as members of Virginia's growing middling and professional classes demonstrates the extent to which this trend had begun to drive the middling ranks of society into partnerships with freedmen and smallholders in a social formation historian Peter Thompson has referred to as the commonalty.[45]

According to Thompson, "As used by Virginians commonalty referred to the actual common people of the colony, often but not always figured as a distinct social and political estate oppressed by corrupt or immoral great planters." Furthermore, the commonalty began to gain a consciousness of its class position in the years following the Third Anglo-Powhatan War. This is the same period in which the planter elite attempted to reinforce hierarchy, prolong servitude, and deny non-elites opportunities for economic and political advancement, as well as to uphold Indians' land and legal rights. Therefore, as this new language of class took hold among the poor, freedmen, smallholders, and even middling planters and officials, they—acting collectively as the commonalty as well as individually—began to evince considerable disregard for the laws, rules, and pronouncements of their social superiors as embodied by the governor, council, assembly, and county commissions. In addition to acts such as border county sheriffs' refusal to post the order against the purchase or lease of Indian land, many Virginians blatantly violated the prohibitions against trading guns to Indians during the 1660s and 1670s. Those who violated these prohibitions usually received illegal Indian slaves in return.[46] In Lancaster County in 1665, an angry mob drawn from the commonalty forced the members of a sitting court to flee for their lives.[47]

The expression of class-based anger by a mob or a crowd represents a well-established tradition of collective social action on the part of non-elites in England and its Atlantic colonies. For E. P. Thompson, the plebeian mob or crowd acted as an economic leveling force and protector of custom when it rose up to enforce customary (non-market) bread prices. The crowd achieved this through the threat, and sometimes the use, of violence. While Thompson focused primarily on the eighteenth-century English crowd in his famous essay "The Moral Economy of the English Crowd in the Eighteenth Century," he traced the origins of that crowd's resort to violence back to the efforts of English plebeians to resist enclosure in the fifteenth century.[48]

However, the lack of a universal definition of riot presents a particularly thorny problem in any study that utilizes riot as an object of analysis. This study employs the definition set forth by Peter Clark in "Popular Protest and Disturbance in Kent, 1558–1640." Clark defines a riot as "the collective action or demonstration of at least five people, joining together to voice a communal grievance or remedy a communal wrong." Under this definition, many different kinds of events, ranging from an assault on a justice of the peace or landowner by a small group of tenants to full-scale uprisings such as Kett's Rebellion in 1549 and the Midland Revolt in 1607, merit inclusion.[49]

Although the larger revolts and rebellions have typically attracted more attention from scholars, they occurred much less frequently than smaller-scale actions. In addition, as Roger Manning has argued, the more frequent smaller disturbances provide a much more effective tool for gauging the viability of popular political consciousness: "Since riots were more numerous than rebellions and have left a larger body of evidence—especially in the records of the Tudor and early Stuart Court of Star Chamber and other equity courts, their study is likely to yield much knowledge about the nature of popular protest."[50]

Manning estimates that between 1530 and 1640, England experienced "hundreds of riots protesting enclosures of commons and wastes, drainage of fens and disafforestation." In addition, the number of individuals prosecuted in the Henley-in-Arden court for riotous disturbances skyrocketed in the first twenty years of the seventeenth century. In Kent, the late sixteenth and early seventeenth centuries saw a marked increase in popular upheavals that did not stop until the 1640s. In seventeenth-century Essex County alone, J. A. Sharpe found a "constant undercurrent of small-scale rioting." Between the years 1640 and 1642, twenty-two violent disturbances occurred in Essex, including two military mutinies and an attack on a local patrician:[51] "Population growth, inflation, and the changing agricultural economy had profound social consequences. Put simply, the conditions of the century before 1640 favored people whose incomes were elastic while their expenditures were inelastic: those who could take advantage of a fluid land market, or produce a surplus at a time of rising prices. People in the opposite situation—those with reduced access to land, or with incomes that failed to keep up with inflation—suffered correspondingly. The result was a heightened polarization of society which makes this period an important stage in the long process of class formation."[52]

What do these traditions of crowd action have to do with Virginia? According to David Hackett Fischer, the South of England constitutes the "cradle of Virginia." In particular, Fischer defines the seedbed of Virginia colonists as the "broad region in the south and west of England, running from the weald of Kent to Devon and north as far as Shropshire and Staffordshire." Fischer also argues that the emigrants to Virginia from this region, both elite and non-elite, sought to reproduce southern and western English culture in Virginia: "Both regions were marked by deep and pervasive inequalities, by a staple agriculture and rural settlement patterns, by powerful oligarchies of large landowners with Royalist politics and an Anglican faith."[53]

In particular, a cross-examination of hotbeds of crowd violence and the origination points for Virginia settlers yields striking results. The Virginia recruiting area delineated by Fischer roughly corresponds with the areas that witnessed the most defiant acts aimed at maintaining customary rights found by the scholars of early English social relations mentioned earlier. Grain riots were rampant in Norfolk, Essex, Kent, Sussex, Hertfordshire, Hampshire, and the Thames Valley during the mid-fifteenth and early sixteenth centuries. Peter Clark's study of Kent revealed "that popular disturbance was a regular phenomenon" in that southeastern county and "that the typical disorder was small-scale, localized and customary." Likewise, much of the social strife over customary rights examined by both Buchanan Sharp and David Underdown occurred in the cloth-making areas of southern England and in London. Finally, the area of England from whence most Virginia colonists came experienced one of its worst periods of dearth in the decade immediately preceding the Jamestown expedition.[54]

Each of the individual instances of popular disturbance mentioned previously occurred within this area. Disorders in Essex, the Forests of Blean and of Dean, Frampton upon Severn, and Falmouth all coincide with the major Virginia emigrant-producing areas of southern and western England. One study of Isle of Wight County in Virginia found that 90 percent of seventeenth-century settlers came from this area.[55]

According to Fisher, this trend changed slightly in the mid-seventeenth century when the western port of Bristol joined London as a major point of departure for Virginia-bound Englishmen. James Horn has produced data for Virginia colonists departing from the two major ports during the second half of the seventeenth century. Horn concurs that Bristol and London served as the main ports of departure for Virginia colonists. Though his study focuses on the period after 1650, the Bristol-London relationship with colonial Virginia existed from the earliest days of the enterprise. In his letter of patent dated April 10, 1606, James I granted the colony to "certain Knights Gentlemen merchants and other Adventurers of our City of London" and to "Knights Gentlemen merchants and other Adventurers of our Cities of Bristol and Exeter."[56]

Bristol, while less heavily involved than London in the early settlement of Virginia, nevertheless echoed the capital city in its penchant for social unrest. The city had what one Quaker corn dealer referred to as a "law-giving mob." Crowds had brought the export of corn from the Wye and Severn River valleys to a complete halt the preceding year out of their desire to fix prices at a customary, non-market rate.[57] Similar situations existed in the various market towns and shires near Bristol, such as Bath and Whitney. Both Frampton upon Severn and the Forest of Dean, which witnessed customary rights riots in 1610 and the 1630s, respectively, were within Bristol's orbit as well. With the importance of both London and Bristol as major ports for future Virginians and their proximity to the major areas of popular protest and disorder, it seems logical that these customary rights disputes did not end at the edge of the pier. Both elite and lesser colonists in early Virginia came from places with a history of plebeian unrest and violent patrician response. Therefore, it appears logical that among this population one would find many veterans of bread riots, enclosure disturbances, and other acts of collective disobedience by members of the English commonalty. Their actions toward their social superiors when they arrived in the Chesapeake, particularly in regard to the colony's Indians, also indicate the extent to which these traditions crossed the Atlantic alongside Virginia adventurers.

Beyond instances of collective disobedience in Virginia, individual members of the commonalty also found themselves emboldened during this period, to the point that they began to sue their current and former masters for the freedom dues promised them at the time of their original indentures. Tenants and hired men increasingly began to bring suits for back wages and other remuneration. Others took it upon themselves to beat overseers whom they deemed unfair or harsh. Still others felt empowered enough to upbraid both masters and other social elites verbally. All of these collective and individual actions demonstrate the extent to which, according to Peter Thompson, "the social imagination of poorer Virginians and their observers after the Restoration . . . were suffused with agency rather than dependency."[58]

By the late 1660s, the rise of the commonalty and the increasing disruptions it caused were wearing Sir William Berkeley down. In a letter to the Earl of Arlington in 1667, he contemplated retirement and lamented, "age and misfortune has withered my desires as well as hopes." His resignation was not accepted, so he continued on.[59] Despite his best efforts, his popularity failed to recover, and he faced several potential uprisings during the 1660s and 1670s. Some of these uprisings demonstrated a real potential to spark a full-scale rebellion, while others are best categorized as an overreaction by the elite. In 1661 a group of servants in York County was apprehended for conspiring to draw up a petition complaining about their masters' failure to provide them with meat on a regular basis. Two years later a group of Gloucester servants was discovered hatching a plot to obtain weapons and march on Jamestown to demand their freedom. The assembly designated September 13 (the day it was informed of this plot by another servant) as a day to "be annually kept holy," which demonstrates the extent to which such plots struck at the deepest fears of Virginians who held tight to the reins of power.[60]

The Lawne's Creek plot in 1673, mentioned in the book's introduction, represents yet another near-rebellion traceable to the growing disaffection among Virginia's commonalty and the growing perception that the planter elite cared only for themselves. The most immediate cause of the Lawne's Creek plot can be traced to Berkeley's attempt to enforce a new levy intended to provide him with enough funds to buy out the group of absentee proprietors to whom King Charles had years before granted the entire Northern Neck (the peninsula between the Rappahannock and Potomac Rivers), despite several existing claims to the area by various Virginia planters.[61] According to Berkeley, he snuffed out not one but two rebellions by "some secret villains that whispered among the People, that there was nothing intended by the fifty pound levy but the enriching of some few people" in 1673 and 1674. Virginia was toppling on the precipice of a violent conflict. Social unrest, much like that which roiled the areas of England from whence many of the colonists had come, was beginning to pop up with increased regularity and ferocity, but even the Lawne's Creek rising failed to push the tottering colony over the edge because it lacked two critical and related elements. The rising ultimately sputtered because the fourteen conspirators failed to break the powerful bonds of dependence binding middling colonists (in this case, the local sheriff and other local planters of more robust means) to their superiors. To paraphrase E. P. Thompson's famous metal shaving metaphor, the Lawne's Creek rising did not contain sufficient power to counteract the elite field of force.[62] A call for the extermination of all Indians constitutes the second critical element missing from the Lawne's Creek rising. The incident demonstrates that the grievances over taxes and political participation were not enough to break the elite hold on middling colonists and create solidarity among all non-elites. Something or someone was needed to break the hegemony of Virginia's planter elite and create the necessary solidarity among Virginia non-elites. Nathaniel Bacon would eventually rise to this challenge in the spring of 1676.[63]

NOTES

1. Warren Billings, *Sir William Berkeley and the Forging of Colonial Virginia* (Baton Rouge: Louisiana State University Press, 2004), 1–5, 12–15.

2. Ibid., 57.

3. Ibid., 39–40.

4. According to Alexander Haskell, "Historians have often seen the years leading up to Bacon's Rebellion as . . . 'a crisis of authority.' Although that view provides an at least seemingly compelling way in which to make sense of Bacon's Rebellion, it fails to recognize the most significant political development during the three decades before that event, the overwhelming perception among colonial leaders that they had finally achieved that elusive goal of establishing authority upon a firm foundation of the people's love. That by the late 1660s Berkeley's administration could only say with conviction that they enjoyed the affections of property-owning Virginians, and not the large numbers of non–property owning settlers, was nevertheless still a claim worth celebrating." See Alexander B. Haskell, " 'The Affections of the People': Ideology and the Politics of State Building in Colonial Virginia, 1607–1754" (PhD diss., Johns Hopkins University, Baltimore, MD, 2004), 214–15.

5. Billings, *Sir William Berkeley and the Forging of Colonial Virginia,* 80–85; J. Frederick Fausz, "Merging and Emerging Worlds: Anglo-Indian Interest Groups and the Development of the Seventeenth-Century Chesapeake," in *Colonial Chesapeake Society,* ed. Lois Green Carr, Philip D. Morgan, and Jean B. Russo (Chapel Hill: University of North Carolina Press, 1989), 85.

6. Fausz, "Merging and Emerging Worlds," 58–64, 84–86.

7. Billings, *Sir William Berkeley and the Forging of Colonial Virginia,* 85–89.

8. Ibid., 91–92.

9. Ibid., 75; Fausz, "Merging and Emerging Worlds," 58–59; William Waller Hening, *The Statutes at Large: Being a Collection of All the Laws of Virginia from the First Session of the Legislature in the Year 1619* (New York: R&W&G Bartow, 1823), 1:262. See also Alan Vance Briceland, *Westward from Virginia: The Exploration of the Virginia-Carolina Frontier, 1650–1710* (Charlottesville: University Press of Virginia, 1987). For more on Virginia's role in the Indian slave trade, see Paul Kelton, *Epidemics and Enslavement: Biological Catastrophe in the Native Southeast, 1492–1715* (Lincoln: University of Nebraska Press, 2007).

10. Billings, *Sir William Berkeley and the Forging of Colonial Virginia,* 92–96.

11. Hening, *Statutes at Large,* 1:290, 293, 328–29; Joseph Frank, "News from Virginny," *Virginia Magazine of History and Biography* 65 (1957): 84–87; Robert Beverley, *The History of the Present State of Virginia* (London: J. W. Randolph, 1705), 60–62; John Ferrar, "A Perfect Description of Virginia," in *Tracts and Other Papers Relating Principally to the Origin, Settlement, and Progress of the Colonies in North America, from the Discovery of the Country to the Year 1776,* ed. Peter Force (Washington, DC: Peter Force, 1835), 2:no. 8, 7–11; Helen Rountree, *Pocahontas's People: The Powhatan Indians of Virginia through Four Centuries* (Norman: University of Oklahoma Press, 1990), 84–88; Edmund S. Morgan, *American Slavery, American Freedom: The Ordeal of Colonial Virginia* (New York: W. W. Norton, 1975), 149, 404.

12. Hening, *Statutes at Large,* 1:323–25.

13. The possibility that the leaders of Virginia actually wanted to prevent further bloodshed for more altruistic reasons constitutes another interpretation of the treaty language.

However, an act passed by the legislature later in 1646 casts doubt on this interpretation. The act reserved the lands north of the York River to the original patentees who had fled them during the war. For them to take up these lands, they would have had to encroach on the territory reserved for Indians in the treaty. Passage of this act by the legislature demonstrates that peace was never its objective, since it never intended to abide by the 1646 treaty. The act also proves that the governor and legislature intended those lands only for a select few (planters who had previously claimed them) and not the general populace. See ibid., 328–29.

14. William Bullock, *Virginia Impartially Examined, and Left to Publick View, to Be Considered by All Judicious and Honest Men* (London: John Hammond, 1649).

15. Billings, *Sir William Berkeley and the Forging of Colonial Virginia*, 96–99.

16. Ferrar, "Perfect Description of Virginia," 2:no. 8.

17. Beverley, *History of the Present State of Virginia*, 60–62.

18. Billings, *Sir William Berkeley and the Forging of Colonial Virginia*, 100–102.

19. Ibid., 99–110.

20. See Wilcomb Washburn, *Virginia under Charles I and Cromwell, 1625–1660* (Williamsburg: Virginia 350th Anniversary Celebration Corporation, 1957), 111.

21. Billings, *Sir William Berkeley and the Forging of Colonial Virginia*, 117–20.

22. Haskell, "Affections of the People," 205.

23. Billings, *Sir William Berkeley and the Forging of Colonial Virginia*, 132–33; Haskell, "Affections of the People," 212.

24. Sir William Berkeley, "A Discourse and View of Virginia," ed. William H. Smith Jr. (Norwalk, CT: William H. Smith Jr., 1914), 12; Billings, *Sir William Berkeley and the Forging of Colonial Virginia*, 145–48, 160–62.

25. Billings, *Sir William Berkeley and the Forging of Colonial Virginia*, 158.

26. Ibid., 175–83, 199–203; York County Court, "Proceedings in York County Court," *William and Mary Quarterly* 11, no. 1 (July 1902): 27–34; Virginia State Historical Society, "Virginia Colonial Records (Continued)," *Virginia Magazine of History and Biography* 15, no. 1 (July 1907): 38–43.

27. Gary B. Nash, *The Urban Crucible: The Northern Seaports and the Origins of the American Revolution* (Cambridge: Harvard University Press, 1986), xii.

28. Beverley Fleet, *Virginia Colonial Abstracts* (Baltimore, MD: Genealogical Publishing, 1988), 1:350.

29. Ibid., 3:200. See also the 1673 case of David Morris in H. R. McIlwaine, ed., *Minutes of the Council and General Court of Colonial Virginia, 1622–1632, 1670–1676* (Richmond: Virginia State Library, 1979), 330.

30. Fleet, *Virginia Colonial Abstracts*, 1:335.

31. Ibid.; William Glover and Mary Newton Stannard, eds., *The Colonial Virginia Register* (Baltimore: Genealogical Publishing, 1965), 67.

32. For more on the "juridico-political" function of punishment in early modern Europe, see Michel Foucault, *Discipline and Punish: The Birth of the Prison* (New York: Vintage, 1995), 48–53.

33. Morgan, *American Slavery, American Freedom,* 216.

34. Hening, *Statutes at Large,* 1:254.

35. Ibid., 216–17. See the cases of James Hugnut in Fleet, *Virginia Colonial Abstracts,* 3:151, and of Wilimot Rogerman in McIlwaine, *Minutes of the Council,* 258. Rogerman's case is of particular interest as another example of elite control over the court system, as she was the servant of Thomas Ludwell who at the time of the case (1670) served as secretary of the colony. See also the 1672 case of John Hull in McIlwaine, *Minutes of the Council,* 293. For specific legislation increasing the penalties for stealing hogs, running away from servitude, harboring runaway servants, and the outlawing of secret marriages between servants, see Hening, *Statutes at Large,* 1:350–51, 401, 403; 2:113–14.

36. Morgan, *American Slavery, American Freedom,* 225.

37. Ibid., 226–30. See also Hening, *Statutes at Large,* 2:274–75.

38. Fleet, *Virginia Colonial Abstracts,* 3:45, 63–64.

39. Hening, *Statutes at Large,* 1:330–31, 336–37; Morgan, *American Slavery, American Freedom,* 218–19.

40. Hening, *Statutes at Large,* 1:355.

41. Ibid., 334.

42. Ibid., 421, 423–24, 435–40, 445, 460.

43. Ibid., 2:280.

44. Billings, *Sir William Berkeley and the Forging of Colonial Virginia,* 204–9; Haskell, "Affections of the People," 223.

45. McIlwaine, *Minutes of the Council and General Court,* 384. See Peter Thompson, "The Thief, the Householder, and the Commons: Languages of Class in Seventeenth-Century Virginia," *William and Mary Quarterly* 63, no. 2 (April 2006): 253–80.

46. Fleet, *Virginia Colonial Abstracts,* 1:338; Kelton, *Epidemics and Enslavement,* 110.

47. Lancaster County Orders, 1655–1666, State Library of Virginia, Richmond, 364, 369.

48. E. P. Thompson, *Customs in Common: Studies in Traditional Popular Culture* (New York: New Press, 1993), 33–35, 122.

49. Peter Clark, "Popular Protest and Disturbance in Kent, 1558–1640," *Economic History Review,* New Series 29, no. 3 (August 1976): 366; Roger Manning, *Village Revolts: Social Protest and Popular Disturbances in England, 1509–1640* (Oxford: Clarendon, 1988), 3.

50. Manning, *Village Revolts,* 1.

51. Ibid., 3; Clark, "Popular Protest and Disturbance in Kent," 365–70; David Underdown, *Revel, Riot and Rebellion: Popular Politics and Culture in England, 1603–1660* (Oxford: Clarendon, 1985), 34; J. A. Sharpe, *Crime in Seventeenth Century England* (New York: Cambridge University Press, 1983), 71, 85.

52. Underdown, *Revel, Riot and Rebellion,* 20.

53. David Hackett Fischer, *Albion's Seed: Four British Folkways in America* (New York: Oxford University Press, 1989), 240–46.

54. John Walter and Keith Wrightson, "Dearth and the Social Order in Early Modern England," *Past and Present* 71 (May 1978): 27; Clark, "Popular Protest and Disturbance in Kent," 381; Buchanan Sharp, *In Contempt of All Authority: Rural Artisans and Riot in the West of England, 1586–1660* (Berkeley: University of California Press, 1980), 3; Underdown, *Revel, Riot and Rebellion,* 12–19; Manning, *Village Revolts,* 12.

55. John Bennet Boddie, *Seventeenth Century Isle of Wight County, Virginia* (Baltimore: Southern Book, 1959), 204.

56. Fischer, *Albion's Seed,* 237; James Horn, *Adapting to a New World: English Society in the Seventeenth-Century Chesapeake* (Chapel Hill: University of North Carolina Press, 1994), 39–48; "Letters Patent to Sir Thomas Gates and Others, April 10, 1606," in *The James-town Voyages under the First Charter: Documents Relating to the Foundation of Jamestown and the History of the Jamestown Colony up to the Departure of John Smith, Last President of the Council in Virginia under the First Charter, Early in October 1609,* 2 vols., ed. Philip Barbour (New York: Cambridge University Press, 1969), 1:24–25, 34.

57. Collins, *Lying Detected* (Bristol: no pub., 1758), 67–74, quoted in Thompson, *Customs in Common,* 209.

58. Fleet, *Virginia Colonial Abstracts,* 3:158, 176; McIlwaine, *Minutes of the Council and General Court,* 214, 245, 254, 267, 293, 295, 297, 349, 354, 367, 371, 377, 379; Charles City County Orders, 1672–1673, State Library of Virginia, Richmond, 527; Thompson, "The Thief, the Householder, and the Commons," 260.

59. "Sir William Berkeley to Henry Bennet, Earl of Arlington, 5 June 1667," in *The Papers of Sir William Berkeley, 1605–1677,* ed. Warren Billings (Richmond: Library of Virginia, 2007), 311.

60. York County Court, "Proceedings in York County Court," 34–37; Hening, *Statutes at Large,* 2:191, 204.

61. "The Lawne's Creek Uprising, 1673," in *The Old Dominion in the Seventeenth-Century: A Documentary History of Virginia, 1606–1689,* ed. Warren Billings (Chapel Hill: University of North Carolina Press, 1975), 258–67.

62. Thompson, *Customs in Common,* 73. For my explanation of the metaphor, see introduction, note 21.

63. Colonial Papers General Series, CO 1/30, 114–16, CO 1/36, 67–68, British National Archive, Kew, England; Billings, *Old Dominion in the Seventeenth-Century,* 243–44; McIlwaine, *Minutes of the Council and General Court,* 367.

Principal Tributary Groups and "Foreign Indians" in 1676

MAP 6.1. Principal tributary groups and foreign Indians, 1676. Map by Ryan Morris.

6

"To Ruin and Extirpate All Indians in General"

The Rebellion of Nathaniel Bacon

Nathaniel Bacon's 1676 rebellion against Governor William Berkeley and the rest of the Virginia government remains one of the most important events of the seventeenth-century Atlantic world. Its role in hardening racial identity, as well as reaffirming the masculinity of white Virginians, has been ably documented, but Bacon's Rebellion was not the only challenge to elite authority in Virginia during the second half of the seventeenth century.[1] Yet none of the other plots generated a full-scale social rebellion resembling Bacon's in 1676. While these plots originated from the same social conflicts that later fed Bacon's Rebellion, they lacked one critical element. It would take more than the abridgment of political rights and the imposition of highly regressive taxes to create the solidarity across all levels of Virginia society required for such a rebellion. One issue in particular united poor, middling, and even some elite Virginians in 1676, and that was their desire to open opportunities for western settlement and trade by driving the remaining Indians from the colony. Nathaniel Bacon realized this, and his willingness to call for such a campaign thrust him into the leadership of one of the most significant rebel movements in American history.

In the aftermath of the rebellion, special commissioners sent to the colony by King Charles II meticulously cataloged the complaints of both entire counties and individual colonists in an effort to understand the causes of the upheaval. The complaints from Henrico County, the home of the rebellion's titular leader, Nathaniel Bacon, provide considerable insight into the rebels' mind-set. In their formal list

DOI: 10.5876/9781607323082.c006

of grievances, the people of the county complained that Virginia's government structure was stacked from top to bottom with a small group of elite men who legislated and adjudicated in their own best interests, oblivious to the effects of their decisions on the general populace. They particularly cited the imposition of poll taxes that fell heaviest on the lower ranks of society as a prime example of this phenomenon. To combat this, they suggested that no decisions about tax policy be considered legitimate "without att least six of the Comonaltie be joined to the Commissioners at the laying [of] the leavye." Furthermore, the citizens of Henrico County protested that the increasingly lucrative trade with western Indians was monopolized by the same elites who made policy "and that in favor of the monopolisers the people are betrayed to the Indians." They suggested that the only remedy to this situation was "an immediate warr with all Indians in Generall."[2]

While the Henrico County grievances and those compiled for other Virginia counties mentioned other possible triggers for the rebellion, the grievances as well as the remedy prescribed by the Henrico residents hit as close to the core of Bacon's Rebellion as anything does. Heretofore disconnected factions of Virginia society had come to feel that the leadership of the colony's government had manipulated it to the point that it served only to benefit the interests of those leaders. Events in 1675 and 1676 drove these parties into a union with one another against Sir William Berkeley and his supporters. The various disaffected blocs included those from all levels of society who objected to the colony's increasingly regressive taxation system: residents whose political and legal rights had been eroded to the point of near nonexistence during the years following the Anglo-Powhatan Wars; former indentured servants who had survived the often brutal existence of servitude only to find that the land, supplies, and opportunity promised them when they indentured themselves was nothing more than a mirage; African slaves whose numbers were on the rise during this period; and elite planters who, for reasons that included their lack of breeding and temperament, their relative newness to the colony, their geographic distance from Jamestown, or their dependence upon either opening up new lands for tobacco cultivation or establishing themselves in the Indian trade, found themselves outside the increasingly isolated inner circle of those who governed the colony. These groups began to coalesce around the notion that the government of Sir William Berkeley valued the rights of Indians over the rights of those outside the highest echelons of the planter elite. Ultimately, these groups were united by their desire to engage in ethnic cleansing against all Indians in Virginia. This unity, established through a shared desire to eradicate all of Virginia's Indians, made Bacon's Rebellion more than a localized riot or crowd action.

Discontent over the government's policies regarding Indians had been growing in Virginia ever since the end of the Anglo-Powhatan Wars in 1646. This period also witnessed several events that indicate that the proper policy toward Indians was fast becoming a divisive issue in the colony. Despite the end of the Anglo-Powhatan Wars, neither Berkeley, the Cromwellian governors, the Council of State, nor the House of Burgesses had succeeded in crafting a policy toward Indians, within or beyond Virginia, that kept the peace and satisfied the majority of the white population. In fact, they often unwittingly provided both encouragement as well as significant frustration to Virginians who advocated unrelenting violence toward Indians as the preferred direction of Virginia's Indian policy.

The first statute passed by the assembly after the end of the Anglo-Powhatan Wars also contributed to the perception that the elite were deliberately picking the pockets of smallholders and freedmen at the expense of an effective defense against Indians. The act, which angered non-elites into the 1670s, turned over maintenance of the colony's network of protective forts to the wealthiest planters of the respective counties. In the preamble language justifying the move, the assembly referred to the forts as "a great burden to be maintained by the public charge." In other words, it cast the decision as a cost-saving move that would still provide security from both Indian and foreign attack.

Had the assembly stopped there, this decision might not have aroused such ire. After all, the law required the planters entrusted with the care of the forts to man the garrisons and maintain the structures at their own expense, but other provisions of the act provided enough compensation to ensure that even the least thrifty of the fort's undertakers would turn a profit. The various men named to control the forts all received title to the fort's grounds, ammunition, buildings, and contents. They also received between 400 and 600 acres of land. Instead of public works designed to ensure the safety of the entire colony, the assembly and the governor transformed the fort system into a plum perquisite to be exploited by enterprising elites, one of whom was the son of Pocahontas and John Rolfe. Thomas Rolfe had returned ten years earlier and quickly established himself in the vocation made possible by his father's introduction of West Indian tobacco to Virginia. The trader Abraham Wood not only received possession of Fort Henry on the Appomattox River, but the 1646 treaty also stipulated Fort Henry as one of only two locations at which the defeated remnants of the Powhatan chiefdom, now referred to as tributary Indians, could go to trade with licensed white Virginians. In less than five years, Wood had successfully exploited both his landholdings and his trading monopoly to the point that he had accumulated nearly 1,600 acres of land in the area. By the early 1670s, he had garnered the title major general and received an appointment to the Governor's Council. Wood's success only perpetuated the belief that one could arrive in Virginia with nothing and rise to a position of prominence. Wood had arrived in Virginia in 1620 as a five-year-old indentured servant, but for every

Abraham Wood there were hundreds of others who never made it out of servitude. Those who did often found substantial barriers to their aspirations erected and perpetuated by men such as Wood and Rolfe.[3]

From almost the moment the western forts were built, the proprietors of those forts, such as the aforementioned Abraham Wood, saw them not simply as a means of defense but as a tremendous economic opportunity. In Paul Kelton's words, "Wood, in fact, represented a vanguard of Virginians, including Cadwallader Jones and Thomas Stegge, who sought profits from something other than tobacco cultivation and looked to the Native trade to make their fortunes." These men were not the only ones, as the famous Byrd family also got its start through trade with Indians.[4]

While we might assume that trade with western Indians would provide the perfect opportunity for those too poor in land and servants to compete in the tobacco trade, Virginia's leaders endeavored to bring the Indian trade under their control as well. For example, while leading men such as Wood, William Byrd I, and others often did not actually conduct the trade missions themselves, they used their tobacco wealth to employ poorer Virginians to undertake the trips to the Siouan- and Iroquoian-speaking groups in the west and south. Often, instead of paying wages, the Indian trade elite would offer to clear the debts owed them by freedmen and other non-elites if they would undertake such a trip and return with a sufficient amount of Indian goods to balance the transaction. In this way, no doubt, the Indian trade became simply one more way in which wealthy and well-connected Virginians exercised significant control over the economic lives of their lesser countrymen.[5]

In addition, through their control of the colony's government, leading Virginians attempted to erect significant legal barriers to non-elite entry into the trade. Even before the advent of the postwar western trade, the Virginia government had long sought to limit trade with Indians to a very few specific locations where it would be conducted by a small number of men handpicked by the governor.[6] These attempts to control trade became even more overt as the trade began to flourish in the 1650s and 1660s.[7] For example, in 1653 the assembly ordered Nathaniel Battson whipped for illegally trading with Indians and promised further whippings if he attempted to enter the Indian trade in the future.[8] In 1659 Richard Parker was fined 2,000 pounds of tobacco by the Charles City County Court for trading one gun to an Indian.[9] Throughout most of the seventeenth century, trading guns, ammunition, or similar items to Indians was of more concern to Virginians than were more mundane economic exchanges and had often been expressly prohibited even in times when other exchanges were permissible. However, the assembly repealed all prohibitions on trading weapons to Indians three months before this case, largely because the Virginia Indians had been receiving guns from the Dutch for several years. Prohibiting Virginians from trading weapons to Indians did nothing to stem the flow of guns and only hurt Virginia's commerce. The fact that the court still punished Parker for this transaction seems to indicate that it had some other reason for punishing him, such as limiting competition from non-elites.[10]

In 1665 the assembly once again prohibited the trading of guns, powder, and shot to Indians.[11] This lurching back and forth between prohibitions on open trade with Indians and a virtually unregulated market for such trade mirrors the confused state of Virginia Indian policy throughout much of the seventeenth century. During the third quarter of the century, this continual swing of the pendulum wore thin with freedmen, smallholders, and middling planters to the point that they joined together in Bacon's Rebellion.

In 1663 Berkeley and the Council of State, acting in their capacity as the colony's General Court, acquitted nine Indian "kings" for murder for their part in a series of attacks in Rappahannock County. The acquittal did not sit well with Rappahannock County residents, who blamed the poor advice Berkeley received from his self-interested Council of State for the decision. In addition, one man promised that if Indians raided the county in the future, the residents of the county would "not be so forward as we have been for public redress of our wrongs." In other words, they would take matters into their own hands.[12]

Three years later, more conflict between Indians, specifically Doegs and Potomacs from Maryland, occasioned the leaders of Rappahannock County to beg Berkeley for help in combating them. Berkeley responded favorably by instructing the militia to destroy the villages of the offending groups and sell the captive women and children into slavery. Whether Berkeley decided on this course in response to the anger over the General Court's decision in the murder case three years earlier or for other reasons is not clear. The Council of State went further and advocated for the destruction of all Doegs and Potomacs, regardless of whether they were affiliated with the villages involved in the attacks. The record is largely silent about the outcome of this incident, and we know that Doegs and Potomacs were not destroyed in 1666, but this incident indicates that Berkeley and the council could indeed be ruthless toward Indians when they wanted to. Ten years later they refused to allow such a campaign when proposed by Nathaniel Bacon, but those were Maryland Indians. Since the end of the beaver trade with northern Indians, Virginians had increasingly focused their Indian trading activities on groups to their west and south, the location of both a continuing beaver trade and the burgeoning trade in Indian slaves. Berkeley and most Virginians did not have a trading relationship with the Maryland groups, so such an expedition had no potential to disrupt their economic activities. However, in Berkeley's case at least, financial considerations seem not to have been the only factors in determining his policies toward military campaigns against Indians, as demonstrated by his behavior during the months leading up to Bacon's Rebellion in regard to the same Doegs from Maryland. Regardless, the incident is important not so much for Berkeley's reasoning as for its potential as a signal to Virginians that extermination of Indians was now the colony's official policy. Given this precedent, though, Bacon's expectation that his campaign to exterminate all Indians would meet with Berkeley's approval seems a more reasonable assumption.[13]

Beyond the contradictory nature of Virginia's Indian policy in general, the individual and collective actions of Virginia Algonquians to maintain their lands and manage their relationship with Virginia to their best advantage also contributed to the view of many non-elites that the colony's leaders valued the rights of Indians above those of common colonists. These efforts began almost simultaneous with their defeat in 1646. Until recently, most scholars have assumed that the reservation (like most throughout history) represented the worst possible and therefore least desirable piece of land in the area. Certainly, from an English standpoint, those accounts are correct. The English had little use for the swampy area at the lower end of the land between the Pamunkey and Mattaponi Rivers known as Pamunkey Neck, which eventually became the Pamunkey Reservation. However, recent work by Helen Rountree argues convincingly that far from "getting stuck" with their particular reservation, the Pamunkeys skillfully selected the site because it offered them the best hope of retaining the greatest amount of their traditional life ways. The Pamunkey Neck area provided ready access to the ecosystems that had produced many of the flora Virginia Algonquians had relied upon as a vital component of their subsistence long before the arrival of the English. The Pamunkeys had also lived in the general area of Pamunkey Neck (albeit on more acreage than they were granted after the Anglo-Powhatan Wars) for generations and were therefore adept at growing crops there. Thus, in this strategic location, the Pamunkeys at least were able to stave off the complete destruction of their culture and life ways that most Virginians likely assumed was imminent.[14]

By 1649 Necotowance, the man recognized as "the King of the Indians" in the treaty that ended the Anglo-Powhatan Wars in 1646, had disappeared from the historical record. Virginia records refer to his successor, a Pamunkey man called Totopotomoy, as "King of the Pamunkey" rather than by the "King of the Indians" moniker they applied to Necotowance. The change in title, as well as a legislative act the same year that redistributed Indian lands equally among all remnants of the Powhatan chiefdom, had to have hammered home the totality of the Pamunkeys rapid fall from power and the depths to which their access to sources of spiritual power had plunged. Less than fifty years before, the Pamunkeys occupied a preeminent place among the leadership of one of the most powerful Native polities in

North America. By the middle of the seventeenth century they were paying tribute to the English governor of the colony of Virginia.[15]

By all accounts, Totopotomoy, fully grasping the reality of the Pamunkeys' situation, saw obedience to the colony's leadership as the surest way to ensure his people's long-term existence. The English failed to appreciate his fealty. By 1656, large numbers of English settlers had invaded the territories of the tributary Indians, further shrinking their land base and, more important, depleting what little game was left on Pamunkey lands. That same year, in his last act of fidelity to his English overlords, Totopotomoy led a group of Pamunkey warriors on a joint expedition with the Virginians against a western Indian group the colonists referred to as Richahecrians, who had recently settled near the falls of the James River. The ensuing battle cost Totopotomoy his life and thrust his wife, Cockacoeske, by all accounts a blood relative of Opechancanough, into the leadership of the Pamunkey people.[16]

Despite the fact that Pocahontas occupies a significant space in Americans' collective memory, Cockacoeske is a more successful example of Algonquian female diplomacy. Specifically, Cockacoeske had two distinct advantages that eluded her ancestral kinswoman. In the fifty years since the English arrived, the Virginia Algonquians had learned a considerable amount about the ways English colonial politics, social relations, familial relations, and economic relationships worked. In addition, Cockacoeske, unlike her late husband, was not content simply to please the Virginians in return for her people's lives. Her goals were much more ambitious. She aimed to restore the Pamunkeys to overlordship of the area tribes and recreate the Paramount chiefdom as much as possible. The knowledge handed down to her over the years regarding English gender relations and political institutions proved invaluable in this mission.

Either immediately after Totopotomoy's death in 1656 or very likely while he was still alive, Cockacoeske gave birth to a son she named John West after the boy's father, Colonel John West, who owned a nearby plantation on Pamunkey Neck. Colonel West was no average tobacco planter. His grandfather, Sir Thomas West, also known as the Third Baron De La Warr, served as governor of Virginia from 1610 to his death in 1618. On the surface, today one might interpret Cockacoeske's sexual relationship with West as nothing more than another example of the unequal power relationship between colonizer and colonized in which a male colonist saw not only the land as his to dominate but also the women of that land. Conversely, many colonists at the time likely viewed her relationship with West as proof of the sexual depravity rampant among heathen savages. A careful examination of the written as well as ethnographic evidence suggests another interpretation.[17]

Cockacoeske's relationship with Colonel John West constituted a culturally based diplomatic strategy on her part, aimed to provide her with a kinship connection to a powerful Virginia figure but one that would not require her to surrender any of her personal autonomy, as Pocahontas had done by marrying Rolfe on Anglo-Christian terms. If Totopotomoy were still alive when she and West conceived their son (and the date of the child's birth compared with that of Totopotomoy's death seem to indicate that he was), he was likely aware of the liaison, which was a common practice among Virginia Algonquians. They not only practiced polygyny, but Virginia Algonquian marriages also allowed women and men considerable sexual freedom. This was particularly the case in chiefly marriages, which were often arranged pairings that according to traditional practice required the couple to separate after the birth of their first child. According to Rountree, "Affairs, permitted to women with husbands' permission (apparently often given) and seemingly free for men to engage in, were less likely to cause jealousy if husband and wife were not even supposed to be emotionally close." Thus, Cockacoeske's engaging in sex with a man outside her marriage was in keeping with Algonquian cultural norms.[18]

Nevertheless, the acceptability of extramarital sexual relationships among the Powhatan does not in itself prove that Cockacoeske's affair with West represented a concerted political strategy on her part. However, combined with Powhatan customs regarding the role of females in establishing political and economic relationships (which in Pocahontas's time were usually only achieved by sponsoring adoptees or through marriage) and the very credible evidence we have of Cockacoeske's considerable political acumen, it seems possible that she engaged in the relationship for more than sex.[19] A relationship with a powerful colonist like West gave her access to inside knowledge of colonial affairs. The product of the relationship, her son John, whether intended or not, provided an opportunity to create a significant go-between who could straddle the line between the cultures. Yet unlike Pocahontas, since the affair was a sexual one and not an English marriage, Cockacoeske did not have to acquiesce to the repressive gender norms regarding marriage codified in European ecclesiastical and legal strictures. Whereas in Pocahontas's time marriage represented a diplomatic and political strategy and extramarital affairs functioned as a way of ameliorating the negatives of that strategy, Cockacoeske's experience points to a new formulation based on her understanding of European legal and social structures. For her, sex represented a viable political strategy when dealing with Virginians, both because it lacked the restrictions that came with English marriage and because of the very real possibility of producing a cultural go-between.[20]

In addition to her knowledge of English gender relations and the perils of becoming enmeshed in them, Cockacoeske demonstrated over the course of thirty years as *weroansqua* a deep understanding of the workings of Virginia's political and legal systems. This represents another area in which she possessed considerable advantages over Pocahontas, Powhatan, and Opechancanough. In addition to acting as the official emissary of her people to the colonial government on several occasions, she seems to have used her trips to Jamestown to cultivate political relationships with such powerful individuals as Deputy Governor Francis Moryson. This relationship would serve her well when he returned in 1677 as a member of the commission sent by King Charles II to deal with the aftermath of Bacon's Rebellion. The fact that Sir William Berkeley called on her for support very early during Bacon's Rebellion also indicates her political connections. Finally, her demeanor when she addressed the assembly in response to Berkeley's request bespeaks a confidence that could only have come from the knowledge that she was a very powerful political figure, not just among her own people but among Virginians as well. However, in this instance she seems to have overestimated that power, which possibly put her life in danger from the elements in Virginia society who came to advocate the destruction of all Indians.[21]

According to a contemporary account, Cockacoeske, dressed in traditional Algonquian ceremonial attire, "entered the chamber with a comportment graceful to admiration." She also brought her son, John West, now twenty years old. During this audience she spoke only through her personal interpreter, despite the fact that she was likely fluent in English. When asked how many warriors she would supply to an expedition against the foreign Indians involved in the initial raids of the rebellion, she let forth with an emotionally charged "harangue [for] about a quarter of an hour, often interlacing with a high shrill voice and vehement passion these words, 'Tatapatamoi Chepiacke,' i.e., Totopotmoy dead." According to one historian, this reference was surely meant to remind the assembly that her husband and his entire party had died under exactly the same circumstances, which seems logical, but the few interpretations we have of this very interesting audience do not go far enough. They fail to answer the question of what exactly Cockacoeske hoped to gain by responding to the assembly's request in this manner. Totopotomoy, a man she had been forced to marry (according to the ethnographic evidence) and therefore felt little emotional connection to, had been dead for twenty years. Surely her emotional reaction to the request did not stem from grief.

Her eventual contribution to the campaign against the Susquehannocks provides a possible clue to her motivations. Despite the fact that she had at her command as many as 150 warriors, Cockacoeske contributed only 12 of them to the campaign, and there are indications that she demanded compensation for them. In this light, her emotional outburst seems more a shrewd political stratagem designed to satisfy the Virginians of her loyalty while at the same time incurring the least possible amount of loss to her own warrior base and ensuring that her people would receive some measure of economic settlement for whatever losses they suffered.

Her husband had done none of these things in 1656 and had nearly destroyed the Pamunkeys as a people as a result. Whereas his goal had been simply to survive by pleasing the English in every way possible, hers was to reconstruct the paramount chiefdom and the Pamunkey role in its leadership structure. She could not accomplish this goal if her warriors took massive casualties every time the Virginians got their blood up against other Native groups. This kind of shrewd political maneuvering foreshadowed the savvy ways Cockacoeske manipulated the Treaty of Middle Plantation, signed after Bacon's Rebellion, to the maximum benefit of herself and her people. However, in the immediate future, this strategy might have caused her more harm than good. It more than likely contributed to the growing perception among non-elite Virginians that Cockacoeske seemed to have gotten away with the kind of impertinence toward the colony's leadership that would have earned any other Virginian a severe reprisal.[22]

Beyond this example of an Indian leader's challenges to non-elite ideas regarding the proper place of Indians in Virginia society, several individual Virginia Algonquians outside the leadership structure as well as collective actions by entire Native groups, particularly during the years immediately preceding Bacon's Rebellion, provided plenty of examples to reinforce this perception among non-elites. As early as 1655, individual Virginia Indians were bringing and winning suits against white Virginians. By 1670 Edmund Scarborough, a prominent Eastern Shore colonist, had been stripped of all civil and military offices based on complaints lodged against him by local Indians. This trend widened further until the eve of Bacon's Rebellion in 1674, when several cases arose in which Native rights were consistently upheld against the claims of various Virginians. On April 4 that year, the Nottoway Indians successfully petitioned the Governor's Council to have white settlers evicted from their territory. Just four days later the council issued a general declaration stating, among other things, that the peace of the entire colony depended on "the preservation o[f] the Indians right and propriety in Those lands which have been Assigned them." Therefore, the council outlawed the sale or lease of any Indian-held lands to anyone. To prevent enterprising Virginians from claiming ignorance of the decree as a defense for disregarding it, the council concluded the pronouncement by requiring that the sheriffs in all counties that bordered Native Americans publish the order in their respective county courts.[23]

The failure of the Lawne's Creek plot demonstrates the extent to which middling planters and officials had remained loyal to Berkeley throughout the first half of 1675. However, renewed raids by Susquehannock and Doeg Indians from Maryland that year provided the shove that sent them into an alliance with their non-elite countrymen and hurtled Virginia toward the abyss of Bacon's Rebellion. Over the next several months, both sides took turns visiting atrocities upon the other.

Bacon's Rebellion began with an attempt by a group of Maryland Indians to gain satisfaction from a Virginian they felt had defrauded them. In July 1675 a group of Doegs and Susquehannocks crossed the river and took some hogs from Thomas Mathew, a trader whom they said had "abused and cheated them, in not paying them for such Indian truck as he had formerly bought of them." Mathew and a group of men gave chase, caught up with some of the raiding party, and beat several of them to death. The Indians who made it back to the Maryland side of the Potomac re-crossed the river and killed two men in Mathew's service as well as his son. This incident, combined with the general Indian fear spawned by the outbreak of King Philip's War in New England, provided an opportunity for a pair of Virginians with a long-standing connection to Anglo-Indian violence to continue their efforts to annihilate Indians.[24]

Despite a 1662 judgment against him for a plot to frame the weroance of the Patawomecks for murder, George Mason now held the title of colonel in the local militia. He and Major George Brent, the son of one of his co-conspirators in the Patawomeck plot, set out with a force of thirty men to punish the Indians for the killings at Mathew's plantation. When the fleeing Indians crossed to what they thought was the inviolable safety of Maryland soil, the Virginians refused to stop and crossed the Potomac themselves. When they caught up to the Indians at their village, Mason and Brent "killed an Indian King and 10 of his men upon the place." According to one account, the killing occurred after the Indians had emerged from their meetinghouse in response to Brent's request for a parley:[25]

> Capt. Brent went to the Doegs Cabin (as it proved to be) Who speaking the Indian Tongue Called to have a *Matchacomicha Weeship* i.e., a Council, called presently Such being the usual manner with Indians. The King came Trembling forth, and would have fled, when Capt. Brent, Catching hold of his twisted Lock (which was all the Hair he wore) told him he was come for the Murderer of Robert. Hen, the King pleaded Ignorance and Slipped loose, whom Brent shot Dead with his Pistol. The Indians Shot Two or Three Guns out at the Door and fled, The English Shot as many as they could, so that they Killed Ten, as Capt. Brent told me, and brought away the Kings Son of about 8 Year old.[26]

For his part, Mason reportedly killed nearly fifteen peaceful Susquehannocks from nearby houses who had come to investigate the noise caused by Brent's attack on the meetinghouse.[27]

Brent and Mason's Maryland sortie sparked not only a war of words between the governments of Virginia and Maryland over the violation of the latter's border but also numerous acts of retaliation perpetrated by both Indians and whites on both sides of the Potomac. Governor Berkeley dispatched a force of nearly

1,000 militia, under the command of Colonel John Washington and Major Isaac Allerton, to deal with the escalating conflict on the Virginia-Maryland border. On September 26 Washington and Allerton's men besieged a party of approximately 100 Susquehannocks who had conducted retaliatory raids into Virginia in response to Mason's "accidental" killing of their brethren earlier in the summer. When the besieged Indians sent a party to negotiate peace, the Virginians "caused them to be (Instantly) Slain." Eventually, the remaining Susquehannocks escaped and made their way across to the Virginia side of the Potomac, where they conducted revenge raids on the frontier settlements of the upper Rappahannock. In January 1676 they killed nearly 40 colonists in an attack on settlements near the falls of the Potomac and Rappahannock Rivers. In response, Governor Berkeley initially ordered Sir Henry Chicheley to command a punitive expedition against the Susquehannocks for the Potomac and Rappahannock River killings. However, as Chicheley and his force were about to set out, the governor abruptly changed his mind and canceled the expedition. In its place, he proposed a defensive rather than an offensive strategy for dealing with this threat. When word of Berkeley's change of heart and his new plan reached the residents of the western counties that bordered the lands of the tributary (peaceful) remnants of the once formidable Powhatan Indian chiefdom, simmering tensions flared into open rebellion.[28]

Key provisions of the defensive strategy smacked of economic profiteering by Virginia's most powerful men. Specifically, the government planned to build a string of defensive forts and man them with soldiers recruited from non-western counties. Westerners objected to the plan on several grounds. First, the forts would certainly be built on lands held by members of the assembly. The government proposed to pay the outsiders who would man the forts more than the typical western smallholder or freeman earned in a year. These funds were to be raised by a general levy of all landholders. Frontier residents resented the fact that they should "be compeld to worke all the day, (nay all the yeare), for to reward those Mole-catchers at the forts." Second, the wave of new explorations beyond the Blue Ridge Mountains had revealed to middling westerners the tremendous potential for trade with the Native groups who inhabited the region. The tributary groups and others such as the Occoneechees, located between the westernmost colonists and the Blue Ridge, represented a significant barrier to the development of this trade. Therefore, many western planters saw the conflict with the Maryland Indians as the perfect opportunity to eliminate the Indian barrier to the western trade.[29]

Nathaniel Bacon eventually emerged as the leader of Virginians who opposed Berkeley's defensive strategy for dealing with the area's Indians. Who was Nathaniel Bacon, and how did he come to lead the makeshift army of plebeians and middling Virginians that attempted to both wipe out the tributary Indians of Virginia and refashion the colony's social structure? In many ways, the details of Bacon's personality remain somewhat of an enigma. He had obviously not been in Virginia long at the time of the rebellion, and he was somewhat young, at age twenty-nine, even by the standards of a deathtrap like seventeenth-century Virginia. While Bacon's father, Thomas, owned a significant amount of land in Suffolk, England, he held no peerage and would probably have been considered a member of the lower gentry or upper middling ranks of English society. He, like most patriarchs of a rising English family, likely hoped that his son would advance the family's fortunes and power within the realm.[30]

By most accounts, the young Nathaniel consistently failed to live up to his father's expectations.[31] Thomas's withdrawal of his only son from Cambridge University after only two-and-a-half years constitutes the first mention of Nathaniel Bacon in the historical record. As reason for the withdrawal, Thomas Bacon cited his son's propensity toward "extravagancies." Bacon's tutor put it more explicitly, praising his "quick wit" but lamenting his lack of dedication, concluding that "his temper will not admit long study."[32]

His forced withdrawal from Cambridge seems to have done little to correct Nathaniel's rebellious behavior. Sometime thereafter, he entered into an affair with Elizabeth Duke, the daughter of Sir Edward Duke of Benhall. By most accounts, the match pleased none of the pair's parents. When word reached Sir Edward that his daughter and the young Bacon had married, he disowned her and never spoke to her again. For Thomas Bacon, his son's involvement in a plot to swindle a neighboring youth's inheritance constituted the last straw, and he put Nathaniel and his young wife on a ship bound for Virginia where his kinsman, also named Nathaniel Bacon, served as the colony's treasurer. Thomas hoped the combination of the elder Nathaniel Bacon's connections and the considerable sum of £1,800 he gave them would set them up comfortably in the colony.[33]

After he arrived in Virginia, Bacon quickly exploited his family connections as well as his wife's friendship with Lady Berkeley to gain a seat on the Governor's Council. Like many of his neighbors, he had recently obtained a commission from Berkeley and constructed a trading post for the purpose of setting himself up in the increasingly lucrative western Indian trade. Bacon and many other ambitious young westerners, like William Byrd I, attempted to benefit from both sides of the economic coin by supplementing their tobacco activities with Indian trading in an effort to gain the kind of wealth that would place them on an even footing with their elite counterparts in the East. Thus, for men on the rise such as Bacon and Byrd, the presence of the tributary Indians in particular presented an obstacle to both activities. First, the Indians' lands, guaranteed them by treaty with the Virginia government, represented good tobacco land wasted. Second, because of their geographic position between the edges of the Virginia settlement and their Native trading partners to the south and the west, the tributary groups were able to set themselves up as middlemen in this burgeoning trading network, thus decreasing the potential profits for intrepid western Virginians.[34]

Eventually, Virginia's leaders began to realize that they, too, could benefit from financing and co-opting this trade. In 1676 Governor Berkeley placed all trade with Indians under his personal control. Only he and those licensed by him could legally engage in the Indian trade. When he learned of Berkeley's decision to assert greater control over the trade, Bacon reacted furiously. During the rebellion, he accused Berkeley of monopolizing "a trade with the Indians" while granting trade licenses to "his creatures . . . to trade with them for which he had every third skin."[35] Furthermore, Bacon and his family personally experienced the effects of the increased Susquehannock raiding. In a letter to her sister, Bacon's wife, Elizabeth, decried the loss of an overseer "at an outward plantation which we had, and we have lost a great stock of cattle, which we had upon it, and a good crop that we should have made there."[36]

Not long before, Bacon had fallen out of favor with Berkeley for arresting a group of Indians whom he accused of stealing corn. His subsequent rebuke by Berkeley seems to have ingrained in him an antagonistic stance toward the governor, in addition to his belief that the removal of the tributary Indians represented the surest path to a successful future for westerners like himself. Beyond his personal rift with Berkeley, Bacon also expressed a marked disdain for Virginia's leadership in general, whom he characterized as "vile" and "whose tottering fortunes have been repaired and supported at the public charge."[37]

According to one account, Bacon and his followers pleaded with the assembly to address all of these grievances: "He [Bacon] pressed hard nigh half an hour's Harangue on the [topics of] Preserving our Lives from the Indians, Inspecting the Public Revenues, the exorbitant Taxes and redressing the Grievances and Calamities of that Deplorable Country, Whereto having no other Answer, He went away Dissatisfied."[38]

Finally, Bacon and his closest associates among the county's planters shared many characteristics.[39] Captain James Crews, Henry Isham, and William Byrd, with whom Bacon was socializing on the day he took over leadership of the rebellion, as well as many of his other closest acquaintances—including Thomas Blayton, Francis Poythress, John Poythress, and John Sturdivant—were ambitious upcountry planters who for various reasons had fallen out of or never curried favor with those who ran the colony and the county. Byrd and Crews were militia officers as well as justices of the peace, but they had recently fallen out of favor with the faction who controlled Henrico County. Blayton, Isham, the Poythress brothers, and Sturdivant were successful planters, but their political opposition to Colonel Edward Hill, one of Berkeley's most trusted allies, had earned them the governor's enmity. Like Bacon, these men harbored an intense desire to eradicate Indians from their midst. Also like Bacon, some of them had lost servants during the recent Susquehannock raids, and none placed any faith in the governor's plans for combating those raids. Many were also relatively new arrivals to Virginia. That, along with the distance of their plantations from Jamestown, placed them outside the inner core of the elite power structure.

According to one account, the four men spent the day drinking and lamenting "the sadness of the times, their discourse and the fear they all lived in, because of the Susquehannocks who had settled a little above the falls of the James River." They also expressed concern at the presence of Virginia's tributary Indians despite the thirty years of peace between the remnants of Powhatan's chiefdom and the Virginia government. While Bacon and his companions pointed to signs they interpreted as preparations for war by the tributary Indians, the men's long-standing disdain for Indians coupled with their desire for Indian land provided cause enough.[40] Sometime during their commiserations, Bacon declared his support for a campaign "against all Indians in general." In response the other men, led by Crews, began to persuade Bacon to cross the James River and take command of a group of former servants, artisans, and landless Virginians that had begun to form there under the leadership of a man named Giles Bland.[41]

The case of Giles Bland is another excellent example of the growing discontent with the government's leadership among wealthy Virginians outside of Berkeley's inner circle. Bland had been removed from his job as a customs collector and barred from ever holding office again because of his vocal disdain for his social superiors. He had even gone so far as to publicly refer to Philip Ludwell, one of the highest-ranking officials in the colony and one of Berkeley's closest advisers, as a "puppy" and a "son of a whore." Like Nathaniel Bacon, the fact that Bland had managed to get himself appointed to a position of leadership placed him among the upper strata of Virginia society. However, also like Bacon, his relative newcomer status and the location of his seat far from Jamestown prevented him from gaining true access to the highest circles of the Virginia elite. Finally, again like Bacon, Bland harbored an intense desire to see the tributary Indians destroyed. He would become one of Bacon's most trusted lieutenants over the coming months.[42]

Interestingly, it seems that at least James Crews, but probably William Byrd and Henry Isham as well, had already broached the idea of Bacon's leadership of the group to Bland. Therefore, the events that led to the three men encouraging Bacon to cross the river seem to have been more the result of a concerted plan than happenstance. Their reasons for pushing Bacon to take leadership of the crowd remain hidden. Some have speculated that they believed Governor Berkeley might be more willing to grant official sanction to such a campaign if it were proposed and headed by one of his own councilors. It is just as likely that the three men sought to encourage the movement but at as little risk to themselves as possible. Bacon's well-known disdain for Indians and his reputed hot temper made him the perfect vehicle through which to act. Whatever the case, the fact that Bacon's decision to head the rebellion was not his own speaks volumes about the nature of the movement among these planters. Previous interpretations of Bacon's Rebellion (beginning with William Berkeley himself) often characterize it as the result of Bacon's hot-tempered and megalomaniacal nature. After all, it is Bacon's Rebellion, not Byrd's or Isham's. However, the critical roles played by members of the planter class such as Crews, Isham, Byrd, and, later, Bland demonstrate the extent to which disaffection for Berkeley's government and a desire for the extirpation of all of Virginia's Indians permeated all levels of Virginia society and spurred the rebellion onward.[43]

Bacon's first actions demonstrate the extent to which he understood that he and his fellow western planters wanted to drive all Indians from Virginia and that he also realized that failure by the planter elite and the government to support such a campaign held the potential to plunge the colony into a full-blown social rebellion. He twice proposed that Governor Berkeley authorize a punitive expedition against all Indians to diffuse the potential for an outright mutiny of the landless against the landed. In other words, Bacon suggested that Berkeley allow the landless frontiersmen who had gathered under Bland's leadership originally to satiate their anger with the blood of various indigenous peoples. This, Bacon argued, would stop them from turning against the planter elite. Twice, Berkeley refused.[44]

On May 2, after having learned that Berkeley denied his requests for a commission against the Indians, Bacon fired off a private letter to the governor informing him of his desire to "seek a more agreeable destiny than you are pleased to design me." Eight days later, Berkeley responded by removing Bacon from the Governor's Council.[45] Bacon then took his case straight to the masses. In "The Humble Appeal of the Volunteers to All Well Minded and Charitable People," he denounced all Indians, including those in a peaceful and tributary relationship with Virginia, as "treacherous thieves . . . his Majesty's enemies and the molesters of the public good." Bacon went on to argue that Indians were not subjects of the king and could hold no legal title to any of Virginia's land. Therefore, the presence of peaceful Indians on Virginia soil represented an affront to the sovereignty of Charles II that cried out for punishment meted out by all good and loyal subjects. In Bacon's mind, killing Indians was not just desirable and permissible but literally a patriotic duty.[46]

Bacon and his army proceeded to a nearby Occoneechee village to make good on these threats. The village, situated on an island in the middle of the Roanoke River, consisted of three palisaded forts and served as a last refuge for the remnants of the once formidable Siouan-speaking Monacan chiefdom. While the Occoneechees constituted the largest element of the population, the village also housed a considerable number of other Siouan-speaking groups. In addition, following the Anglo-Indian conflagrations on the Virginia-Maryland border, many of the Susquehannocks who escaped Washington and Allerton's siege made their way to the presumptive safety of the Virginia-Carolina border and the settlements of their former Monacan allies. As a community made up of both weakened Indian nations and Occoneechees who had been valuable trading partners of the Virginians, it likely never occurred to the villagers to deny Bacon entry.[47]

When he arrived in the village, Bacon demanded that the Siouans capture and kill the Susquehannocks they had allowed to shelter in the area. The Occoneechees, now more than likely fearful of the consequence if they did not comply, proceeded to apprehend approximately 30 Susquehannock warriors and torture them to death. Bacon then demanded that they provide him and his men with food and provisions. According to Bacon's account, as well as that of one of his men, the Occoneechees hesitated to provide the supplies Bacon demanded and a standoff ensued, with the Siouans retreating inside their palisades and Bacon and his men falling back to siege positions near the riverbank. All sources agree that eventually a shot rang out from behind Bacon, killing one of his men. Though no evidence exists to suggest that the shot was fired from an Indian weapon, the Virginians assumed that the Siouans' delay in bringing them supplies represented a ruse designed to buy time for the assailant or assailants to move into position behind them. The death of one of their men sent Bacon and his army into a rage. According to one account, "We quickly repaid them, firing in at all their . . . ports holes, and other places so thick that the groans of Men, Women & Children were so loud." Having trapped the remaining Indians inside the palisades, Nathaniel Bacon and his people's army then set fire to the fort. One participant remarked at the sounds that emanated from inside the village as the remaining Siouans burned to death: "A great number of Men, Women and Children, whose groans were heard, but they all burnt, except 3 or 4 men, who hoping to escape, broke out, and had a welcome by a liberal volley of shot from our men." When the screaming stopped, 150 Siouans lay dead, and the longtime alliance between the Siouans of western Virginia and the Iroquoian-speaking Susquehannocks to their north was smoking in the ashes of the burned-out village.[48]

This episode represents a critical juncture in the history of Bacon's Rebellion. When the Siouans began to torture the Susquehannock prisoners, they offered the Virginians the opportunity to join in, but according to the most detailed account left behind by them, Bacon and his men flatly rejected the offer out of a seeming sense of disgust. Specifically, the writer states, "Several of the Susquehannocks [were] put to death, after their way, for that we refused to take that office." The Virginians' refusal to take part in the torture of the Susquehannocks, combined with their willingness to destroy the Siouans shortly thereafter, signifies two critical factors inherent in understanding the goals and beliefs of Bacon and his followers. Given the tremendous enthusiasm with which Bacon's army killed the Siouans (who had not attacked Virginia settlements and had just captured the Susquehannocks for them), it seems unlikely that the Virginians' refusal to take part in the torture of the Susquehannocks stemmed from any misgivings about killing itself; rather, it emanated from an inherent disgust and hatred of Indians in general. Ritualized torture represented an Indian cultural practice. Therefore, to engage in it would have constituted a tacit recognition of a general equality between colonists and Indians. Since the exact opposite idea was at the heart of Bacon's Rebellion, he and his followers would not have dared to engage in anything that smacked of Native culture and traditions.[49]

Second, the killings on the Roanoke River illuminate one of the ultimate purposes of the rebellion in the minds of Bacon and his followers. The member of the expedition quoted previously closed his account by expressing extreme satisfaction at the achievements of the engagement in the village. While he listed the killing of three Indian "Kings" as well as the taking of a few prisoners as important objectives met, they were not, in his estimation, the most significant achievements: "What we reckon most material, is that we have left all nations of Indians, where we have been engaged in a civil war amongst themselves, so that with great ease we hope to manage this advantage, to their utter ruin and destruction." In other words, Bacon and his men hoped to divide the Indians to the point that they did the work of destroying one another for him.[50]

Meanwhile, Sir William Berkeley undertook drastic steps designed to undercut the burgeoning movement forming around Nathaniel Bacon. In particular, the governor promised that Virginians who joined him against Bacon "for 21 years should be discharged from all imposition, excepting Church dues." He called for the election of a new assembly for the express purpose of allowing the representatives of the people to present their grievances against Bacon. He then invited Bacon to submit himself and implied that he would be willing to pardon him or allow him to go to England to state his case directly to the king. Berkeley also declared that all Indians were hostile to the colony. However, while Berkeley now agreed with Bacon and his followers that all Indians were Virginia's enemies, he strongly insisted that only those given express permission by the Crown, through himself as the Crown's direct representative in the colony, could inflict punishment on them for that hostility. Since he had denied Bacon and the westerners that permission and they had proceeded anyway, they were in open rebellion against the king.[51]

By the beginning of June, however, there were signs that the seventy-year-old governor's will to fight was waning. Berkeley had captured Opechancanough, the last paramount chief of the Powhatan chiefdom, and forced the Powhatans into submission. He had survived the Cromwellian Protectorate and fended off more than one attempted uprising, but he could not bring a twenty-nine-year-old ne'er-do-well to heel. Confronted with a legislature he believed was predisposed to thwart him and the news that Bacon had refused his request to submit to the governor's mercy, Berkeley wrote to Henry Coventry, secretary of state in charge of England's American colonies, asking to be relieved. As it turned out, Berkeley did not have to find the rebel leader; Bacon came to him. On June 8, a scant five days after Berkeley penned what was in effect his resignation letter, Bacon was brought before Berkeley in chains.[52]

In the May elections, the people of New Kent County had elected Nathaniel Bacon to represent them as burgess. After he returned from the massacre on the Roanoke River, Bacon boarded his personal sloop and sailed down the James to the capital. Certain that he could convince Berkeley to see things his way, Bacon anchored upriver and sent word asking permission to enter Jamestown. Berkeley responded by ordering the guns of the fort to fire on Bacon's sloop. He also dispatched Thomas Gardner, a ship captain and one of Berkeley's most loyal followers, to pursue Bacon as he fled the bombardment. Gardner succeeded in catching Bacon, disabling his vessel, and taking the rebel leader prisoner.[53]

In a dramatic scene described by several contemporaries, Berkeley and Bacon finally confronted one another face to face. His defiance and bluster gone, Bacon made a full "acknowledgment of his so late crimes and disobedience, imploring thereby the Governor's pardon and favor." Berkeley set Bacon free and restored him to full membership on the Governor's Council. Furthermore, he promised Bacon a proper commission to proceed against the Indians.[54]

Having obtained the governor's pardon, Bacon left to reunite with his wife. Over the next several days, the new assembly proceeded to right everything it perceived as wrong in Virginia. Among other things, the assembly granted suffrage to landless freemen, placed checks on the ability of appointed magistrates to levy taxes, and removed the tax exemptions granted to members of the governing council. While Berkeley offered little or no resistance to these measures, his continued resistance to violence against Indians signifies the issue's crucial importance to all sides of the conflict. In one address to the assembly, the seventy-year-old knight vented frustration over the killing of some surrendering Susquehannocks by a Virginia militia expedition, exclaiming "if they had killed my Grandfather and Grandmother, my father and Mother and all my friends, yet if they had come to treat of Peace, they ought to have gone in Peace!" His resistance to measures calling for the indiscriminate destruction of all Indians succeeded in forcing the assembly to admit to the possibility that not all Indians harbored murderous intentions toward the colony. While the preamble to one act regarding the Indian conflict differentiated between those who were friendly and those unfriendly to Virginia, the provisions of the act made little distinction. The act defined any Indians who left their village without express permission from the Virginians as enemies. Furthermore, the assembly swept away Berkeley's defensive plans and authorized a force of 1,000 men to take the fight directly to the Indian villages. The legislation also granted the members of this force "the benefit of all plunder [of] either Indians or otherwise." Specifically, the members of the expedition would be paid with both Indian possessions and individual Indians to be "held and accounted slaves during life."[55]

This last provision, as well as another incident from Bacon's Rebellion, further demonstrates the centrality of Indian extermination for Bacon and those he led. During the period after he was pardoned by Berkeley in the summer of 1676, Bacon's status as a rallying point for those intent on fomenting genocide against Virginia's Indians reached a fever pitch. According to one source, "He no sooner was come to the upper parts of [the] James River, but the impatient people run to him." When frontier residents learned that Berkeley had yet to provide Bacon with the promised commission to proceed against the area tribes, they "began to set up their throats in one common cry . . . that they would either have a commission for Bacon or else they would pull down the town or do worse." On June 22 Bacon reentered Jamestown at the head of nearly 500 like-minded frontiersmen. Berkeley, enraged that Bacon seemed to have quickly forgotten his recent pledge of loyalty, offered to face him in individual combat to end their contest once and for all, but Bacon refused the challenge. He told Berkeley that his sole purpose was to obtain "a commission to save our lives from the Indians, which you have so often promised, and now we will have it before we go." Under the threat of death, Berkeley finally produced Bacon's coveted orders. Bacon, thus armed with his coerced commission, set out to take his extermination campaign to the peaceful remnants of the formerly powerful Powhatan chiefdom.[56]

The fact that both Bacon and the assembly obstinately refused to compromise concerning the campaign against the Indians signifies the issue's overwhelming importance for Bacon and his followers. If firmly establishing their perceived right to kill Indians for land had not been so central to their cause, they would have gladly sacrificed both Bacon's commission and the new offensive-minded Indian legislation in favor of compromises Berkeley offered them regarding suffrage and taxes, but they did the opposite. Voting rights and smaller tax levies could be taken away with a simple vote of the next assembly, but public acknowledgment of a right to take Indian land by force carried long-term prospects for the acquisition of political and economic power. On that point, frustrated Virginians refused to compromise.

Bacon proved as much almost immediately after leaving Jamestown by issuing his "Declaration of the People" on July 30, in which he cast himself as the true protector of the king's interests in Virginia as opposed to Berkeley and his self-serving cronies. The declaration also spelled out Bacon's intent to "not only ruin and extirpate all Indians in general, but all manner of trade and commerce with them." He then set out for the falls of the James River and from there to the Great Dragon Swamp, where he intended to visit his wrath upon Cockacoeske and her Pamunkeys who had taken refuge there.[57]

Heavy rain fell on the upper Pamunkey River area in early August 1676. Despite the mucky conditions created by the deluge, the Indians encamped in the Great Dragon Swamp did not welcome the return of dry weather. More than the intense Virginia humidity, the small group of Pamunkeys hiding in the swamp feared Bacon and his "army" of Virginians. Having once formed the backbone of the mighty Algonquian-speaking Powhatan chiefdom, the Pamunkeys now numbered under 200 warriors and had lived in a state of dependence and subjection to the Virginia government since the end of the Anglo-Powhatan Wars in 1646. From the time of her accession to the position of Pamunkey weroansqua in 1656, their leader, Cockacoeske, had resiliently attempted to reestablish her people's place as the dominant Indian group of the Virginia coastal plain. Recognizing the futility of continued armed resistance to English colonialism, the "Queen of the Pamunkey" had spent the last twenty years navigating the tangle of policies, proclamations, customs, and expectations that constituted Virginia's complex political and legal system to achieve her ends. Now in the space of a few short weeks, an army made up of nearly 600 western Virginians who blamed her people for the attacks of Iroquoian Indian groups from Maryland had nearly destroyed all of her progress.[58]

When they learned of Bacon's malice toward all Indians, Cockacoeske and her people deserted the reservation granted them in 1646 and took shelter in the Great Dragon Swamp. However, the swamp's remote location and the stormy beginning to August could only protect them for so long. Soon after the storms ended, Bacon and his "People's Army" found the Pamunkey camp. In the first assault on the camp, the swampy terrain (made worse by the recent rains) slowed Bacon and his men enough to allow Cockacoeske to issue orders to her people. She instructed them to flee and not to fire on the Virginians under any circumstance. Having lived up to their treaty obligations for more than thirty years, the Pamunkeys refused to play the aggressors now. Bacon and his army failed to appreciate the gesture. While the majority of the Indians in the camp escaped, Bacon captured as many as 45 Pamunkeys and killed 8, including one of Cockacoeske's retainers whom they had captured and ordered to lead them to the weroansqua, who had fled. After a day and a half in which the woman led them in every direction but the one in which the Pamunkeys had fled, the Virginians decided they had little use for her. According to one eyewitness, "Bacon gave command to his Soldiers to knock her in the head, which they did, and they left her dead on the way." Cockacoeske wandered in the swamp for nearly two weeks before she dared reemerge for fear of suffering the same fate as her former servant. Fortunately for her, Bacon had left the swamp long before she emerged from hiding. News that Berkeley was moving against him ratcheted the rebel leader's attention back to the east. His efforts to defeat Berkeley prevented him from instituting further attacks against Indians.[59]

Meanwhile, Berkeley refused to give up, and he invalidated Bacon's commission immediately. He fled to the countryside to recruit a volunteer force to pursue the rebel leader. By one account, Berkeley initially succeeded in recruiting nearly 1,200 men, but when they learned that their objective was Nathaniel Bacon and not Indians, they refused to fight. When Bacon learned of Berkeley's plans to march against him, he changed course and took the fight back to the aging governor. With no troops to defend him, Berkeley once again officially declared Bacon a rebel and fled by boat to the relative safety of Virginia's Eastern Shore.[60]

Unbeknownst to him at the time, Berkeley's decision to seek refuge on the Eastern Shore revived his sagging cause. He found the colonists there much less rebellious and more willing to aid him. When Bacon dispatched two of his lieutenants, Giles Bland and William Carver, to sail to the Eastern Shore and apprehend the governor, Berkeley, with the help of Eastern Shore colonists, managed to capture Bland and Carver instead. The news of his success allowed the governor to recruit a force of nearly 600 men, and on September 8 he and his force regained Jamestown.[61]

Fresh from his attack on the Indians at the Great Dragon Swamp, Bacon learned of Bland and Carver's captivity as well as the fall of Jamestown. He ordered a forced march to the capital. Along the way, Bacon paused long enough to abduct the wives of men who remained loyal to Berkeley. When he besieged Jamestown after he arrived there in mid-September, he displayed both the Indian captives he had taken and the female loyalists, many of whose husbands looked down upon them from inside Jamestown's walls. This display, as well as the fact that Bacon's forces still outnumbered Berkeley's, convinced the governor to once again retreat to the Eastern Shore by way of the water. On September 19 Bacon burned Jamestown, the symbol of English permanence in North America, to the ground.[62]

In the wake of Berkeley's supposed final defeat, Bacon's men partook in an orgy of debauchery, including heavy drinking as well as the looting of loyalist estates. By some accounts, Nathaniel Bacon seems to have been troubled by his men's actions, but his death from dysentery in late October 1676 prevented him from acting on those concerns. The actual end of the rebellion, as well as Bacon's death, came rather swiftly. On October 26, 1676, Bacon died from what one of his men described as "the Bloody Flux . . . accompanied with a Lousey Disease; so that swarms of vermin that bred in his Body he could not destroy but by throwing his shirts into the Fire as often as he shifted himself."[63] By all accounts, Bacon died in great distress over the future of the rebellion. In terms of the immediate future of his movement, his concerns proved well-founded. Within three months, Sir William Berkeley regained control of Virginia. The loss of the rebellion's leader immediately threw the movement into chaos and opened up the opportunity Berkeley needed to reestablish control. By early November he had returned from his exile on the Eastern Shore and defeated several rebel bands. Soon after this turn of events, Berkeley condemned Thomas Hansford to death by hanging. Hansford insisted to the very end that the purpose of the entire rebellion had been "for the destruction of the Indians."[64]

On January 11, 1677, Berkeley presided over a court-martial onboard his sloop anchored in the York River. During that day and the next, he sentenced additional men to death. Having already hanged five other prisoners, he condemned four more individuals before he was stopped by the arrival from England of Colonel Francis Moryson, Colonel Herbert Jeffreys, and Sir John Berry, charged by King Charles II with investigating the causes of the unrest. The record of their inquiry further demonstrates both the unifying role Indian hatred played in fueling Bacon's Rebellion and the way the rebellion helped establish the right of all Virginians to use violence against Native Americans whenever they deemed it necessary.[65]

NOTES

1. See Edmund S. Morgan, *American Slavery, American Freedom: The Ordeal of Colonial Virginia* (New York: W. W. Norton, 1975); Kathleen Brown, *Good Wives, Nasty Wenches, and Anxious Patriarchs: Gender, Race, and Power in Colonial Virginia* (Chapel Hill: University of North Carolina Press, 1996). Specifically, see plots in York County in 1661 and in Gloucester County in 1663, as well as the Lawne's Creek Uprising discussed in the introduction. See York County Court, "Proceedings in York County Court," *William and Mary Quarterly* 11, no. 1 (July 1902): 28–38; Virginia State Historical Society, "Virginia Colonial Records (Continued)," *Virginia Magazine of History and Biography* 15, no. 1 (July 1907): 38–43; "The Warrants for the Arrest of the Dissidents, January 3, 1674," in *The Old Dominion in the Seventeenth-Century: A Documentary History of Virginia, 1606–1689,* ed. Warren Billings (Chapel Hill: University of North Carolina Press, 1975), 263–64.

2. Public Record Office, Colonial Office, CO 5/1371, "Henrico County Grievances," October 15, 1677, British National Archives, Kew, England (hereafter CO), 163.

3. William Waller Hening, *The Statutes at Large: Being a Collection of All the Laws of Virginia from the First Session of the Legislature in the Year 1619* (New York: R&W&G Bartow, 1823), 1:326–27; Helen Rountree, *Pocahontas's People: The Powhatan Indians of Virginia through Four Centuries* (Norman: University of Oklahoma Press, 1990), 84, 86; Alan Vance Briceland, *Westward from Virginia: The Exploration of the Virginia-Carolina Frontier, 1650–1710* (Charlottesville: University Press of Virginia, 1987), 23–27.

4. Paul Kelton, *Epidemics and Enslavement: Biological Catastrophe in the Native Southeast, 1492–1715* (Lincoln: University of Nebraska Press, 2007), 109; Hening, *Statutes at Large*, 1:381.

5. Kelton, *Epidemics and Enslavement*, 109–10.

6. Hening, *Statutes at Large*, 1:255, 325. See also Kelton, *Epidemics and Enslavement*, 111.

7. Hening, *Statutes at Large*, 1:377.

8. Ibid., 385.

9. Beverley Fleet, *Virginia Colonial Abstracts* (Baltimore: Genealogical Publishing, 1988), 3:218.

10. Hening, *Statutes at Large*, 1:525.

11. Ibid., 2:215.

12. Billings, *Sir William Berkeley and the Forging of Colonial Virginia*, 200; John Catlett's Letter to Thomas Catlett, April 1, 1664, Manuscript #1931.16, Rockefeller Jr. Library, Williamsburg, VA (quotation); Hening, *Statutes at Large*, 2:193–94.

13. Rappahannock Deeds and Wills, 1663–1668, June 22, 1666, Rappahannock County (Old) Microfilm Reel 3, Library of Virginia, Richmond, 57. See also Billings, *Sir William Berkeley and the Forging of Colonial Virginia*, 201.

14. Helen Rountree, "How Natural Resources Have Directly Affected Pamunkey Indian History" (paper presented at the annual meeting of the American Society of Ethnohistory, Williamsburg, VA, November 1–5, 2006); Rountree, *Pocahontas's People*, 110–13.

15. Martha McCartney, "Cockacoeske, Queen of Pamunkey," in *Powhatan's Mantle: Indians in the Colonial Southeast*, ed. Gregory Waselkov, Peter H. Wood, and Tom Hatley (Lincoln: University of Nebraska Press, 2006), 245; Rountree, *Pocahontas's People*, 91.

16. Hening, *Statutes at Large*, 402–3; McCartney, "Cockacoeske, Queen of Pamunkey," 245; Rountree, *Pocahontas's People*, 93.

17. McCartney, "Cockacoeske, Queen of Pamunkey," 255; Rountree, *Pocahontas's People*, 112.

18. Helen Rountree, "Powhatan Indian Women: The People Captain John Smith Barely Saw," *Ethnohistory* 45, no. 1 (Winter 1998): 22.

19. Ibid. For more on the rise of the "go-between" form of diplomacy, see James Merrell, *Into the American Woods: Negotiators on the Pennsylvania Frontier* (New York: W. W. Norton, 2000).

20. The evidence seems to indicate that Colonel John West was actually more invested in the emotional aspects of the relationship than Cockacoeske was. In fact, his descendants

acknowledge a family story handed down through the years that West's English wife left him because of his continuing attachment to the Queen of Pamunkey. See Rountree, *Pocahontas's People,* 112. Rountree cites the fact that both Cockacoeske and her son used a "W" as their official mark as evidence of a similar emotional attachment on their part. While I do not discount this possibility, it could just as easily signify Cockacoeske's realization that displaying hers and her son's relationship to West represented their entrée into the colony's political power structure.

21. McCartney, "Cockacoeske, Queen of Pamunkey," 246–47; Peter Force, ed., *Tracts and Other Papers Relating Principally to the Origin, Settlement, and Progress of the Colonies in North America, from the Discovery of the Country to the Year 1776* (Washington, DC: Peter Force, 1835), 1, book 8:14–16.

22. Force, *Tracts,* 1, book 8:14–16 (quotations); McCartney, "Cockacoeske, Queen of Pamunkey," 246–47; America and the West Indies Original Correspondence, CO 5/1371, 187–205; Thomas Mathew, "The Beginning, Progress, and Conclusion of Bacon's Rebellion, 1675–1676," reprinted in Charles McLean Andrews, ed., *Narratives of the Insurrections, 1675–1690* (New York: Charles Scribner's Sons, 1915), 25–27; Hening, *Statutes at Large,* 2:341–65; Wilcomb Washburn, *The Governor and the Rebel: A History of Bacon's Rebellion in Virginia* (Chapel Hill: University of North Carolina Press, 1957), 54–55; Morgan, *American Slavery, American Freedom,* 263–64.

23. Fleet, *Virginia Colonial Abstracts,* 1:365; McIlwaine, *Minutes of the Council and General Court,* 238, 365, 370.

24. CO 5/1371, "A True Narrative of the Rise, Progress and Cessation of the Late Rebellion in Virginia Most Humbly and Impartially Reported by His Majesty's Commissioners Appointed to Enquire into the Affairs of the Said Colony," 187–205.

25. Ibid.

26. Mathew, "The Beginning, Progress, and Conclusion of Bacon's Rebellion," 17.

27. Ibid.

28. Ibid. (quotation); Morgan, *American Slavery, American Freedom,* 250–53; CO 5/1371, 187–205.

29. *Strange News from Virginia* (London: William Harris, 1677), 2; Morgan, *American Slavery, American Freedom,* 253; "The History of Bacon's and Ingram's Rebellion, 1676," in Andrews, *Narratives of the Insurrections,* 51 (quotation); Hening, *Statutes at Large,* 2:326–38. For more on the connection between the potential western trade and Bacon's Rebellion, see Briceland, *Westward from Virginia.*

30. Virginia State Historical Society, "The Family of Nathaniel Bacon, the Rebel," *Virginia Magazine of History and Biography* 14 (1907): 411–19.

31. Washburn, *Governor and the Rebel,* 18–19, 181; Virginia State Historical Society, "Family of Nathaniel Bacon," 411–19.

32. Washburn, *Governor and the Rebel,* 18, 181; "John Ray to Peter Courthope," in *The Further Correspondence of John Ray,* ed. Robert W.T. Gunther (London: Ray Society, 1928), 34–35.

33. Washburn, *Governor and the Rebel,* 18, 181; Virginia State Historical Society, "Family of Nathaniel Bacon," 65–70, 306–12; American Council of Learned Societies, Coventry MSS, Microfilm Copy (Washington, DC: American Council of Learned Societies, 1940) 77: 41; Morgan, *American Slavery, American Freedom,* 254.

34. Morgan, *American Slavery, American Freedom,* 254; See also Clarence Alvord and Lee Bidgood, *The First Explorations of the Trans-Allegheny Region by the Virginians, 1650–1674* (Cleveland: Arthur H. Clark, 1912); Briceland, *Westward from Virginia.*

35. Virginia State Historical Society, "Mr. Bacon's Account of Their Troubles in Virginia by the Indians, June 18, 1676," *William and Mary Quarterly* 9, no. 1 (July 1900): 6–8.

36. "A Copy of Mrs. Bacon's Letter, the Wife of Nathaniel Bacon, in Virginia, June 29, 1676, Sent to Her Sister, Concerning a Murder Committed by the Indians," *William and Mary Quarterly* 9, no. 1 (July 1900): 4–5.

37. Nathaniel Bacon, "Manifesto Concerning the Present Troubles in Virginia," *Virginia Magazine of History and Biography* 1 (1894): 55–58.

38. Mathew, "Beginning, Progress, and Conclusion of Bacon's Rebellion," 30.

39. American and the West Indies Original Correspondence, CO 5/1371, 187–205; Morgan, *American Slavery, American Freedom,* 254–55.

40. Billings, *Sir William Berkeley and the Forging of Colonial Virginia,* 234–35; American and the West Indies Original Correspondence, CO 5/1371, 187–205; Andrews, *Narratives of the Insurrections,* 110 (quotation); Morgan, *American Slavery, American Freedom,* 255; Coventry MSS, Microfilm Copy, 77:89–101.

41. Colonial Papers General Series, CO 1/37, 178–79; American and the West Indies Original Correspondence, CO 5/1371, 187–205.

42. Colonial Papers General Series, CO 1/37, 178–79; American and the West Indies Original Correspondence, CO 5/1371, 187–205; McIlwaine, *Minutes of the Council and General Court,* 390, 398–99, 423.

43. Colonial Papers General Series, CO 1/37, 178–79; American and the West Indies Original Correspondence, CO 5/1371, 187–205; McIlwaine, *Minutes of the Council and General Court,* 390, 398–99, 423; Morgan, *American Slavery, American Freedom,* 255.

44. Colonial Papers General Series, CO 1/37, 178–79; American and the West Indies Original Correspondence, CO 5/1371, 187–205.

45. American and the West Indies Original Correspondence, CO 5/1371, 187–205; Hening, *Statutes at Large,* 1:323–26; Morgan, *American Slavery, American Freedom,* 259 (quotation); Colonial Papers General Series, CO 1/37, 2.

46. American and the West Indies Original Correspondence, CO 5/1371, 187–205; Hening, *Statutes at Large,* 1:323–26; Morgan, *American Slavery, American Freedom,* 259; Colonial Papers General Series, CO 1/37, 2. See also Alexander B. Haskell, "'The Affections of the

People': Ideology and the Politics of State Building in Colonial Virginia, 1607–1754" (PhD diss., Johns Hopkins University, Baltimore, MD, 2004), 229–36.

47. Mathew, "Beginning, Progress, and Conclusion of Bacon's Rebellion," 17–19; Morgan, *American Slavery, American Freedom*, 250–53; American and the West Indies Original Correspondence, CO 5/1371, 187–205; "Nova Britannia," in Force, *Tracts*, 1, no. 6.

48. American and the West Indies Original Correspondence, CO 5/1371, 187–205 (quotations); Mathew, "Beginning, Progress, and Conclusion of Bacon's Rebellion," 21; Rountree, *Pocahontas's People*, 97; Morgan, *American Slavery, American Freedom*, 259.

49. American and the West Indies Original Correspondence, CO 5/1371, 187–205.

50. Ibid.

51. "History of Bacon's and Ingram's Rebellion," 57–58.

52. "Henry Coventry to Sir William Berkeley, November 15, 1676," Henry Coventry Papers, British Museum Additional Manuscripts Series, Bundle 25120, 94–95, Library of Congress, Washington, DC.

53. American and the West Indies Original Correspondence, CO 5/1371, 187–205.

54. Ibid; Mathew, "Beginning, Progress, and Conclusion of Bacon's Rebellion," 22–24.

55. Mathew, "Beginning, Progress, and Conclusion of Bacon's Rebellion," 25–27 (Berkeley quotation); Hening, *Statutes at Large*, 2:341–65; Washburn, *Governor and the Rebel*, 54–55; Morgan, *American Slavery, American Freedom*, 263–64; American and the West Indies Original Correspondence, CO 5/1371, 187–205 (last two quotations).

56. American and the West Indies Original Correspondence, CO 5/1371, 187–205 (first two quotations); Mathew, "Beginning, Progress, and Conclusion of Bacon's Rebellion," 29 (last quotation).

57. American and the West Indies Original Correspondence, CO 5/1371, 187–205; Colonial Papers General Series, CO 1/37, 173.

58. American and the West Indies Original Correspondence, CO 5/1371; Washburn, *Governor and the Rebel*, 74–75; Morgan, *American Slavery, American Freedom*, 268; "A Narrative of the Indian and Civil Wars in Virginia, in the Years 1675 and 1676," Massachusetts Historical Society (Boston: John Eliot, 1814), 23.

59. American and the West Indies Original Correspondence, CO 5/1371, 187–205 (quotation); Washburn, *Governor and the Rebel*, 76; "Narrative of the Indian and Civil Wars in Virginia," 21–31.

60. Mathew, "Beginning, Progress, and Conclusion of Bacon's Rebellion," 34; "History of Bacon's and Ingram's Rebellion," 56–57; American and the West Indies Original Correspondence, CO 5/1371, 187–205; Aspinwall Papers, *Collections*, 4th series, 4 (Boston: Massachusetts Historical Society, 1871): 173, 181–84, Boston.

61. American and the West Indies Original Correspondence, CO 5/1371, 187–205; Aspinwall Papers, *Collections*, 174–75; Mathew, "Beginning, Progress, and Conclusion of Bacon's Rebellion," 36–37; "History of Bacon's and Ingram's Rebellion," 64–67.

62. American and the West Indies Original Correspondence, CO 5/1371, 187–205.

63. Ibid.; Washburn, *Governor and the Rebel,* 77–85.

64. "History of Bacon's and Ingram's Rebellion," 79–80.

65. Morgan, *American Slavery, American Freedom,* 257–72; "History of Bacon's and Ingram's Rebellion," 65; Force, *Tracts,* 1, no. 10.

EPILOGUE

White Unity and Indian Survival

Almost thirty years after Bacon's Rebellion, Robert Beverley penned his *History of the Present State of Virginia*. Beverley's description of the history and condition of the colony, published nearly 100 years after its founding, reveals the extent to which Bacon's Rebellion had dramatically altered Virginia society. A passage describing the role of local county militias demonstrates the most noteworthy of these changes. According to Beverley, "Instead of the soldiers they formerly kept constantly in forts, and of the others after them by the name of rangers, to scour the frontiers clear of the Indian enemy, they have by law appointed the militia to march out upon such occasions, under the command of the chief officer of the county, where any incursion shall be notified."[1] In other words, not only had the hated defensive fort system been abandoned, but the power to decide whether to use violence against Indians now resided at the local level rather than with the colonial government.

We need not take Beverley's word alone. Modern historians have likewise documented considerable shifts in Virginia social relations stemming directly from Bacon's Rebellion that, when examined together, support Beverley's interpretation. According to one such historian, Bacon's Rebellion ushered in an era characterized by the "possession of a gun, the right to kill Indian trespassers, and the ability of lesser men, collectively, to resist injustice at the hands of their betters."[2] Those who occupied the highest echelon of the planter elite now realized that they had to deal with the concerns of lesser planters and landholders if they were to avoid a repeat of the chaos of 1676. This became even more important as they realized that

DOI: 10.5876/9781607323082.c007

Bacon's Rebellion had critically altered the colony's relationship with the Crown. In short, Bacon's Rebellion gave Charles II and his advisers the excuse they needed to attempt to gain much greater control of the colony's internal affairs. This, they assumed, would allow them to direct Virginia's development in directions designed to further their overall goal of creating a trans-Atlantic English commercial empire. Virginia's leaders, having become used to managing the colony's economy for their own benefit as opposed to that of England, sought to resist Whitehall's intrusion in these matters in the years following the rebellion. To do so, they had to have the support of the populace. Hence, the government of Virginia became much more responsive to the public at large than it had been in the first three-quarters of the seventeenth century.[3]

An analysis of the changes in the House of Burgesses during the second half of the seventeenth century also supports these findings. Prior to Bacon's Rebellion, wealthy and well-connected immigrants made up the majority of the assembly. After 1676, men born in Virginia not only increasingly populated the assembly, but the House of Burgesses also became more distanced from the Council of State and the governor. The governor and council could no longer count on the House of Burgesses for unquestioning approbation of their agenda. For their part, the burgesses increasingly came to represent the wishes of the public at large. Therefore, by extension, Virginia's tobacco elites were now forced to court the public much more than ever before, and that public was clamoring for the destruction and removal of all Indians.[4]

The grievances recorded by the King's commissioners (once they finally convinced a recalcitrant and vengeful William Berkeley to stop obstructing their work) bear a striking resemblance to the complaints that had presaged events such as the Lawne's Creek Uprising. They also demonstrate that the right to kill Indians had achieved equal status with traditional issues of contention, such as subsistence, suffrage, taxes, and land ownership. The residents of Henrico County, the home of Nathaniel Bacon and his associates, registered six complaints with the commissioners between late October 1677 and the beginning of 1678. All of their grievances concerned either Indians or taxes. The first complaint expressed their anger over the monopolization of the Indian trade. In addition to their general anger over the fact that they were not allowed to participate in that trade, the residents of Henrico County further declared it tyranny that "in favor of the monopolists, the people are betrayed to the Indians." They registered extreme disgust at the decision to build forts for protection against Indians and the 60-pound poll tax levied to pay for them. Finally, another of their complaints epitomizes the extent of non-elite adherence to a right to violence against all Native people and that such violence should be led and carried out at the grassroots level: "It is their desire and request to have an immediate war with all Indians in general and that the charge may be borne by voluntary aids and contributions of men and provision and commanders appointed who have interest in the people's affections to encourage and forward this design." In other words, while Bacon's Rebellion had ended, the desire for recognition of the people's right to "ruin and extirpate all Indians in general" had not.[5]

The grievances registered by other Virginia counties echo many of the same sentiments. James City County complained of the "slow prosecution of the Indian War" and the tax exemptions granted to members of the assembly as main causes "of the late rebellion and civil commotions in Virginia." Gloucester County complained that Major Robert Beverley had attempted to utilize the militia as his personal workforce rather than as a defense against Indians.[6] Isle of Wight County residents pleaded with the commissioners for a "continual war with the Indians," while Nansemond County argued for "a war with all nations and families of the Indians whatsoever without favoring any."[7] Finally, Surry County residents pled "their extreme poverty" and proposed that they be allowed to enslave the Indians taken prisoner during the rebellion as a means of easing that poverty.[8]

Even Philip Ludwell, one of Governor Berkeley's most fervent supporters, came to realize sometime after the rebellion that in the end the desires of westerners, both great and small, for Indian land represented the root cause of the conflict. In 1678 he penned a letter to Henry Coventry stating as much. In the letter, Ludwell complained of westerners' current rapaciousness in their pursuit of Indian land and argued that Bacon's Rebellion had been caused by a similar situation in which westerners provoked Indians by taking their land and then clamored for permission to eradicate them when the Indians struck back: "This was a great cause of this last war, and most of those [who] had thus intruded and were consequently the principal cause of it were notwithstanding amongst the forwardest in the rebellion and complained most of grievances."[9]

Nathaniel Bacon himself, on many occasions, declared that the rebellion's purpose had always been to drive all Indians from Virginia and open up their land for settlement. When offered a pardon by Berkeley if he would desist from his campaign against the tributary Indians, Bacon replied that he would not do so, "for they were all Enemies." Bacon also sought to convince Berkeley that he was not acting of his own volition but was simply responding to the wishes of the overwhelming majority of the populace when he claimed "the discourse and earnestness of the people is against the Indians."[10]

Perhaps more than his words, however, the ultimate fate of the rebellion he led provides the surest proof of the importance of the destruction of Virginia's Indian population to Bacon and his followers. As demonstrated in chapter 6, when Sir William Berkeley refused to authorize an extermination campaign against all

Indians, he lost the support of the majority of property-owning Virginians, particularly those in the west. They then united with the landless under Bacon's command and took matters into their own hands. However, in the fall of 1676 Bacon turned to attack Berkeley's supporters, and his men, either in violation of his orders or in accordance with them, looted the estates of many of Virginia's great planters. In response, many of the property holders whose support had made his rebellion possible deserted Bacon and thus doomed the rebellion. In other words, when the rebellion ceased to be about killing Indians and instead became an attack on wealth in general, Bacon's Rebellion suffered the same fate as the Lawne's Creek Uprising and several others before it. Only the destruction of Indians could maintain the brief unity forged across all ranks of Virginia society during 1676. The anger over taxes, political rights, and economic opportunity was not enough.[11]

The much closer relationship between the House of Burgesses and the populace, as well as the need of the governor and Council of State to enlist popular support for their resistance to the Stuarts and their imperial designs, created a very different dynamic in post-rebellion Virginia. As early as 1679, we can see evidence of the impact of this new reality. In that year the assembly took a much more proactive stance in response to new raids by Indians from outside the colony. Whereas in 1676 Sir William Berkeley had resolved to employ a defensive strategy commanded largely by the governing elite for dealing with the attacks of the Doegs and Susquehannocks, in 1679 Virginia's government chose a decidedly different path. The assembly authorized Major Laurence Smith to gather as many as 250 men and proceed to the Rappahannock River. While there, if he, his lieutenants, his men, or any inhabitants of the area detected any Indians, Smith was to "kill, pursue, resist, destroy or take any and every such enemy and enemies."[12] He did not need to wait for a commission from the governor. The word of one of the county's residents would be sufficient cause for him to take action. Though men like Nathaniel Bacon, Sir William Berkeley, and Thomas Hansford did not live to see it, the core element of Bacon's program had been enacted. The new regime in which any Virginian could potentially sound the alarm and initiate a campaign against Virginia Indians implicitly acknowledged a right to violence against Native people.

The tremendous increase in the ranks of those with enough land to be considered members of the planter elite during this time also indicates the changes wrought by Bacon's Rebellion. According to Lorena Walsh, only 54 colonists could be considered large planters in 1640. By 1680 that number had increased to 250. By 1700 there were 315 such planters. The fact that so many more Virginians now possessed the requisite land and wealth to be included in this number, combined with the changes in Indian policy mentioned earlier, demonstrates the extent to which restraints on the acquisition of Indian land had been lifted.[13]

17th Century Virginia Counties

MAP 7.1. Seventeenth-century Virginia counties. Map by Ryan Morris.

The fate of Virginia's tributary Indians during the last quarter of the seventeenth century provides the final evidence of the extent to which Virginians now enjoyed nearly unfettered permission to deprive Indians of their land. By 1697 the total tributary Indian population in Virginia, including the Meherrins and Nottoways who had never been a part of the Powhatan chiefdom, had declined to fewer than 1,450. In 1699 the Virginia government reduced the amount of tribute they owed the government in recognition that they were unable to pay the previously agreed-upon amount. By 1705 the total population of tributary Indians in Virginia had fallen as low as 600. Finally, a law passed in 1705 deprived the tributary groups of the one element that had allowed them to maintain some semblance of their traditional life ways. In the treaty signed at the close of the Anglo-Powhatan Wars in 1646, the tributary groups had managed to get the Virginians to grant them reservations situated on both banks of several navigable waterways. This arrangement coincided with the patterns of Algonquian settlement that had existed before the English arrived and allowed at least the women of the village to continue to engage in the same agricultural activities they had pursued for centuries.

However, in 1705 the assembly ordered that Englishmen would be allowed to settle within the bounds of these reservations so long as they settled along the opposite bank from an Algonquian village, which was usually situated on only one shore of the river. This transferred nearly half of the land granted to the remnants of the Powhatan chiefdom in 1646 to Virginians, and its effect on the ability of tributary Indian women to maintain their traditional way of life was catastrophic. Barred from venturing onto the territory now controlled by whites, Algonquian women could no longer gather the roots, berries, and other wild produce that had formed the bedrock of their subsistence from time immemorial. During the early years of the eighteenth century, working for white Virginians became the only option for survival available to many members of what had once been a powerful chiefdom. For many white Virginians, the eventual disappearance of Virginia Indians altogether must have seemed certain.[14]

Yet despite the now recognized right of Virginians to eradicate Indians wholesale and the growing propensity of outside Indian groups such as the Seneca to raid the tributary groups, Virginia Indians in general, and the Pamunkeys in particular, managed to persist. While the aftermath of Bacon's Rebellion gave all white Virginians license to kill Indians, it also saw the Pamunkeys, under the leadership of Cockacoeske, reestablish nominal (if temporary) control over the remnants of the Powhatan chiefdom. In doing so, they established the basis for their continuing legal relationship with the Commonwealth of Virginia and thus their survival.

Virginia Indians did not completely disappear but managed to maintain a legal foothold for continued existence there. The origins of this persistence lie in the 1677 Treaty of Middle Plantation, which served as the official negotiated settlement between Virginians of all classes and Indians at the close of Bacon's Rebellion. In the negotiations that led to the signing of the treaty, Cockacoeske used her recognized stature as a spokesperson for Virginia's tributary Indians, her son's status as a cultural go-between, and her previous relationship with Francis Moryson to win the King's commissioners to her position that the other tributary groups should be placed under her leadership. In their official report, Jeffreys, Moryson, and Berry referred to her as "a faithful friend to and lover of the English." Two months after that report, Cockacoeske was summoned to the official signing of the Treaty of Middle Plantation. Article XII of the treaty held particular interest for her:[15] "That each Indian King and Queen have equal power to govern their own people, except the Queen of Pamunkey to whom several scattered Indians do now again own their ancient Subjection and are agreed to come in and plant themselves under power and government who with her are also hereby included in this present *League and treaty of* peace and are to keep and observe the same toward the said Queen in all things as her subjects as well as toward the English."[16]

In addition to this provision, an earlier one stipulated that Cockacoeske and the other Indian leaders held their land and their titles as so-called kings and queens as dependents of the king of England. Therefore, the two passages taken together demonstrate that Cockacoeske had managed to reestablish her people's leadership over the remnants of Powhatan's chiefdom by careful manipulation of English legal and political structures. Rather than reestablish the chieftainship by force, as Powhatan or Opechancanough might have done under the same circumstances, she skillfully maneuvered the English government into doing it for her. Obviously, the nature and extent of her rule over the former Powhatan groups differed considerably from that of her forebears. She experienced considerable resistance from the groups she was to rule over and from various colonists who refused to live up to their part of the agreement. However, the simple act of getting the language inserted into the treaty represents a significant victory for a people many historians considered completely dominated and without recourse and for an oft-forgotten woman operating in the extremely foreign and male-dominated world of late-seventeenth-century Virginia politics. Even tacit permission for all Virginians to displace her people with the use of violence could not completely dislodge her people's hold on their ancestral homeland.[17] According to anthropologist Helen Rountree, the descendants of the Powhatan chiefdom still reside today in the land Cockacoeske's kinsman Powhatan once ruled as paramount chief.

Today, the Powhatan core people remain proudly Indian. Their identity is based on their descent from the aborigines who once owned all of Virginia, official recognition as Indians by the Commonwealth of Virginia, possession of reservations (in the case of the Pamunkeys and Mattaponis), formally organized tribal governments (with the reservation ones still replacing the county government for people in residence there), tribal churches, participation in some intertribal events (e.g., the Virginia Council on Indians), and the winning of federal grant funds specifically for "Indian" purposes (e.g., crafts education) and for community improvement in general.[18]

FIGURE 7.1. Cockacoeske's mark on the Treaty of Middle Plantation, 1677. Courtesy, Earl Gregg Swem Library, Special Collections, College of William and Mary, Williamsburg, VA.

Perhaps this represents the most important lesson to be learned from Bacon's Rebellion when we place Indians and the role of violence directed against them at the center of the analysis: despite the best attempts of Nathaniel Bacon, Thomas Hansford, and their followers, as well as the floodgates of white settlement unleashed during the aftermath of the rebellion, Cockacoeske's people have endured. To do so is to be neither Indian nor white nor Algonquian nor Powhatan but instead to be human.

NOTES

1. Robert Beverley, *The History of the Present State of Virginia in Four Parts,* part 4 (Richmond, VA: J. W. Randolph, 1855), 218.

2. Kathleen Brown, *Good Wives, Nasty Wenches, and Anxious Patriarchs: Gender, Race, and Power in Colonial Virginia* (Chapel Hill: University of North Carolina Press, 1996), 139.

3. Warren Billings, Thad Tate, and John Selby, *Colonial Virginia: A History* (White Plains, NY: KTO, 1986), 96–101.

4. Martin Quitt, *Virginia House of Burgesses, 1660–1706: The Social, Educational and Economic Bases of Political Power* (New York: Garland, 1989).

5. America and the West Indies Original Correspondence, CO 5/1371, 157–58, 163.

6. Ibid., 165–66.

7. Ibid., 160–62, 167–69.

8. Ibid., 152–56.

9. American Council of Learned Societies, Coventry MSS, Microfilm Copy (Washington, DC: American Council of Learned Societies, 1940), 77:89, 99.

10. Ibid., 78:204.

11. Alexander B. Haskell, "'The Affections of the People': Ideology and the Politics of State Building in Colonial Virginia, 1607–1754" (PhD diss., Johns Hopkins University, Baltimore, MD, 2004), 265–77.

12. William Waller Hening, *The Statutes at Large: Being a Collection of All the Laws of Virginia from the First Session of the Legislature in the Year 1619* (New York: R&W&G Bartow, 1823), 2:448–49.

13. See Lorena S. Walsh, *Motives of Honor, Pleasure and Profit: Plantation Management in the Colonial Chesapeake, 1607–1763* (Chapel Hill: University of North Carolina Press, 2010), 16–19.

14. Helen Rountree, *Pocahontas's People: The Powhatan Indians of Virginia through Four Centuries* (Norman: University of Oklahoma Press, 1990), 104–5, 128.

15. Martha McCartney, "Cockacoeske, Queen of Pamunkey," in *Powhatan's Mantle: Indians in the Colonial Southeast,* ed. Gregory Waselkov, Peter H. Wood, and Tom Hatley (Lincoln: University of Nebraska Press, 2006), 249–51.

16. "Treaty of Middle Plantation," in *Samuel Wiseman's Book of Record,* ed. Michael Leroy Oberg (Lanham, MD: Lexington Books, 2005), 134–41.

17. Ibid; McCartney, "Cockacoeske, Queen of Pamunkey," 250.

18. Rountree, *Pocahontas's People,* 276.

Bibliography

MANUSCRIPT SOURCES

America and the West Indies Original Correspondence, 1606–1822 (CO5). United Kingdom National Archives, Kew, England.

American Council of Learned Societies. "The Family of Nathaniel Bacon." In Coventry MSS, Microfilm Copy. Washington, DC: American Council of Learned Societies, 1940.

Aspinwall Papers. *Collections* 4. Boston: Massachusetts Historical Society, 1871.

Ayer Manuscript Collection, NA MS 446. Newberry Library, Chicago, IL.

Bacon's Rebellion, Miscellaneous Papers, 1676–1677. Rockefeller Library, Williamsburg, VA, 1676.

Charles City County Papers, Virginia Counties Collection, Manuscript and Rare Books Department. Swem Library, College of William and Mary, Williamsburg, VA.

Charles City County Papers, 1639–1819. Rockefeller Library, Williamsburg, VA.

Charles City County Orders, 1672–1673. State Library of Virginia, Richmond.

Colonial Papers General Series, 1574–1757 (CO1). United Kingdom National Archives, Kew, England.

Egerton MSS. N.d. British Library, London, United Kingdom.

Gloucester County Papers, 1669–1878. Rockefeller Library, Williamsburg, VA.

Henry Coventry Papers, British Museum Additional Manuscripts Series, Bundle 25120, 94–95, Library of Congress, Washington, DC.

Indian Records, 1722–1855. Rockefeller Library, Williamsburg, VA.

Lancaster County Orders, 1655–1666. State Library of Virginia, Richmond.

Landsdowne MSS. N.d. British Library, London, United Kingdom.

Ludwell Family Papers, 1676–1879. Rockefeller Library, Williamsburg, VA.

Middlesex County Papers, 1676–1781. Rockefeller Library, Williamsburg, VA.

Middlesex County Papers, Virginia Counties Collection, Manuscripts and Rare Books Department. Swem Library, College of William and Mary, Williamsburg, VA.

New York Historical Society. *Collections*, 2nd series, 3. New York: New York Historical Society, 1857.

Norfolk County Minute Book, 1637–46. Library of Virginia, Richmond.

Rappahannock Deeds and Wills, 1663–68, Rappahannock County (Old) Microfilm Reel 3. Library of Virginia, Richmond.

Sir Nathaniel Rich Papers, 1616–42. Rockefeller Library, Williamsburg, VA.

Special Collections. Spencer Research Library, University of Kansas, Lawrence.

State Government Records Collection. Library of Virginia, Richmond.

Virginia (Colony), Colonial Papers, State Government Records Collection, 1630. Library of Virginia, Richmond.

Virginia (Colony) Original Miscellaneous Records, 1606–26. Library of Congress, Washington, DC.

William Blathwayt Papers, 1631–1722. Rockefeller Library, Williamsburg, VA.

PRINTED SOURCES

Alvord, Clarence, and Lee Bidgood, eds. *The First Explorations of the Trans-Allegheny Region by the Virginians, 1650–1674*. Cleveland: Arthur H. Clark, 1912.

Andrews, Charles McLean, ed. *Narratives of the Insurrections, 1675–1690*. New York: Charles Scribner's Sons, 1915.

Andrews, K. R. "Christopher Newport of Limehouse, Mariner." *William and Mary Quarterly* 11, no. 1 (1954): 28–41. http://dx.doi.org/10.2307/1923147.

Axtell, James. *The European and the Indian: Essays in the Ethnohistory of Colonial North America*. New York: Oxford University Press, 1981.

Bacon, Nathaniel. "Manifesto Concerning the Present Troubles in Virginia." *Virginia Magazine of History and Biography* 1 (1894): 55–58.

Bailyn, Bernard. *Atlantic History: Concept and Contours*. Cambridge: Harvard University Press, 2005.

Bailyn, Bernard. "Politics and Social Structure in Virginia." In *Seventeenth Century America: Essays in Colonial History*, ed. James Morton Smith. Chapel Hill: University of North Carolina Press, 1959, 90–115.

Bamforth, Douglas. "Indigenous People, Indigenous Violence: Precontact Warfare on the North American Great Plains." *Man*, New Series 29, no. 1 (March 1994): 95–115. http://dx.doi.org/10.2307/2803512.

Barbour, Philip, ed. *The Complete Works of Captain John Smith.* 2 vols. Chapel Hill: University of North Carolina Press, 1986.

Barbour, Philip, ed. *The Jamestown Voyages under the First Charter: Documents Relating to the Foundation of Jamestown and the History of the Jamestown Colony up to the Departure of John Smith, Last President of the Council in Virginia under the First Charter, Early in October 1609.* 2 vols. New York: Cambridge University Press, 1969.

Barr, Juliana. *Peace Came in the Form of a Woman: Indians and Spaniards in the Texas Borderlands.* Chapel Hill: University of North Carolina Press, 2007.

Beier, A. L. *Masterless Men: The Vagrancy Problem in England, 1560–1640.* New York: Methuen, 1985.

Benton, Lauren. *A Search for Sovereignty: Law and Geography in European Empires, 1400–1900.* New York: Cambridge University Press, 2010.

Berkeley, William. "A Discourse and View of Virginia." Ed. William H. Smith Jr. Norwalk, CT: William H. Smith Jr., 1914.

Beverley, Robert. *The History of the Present State of Virginia.* London: J. W. Randolph, 1705.

Billings, Warren. *A Little Parliament: The Virginia General Assembly in the Seventeenth-Century.* Richmond: Library of Virginia, 2007.

Billings, Warren, ed. *The Papers of Sir William Berkeley, 1605–1677.* Richmond: Library of Virginia, 2007.

Billings, Warren. *Sir William Berkeley and the Forging of Colonial Virginia.* Baton Rouge: Louisiana State University Press, 2004.

Billings, Warren, ed. *The Old Dominion in the Seventeenth-Century: A Documentary History of Virginia, 1606–1689.* Chapel Hill: University of North Carolina Press, 1975.

Billings, Warren, Thad Tate, and John Selby. *Colonial Virginia: A History.* White Plains, NY: KTO, 1986.

Binford, Lewis. "Archaeological and Ethnohistorical Investigation of the Cultural Diversity and Progressive Development among Aboriginal Cultures of Coastal Virginia and North Carolina." PhD diss., University of Michigan, Ann Arbor, 1961.

Boddie, John Bennet. *Seventeenth Century Isle of Wight County, Virginia.* Baltimore: Southern Book, 1959.

Bouwsma, William. *The Waning of the Renaissance, 1550–1640.* New Haven, CT: Yale University Press, 2000.

Brathwaite, Richard. *The English Gentleman and the English Gentlewoman.* Sanford, NC: Microfilming Corporation of America, 1980.

Brenner, Robert. *Merchants and Revolution: Commercial Change, Political Conflict, and London's Overseas Traders, 1550–1653.* Princeton, NJ: Princeton University Press, 1993.

Briceland, Alan Vance. *Westward from Virginia: The Exploration of the Virginia-Carolina Frontier, 1650–1710.* Charlottesville: University Press of Virginia, 1987.

Brooke, Christopher. "A Poem on the Late Massacre in Virginia." *Virginia Magazine of History and Biography* 72, no. 3 (July 1964): 259–92.

Brooks, James F. *Captives and Cousins: Slavery, Kinship, and Community in the Southwest Borderlands*. Chapel Hill: University of North Carolina Press, 2002.

Brown, Alexander. *The Genesis of the United States*. 2 vols. Boston: Houghton Mifflin, 1890.

Brown, Kathleen. *Good Wives, Nasty Wenches, and Anxious Patriarchs: Gender, Race, and Power in Colonial Virginia*. Chapel Hill: University of North Carolina Press, 1996.

Brown, Kathleen. "In Search of Pocahontas." In *The Human Tradition in Colonial America*, ed. Ian Steele and Nancy Rhoden. Wilmington, DE: Scholarly Resources, 1999, 71–95.

Bullock, William. *Virginia Impartially Examined, and Left to Publick View, to Be Considered by All Judicious and Honest Men*. London: John Hammond, 1649.

Canny, Nicholas. "The Ideology of English Colonization: From Ireland to America." *William and Mary Quarterly* 30, no. 4 (October 1973): 575–98. http://dx.doi.org/10.2307/1918596.

Carr, Lois Green, and Lorena S. Walsh. "The Planter's Wife: The Experience of White Women in Seventeenth-Century Maryland." *William and Mary Quarterly* 34 (October 1977): 542–71. http://dx.doi.org/10.2307/2936182.

Cave, Alfred. *Lethal Encounters: Englishmen and Indians in Colonial Virginia*. Santa Barbara, CA: Praeger, 2011.

Cave, Alfred. *The Pequot War*. Amherst: University of Massachusetts Press, 1996.

Charles I, King of England. *A Proclamation for the Better Discovery and Apprehension of Those Malefactors, Who Were Actors in the Late Insolent Riots and Murders*. London: Bonham, Norton and John Bill, 1629.

Charles II, King of England. *A Proclamation Concerning the Students in the College of Edinburgh*. Edinburgh: Printed by the Heir of Andrew Anderson, 1681.

Clark, Peter. "Popular Protest and Disturbance in Kent, 1558–1640." *Economic History Review*, New Series 29, no. 3 (August 1976): 365–82.

Coombs, John C. "Beyond the 'Origins Debate': Rethinking the Rise of Virginia Slavery." In *Early Modern Virginia: Reconsidering the Old Dominion*, ed. Douglas Bradburn and John C. Coombs. Charlottesville: University of Virginia Press, 2011, 239–78.

Coombs, John C. "'Building the Machine': The Development of Slavery and Slave Society in Early Colonial Virginia." PhD diss., College of William and Mary, Williamsburg, VA, 2004.

Craven, Wesley Frank. *The Dissolution of the Virginia Company*. Gloucester, MA: P. Smith, 1964.

Craven, Wesley Frank, ed. *A Good Speed to Virginia*. New York: Scholars Facsimiles and Reprints, 1937.

Davis, Richard Beale. *George Sandys, Poet-Adventurer: A Study in Anglo-American Culture in the Seventeenth Century*. London: The Bodley, 1955.

Davis, Richard Beale. *William Fitzhugh and His Chesapeake World, 1676–1701.* Chapel Hill: University of North Carolina Press, 1963.

de la Vega, Garcilaso. *Florida of the Inca.* Ed. and trans. John Varner and Jeannette Varner. Austin: University of Texas Press, 1951.

Fausz, J. Frederick. "An Abundance of Blood Shed on Both Sides: England's First Indian War, 1609–1614." *Virginia Magazine of History and Biography* 98, no. 1 (January 1990): 3–56.

Fausz, J. Frederick. "Merging and Emerging Worlds: Anglo-Indian Interest Groups and the Development of the Seventeenth-Century Chesapeake." In *Colonial Chesapeake Society,* ed. Lois Green Carr, Philip Morgan, and Jean B. Russo. Chapel Hill: University of North Carolina Press, 1989, 47–98.

Fausz, J. Frederick. "The Powhatan Uprising of 1622: A Historical Study of Ethnocentrism and Cultural Conflict." PhD diss., College of William and Mary, Williamsburg, VA, 1977.

Fischer, David Hackett. *Albion's Seed: Four British Folkways in America.* New York: Oxford University Press, 1989.

Fitzmaurice, Andrew. *Humanism and America: An Intellectual History of English Colonization, 1500–1625.* New York: Cambridge University Press, 2003.

Fleet, Beverley. *Virginia Colonial Abstracts.* Baltimore: Genealogical Publishing, 1988.

Foucault, Michel. *Discipline and Punish: The Birth of the Prison.* New York: Vintage, 1995.

Force, Peter, ed. *Tracts and Other Papers Relating Principally to the Origin, Settlement, and Progress of the Colonies in North America from the Discovery of the Country to the Year 1776.* Washington, DC: Peter Force, 1835.

Frank, Joseph. "News from Virginny." *Virginia Magazine of History and Biography* 65 (1957): 84–87.

Galenson, David. *White Servitude in Colonial America: An Economic Analysis.* New York: Cambridge University Press, 1981.

Gallivan, Martin T. *James River Chiefdoms: The Rise of Social Inequality in the Chesapeake.* Lincoln: University of Nebraska Press, 2003.

Gatford, Lionel. *Public Good without Private Interest, or, a Compendious Remonstrance of the Present Sad State and Condition of the English Colony of Virginia.* London: Henry Marsh, 1657.

Gibson, John L. "Aboriginal Warfare in the Protohistoric Southeast: An Alternative Perspective." *American Antiquity* 39 (January 1974): 130–33.

Gleach, Frederic W. *Powhatan's World and Colonial Virginia: A Conflict of Cultures.* Lincoln: University of Nebraska Press, 1997.

Glover, William, and Mary Newton Stannard, eds. *The Colonial Virginia Register.* Baltimore: Genealogical Publishing, 1965.

Grenier, John. *The First Way of War: American War-Making on the Frontier, 1607–1814.* New York: Cambridge University Press, 2008.

Gunther, Robert W.T., ed. *The Further Correspondence of John Ray*. London: Ray Society, 1928.

Hakluyt, Richard. *A Discourse of Western Planting*. London: Hakluyt Society, 1993.

Hakluyt, Richard. *The Principal Navigations, Voyages, Traffics, and Discoveries of the English Nation*, vol. 1–8. Glasgow: University of Glasgow Press, 1904.

Hakluyt, Richard. *The Writings and Correspondence of the Two Richard Hakluyts*. London: Hakluyt Society, 1935.

Hallowell, A. Irving. "Ojibwa Ontology, Behavior and World View." In *Contributions to Anthropology: Selected Papers of A. Irving Hallowell*, ed. Raymond D. Fogelson. Chicago: University of Chicago Press, 1976, 357–90.

Hämäläinen, Pekka. *The Comanche Empire*. New Haven, CT: Yale University Press, 2009.

Hamor, Ralph. *A True Discourse of the Present State of Virginia*. Richmond: Virginia State Library, 1957.

Hantman, Jeffrey. "Between Powhatan and Quirank: Reconstructing Monacan Culture and History in the Context of Jamestown." *American Anthropologist*, New Series 92, no. 3 (September 1990): 676–90. http://dx.doi.org/10.1525/aa.1990.92.3.02a00080.

Hartwell, Henry. *The Present State of Virginia and the College, Williamsburg Restoration*. Williamsburg, VA: Colonial Williamsburg, 1940.

Haskell, Alexander B. " 'The Affections of the People': Ideology and the Politics of State Building in Colonial Virginia, 1607–1754." PhD diss., Johns Hopkins University, Baltimore, MD, 2004.

Hatfield, April Lee. *Atlantic Virginia: Intercolonial Relations in the Seventeenth Century*. Philadelphia: University of Pennsylvania Press, 2003.

Hening, William Waller. *The Statutes at Large: Being a Collection of All the Laws of Virginia, from the First Session of the Legislature in the Year 1619*. 13 vols. New York: R&W&G Bartow, 1810–23.

Hill, Christopher. *The Century of Revolution, 1604–1714*. New York: W. W. Norton, 1966.

Hill, Christopher. *The World Turned Upside Down: Radical Ideas during the English Revolution*. London: Temple Smith, 1972.

His Majesty's Council for Virginia. *A Declaration of the State of the Colony and Affairs in Virginia*. London: T.S., 1620; reprint, Cambridge: Da Capo, 1973.

Holton, Woody. *Forced Founders: Indians, Debtors, Slaves and the Making of the American Revolution in Virginia*. Chapel Hill: University of North Carolina Press, 1999.

Horn, James. *Adapting to a New World: English Society in the Seventeenth-Century Chesapeake*. Chapel Hill: University of North Carolina Press, 1994.

Horn, James. *A Land as God Made It: Jamestown and the Birth of America*. New York: Basic Books, 2005.

Horn, James. "Leaving England: The Social Background of Indentured Servants in the Seventeenth Century." *Virtual Jamestown*, n.d., at http://www.virtualjamestown.org /essays/horn_essay.html.

Jennings, Francis. *The Invasion of America: Indians, Colonialism, and the Cant of Conquest.* New York: W. W. Norton, 1975.

Johnson, Robert. *The New Life of Virginia: Declaring the Former Successes and Present Estate of That Plantation, Being the Second Part of Nova Britannia.* London: Feliz Kyngston, 1612; reprint, Cambridge: Da Capo, 1971.

Johnson, Robert. "*Nova Britannia.*" London: Samuel Macham, 1609; reprint, Cambridge: Da Capo, 1969.

Johnson, Robert C., and Joseph Mead. "The Indian Massacre of 1622: Some Correspondence of the Reverend Joseph Mead." *Virginia Magazine of History and Biography* 71, no. 4 (October 1963): 408–10.

Jones, Hugh. "Part of a Letter from the Reverend Mr. Hugh Jones to the Reverend Dr. Benjamin Woodroofe, F.R.S. Concerning Several Observables in Maryland." *Philosophical Transactions (1683–1775)* 21 (1699): 439. http://dx.doi.org/10.1098/rstl.1699 .0078.

Karr, Ronald Dale. "'Why Should You Be So Furious?': The Violence of the Pequot War." *Journal of American History* 85, no. 3 (December 1998): 876–909.

Kelton, Paul. *Epidemics and Enslavement: Biological Catastrophe in the Native Southeast, 1492–1715.* Lincoln: University of Nebraska Press, 2007.

Kenny, Kevin. *Peaceable Kingdom Lost: The Paxton Boys and the Destruction of William Penn's Holy Experiment.* New York: Oxford University Press, 2009.

Kingsbury, Susan Myra, ed. *The Records of the Virginia Company of London.* Washington, DC: Government Printing Office, 1906–35.

Kroeber, Alfred. *Cultural and Natural Areas of Native North America.* Berkeley: University of California Press, 1953.

Kulikoff, Allan. *From British Peasants to Colonial American Farmers.* Chapel Hill: University of North Carolina Press, 2000.

Kupperman, Karen Ordahl. *Indians and English: Facing Off in Early America.* Ithaca, NY: Cornell University Press, 2000.

Kupperman, Karen Ordahl. *Roanoke: The Abandoned Colony.* Totowa, NJ: Rowman and Allenheld, 1984.

Land, Aubrey C. "Economic Behavior in a Planting Society: The Eighteenth-Century Chesapeake." *Journal of Southern History* 33, no. 4 (November 1967): 469–85. http:// dx.doi.org/10.2307/2204472.

Larson, Lewis. "Functional Consideration of Warfare in the Southeast during the Mississippi Period." *American Antiquity* 37 (July 1972): 383–92.

Las Casas, Bartolomé. *Devastation of the Indies: A Brief Account.* New York: Seabury, 1974.

Lawson, John. *A New Voyage to Carolina*. Ed. Hugh T. Lefler. Chapel Hill: University of North Carolina Press, 1967.

Lefroy, J. H. *Memorials of the Discovery and Early Settlement of the Bermudas*. London: Bermuda Historical Society, 1981.

Lepore, Jill. *The Name of War: King Philip's War and the Origins of American Identity*. New York: Vintage Books, 1999.

Levy, Philip. "A New Look at an Old Wall: Indians, Englishmen, Landscape and the 1634 Palisade at Middle Plantation." *Virginia Magazine of History and Biography* 112, no. 3 (2004): 226–65.

Lewis, Clifford M., and Albert J. Loomie, eds. *The Spanish Jesuit Mission to Virginia, 1570–1572*. Chapel Hill: University of North Carolina Press, 1953.

Linebaugh, Peter. *The London Hanged: Crime and Civil Society in the Eighteenth Century*. New York: Verso, 2006.

Linebaugh, Peter, and Marcus Rediker. *The Many-Headed Hydra: Sailors, Slaves, Commoners, and the Hidden History of the Revolutionary Atlantic*. Boston: Beacon, 2000.

Mallios, Seth. *The Deadly Politics of Giving: Exchange and Violence at Ajacan, Roanoke, and Jamestown*. Tuscaloosa: University of Alabama Press, 2006.

Mancall, Peter. *Envisioning America: English Plans for the Colonization of North America, 1580–1640*. Boston: Bedford Books, 1995.

Manning, Roger. *Village Revolts: Social Protest and Popular Disturbances in England, 1509–1640*. Oxford: Clarendon, 1988.

McIlwaine, H. R., ed. *Executive Journals of the Council of Colonial Virginia*. 6 vols. Richmond, VA: D. Bottom, 1925.

McIlwaine, H. R., ed. *Journals of the House of Burgesses of Virginia*, vol. 1–3. 13 vols. Richmond: Virginia State Library, 1915.

McIlwaine, H. R., ed. *Minutes of the Council and General Court of Colonial Virginia, 1622–1632, 1670–1676*. Richmond: Virginia State Library, 1979.

Milton, Giles. *Big Chief Elizabeth: The Adventures and Fate of the First English Colonists in America*. New York: Picador USA, 2000.

More, Thomas. *Utopia*. Ed. David Harris Sacks. Boston: Bedford/St. Martin's, 1999.

More News from Virignia: Being a True and Full Relation of All Occurrences in That Countrey, Since the Death of Nathaniel Bacon. London: William Harris, 1677.

Morgan, Edmund S. *American Slavery, American Freedom: The Ordeal of Colonial Virginia*. New York: W. W. Norton, 1975.

Morgan, Edmund S. "Slavery and Freedom: The American Paradox." *Journal of American History* 59, no. 1 (June 1972): 5–29. http://dx.doi.org/10.2307/1888384.

"A Narrative of the Indian and Civil Wars in Virginia, in the Years 1675 and 1676." Massachusetts Historical Society. Boston: John Eliot, 1814.

Nash, Gary B. *The Urban Crucible: The Northern Seaports and the Origins of the American Revolution*. Cambridge: Harvard University Press, 1986.

Neill, Edward. *Virginia Carolorum: The Colony under the Rule of Charles the First and Second, A.D. 1625–A.D. 1685*. Albany, NY: Joel Munsell's Sons, 1886.

Nugent, Nell Marion. *Cavaliers and Pioneers: Abstracts of Virginia Land Patents and Grants, 1623–1800*. Richmond, VA: Dietz, 1934.

Oberg, Michael Leroy. *Dominion and Civility: English Imperialism and Native America, 1585–1685*. Ithaca, NY: Cornell University Press, 1999.

Oberg, Michael Leroy, ed. *Samuel Wiseman's Book of Record*. Lanham, MD: Lexington Books, 2005.

Pagan, John Ruston. *Anne Orthwood's Bastard: Sex and Law in Early Virginia*. New York: Oxford University Press, 2003.

Parent, Anthony. *Foul Means: The Formation of a Slave Society in Virginia, 1660–1740*. Chapel Hill: University of North Carolina Press, 2003.

Pencak, William, Matthew Dennis, and Simon P. Newman, eds. *Riot and Revelry in Early America*. University Park: Pennsylvania State University Press, 2002.

Percy, George. "A Trewe Relacyon of the Proceedings and Occurances of Moment Which Have Happened in Virginia." *Tyler's Historical Quarterly and Genealogical Magazine* 3 (1922): 263.

Perdue, Theda. *Cherokee Women: Gender and Culture Change, 1700–1835*. Lincoln: University of Nebraska Press, 1999.

Potter, Stephen R. *Commoners, Tribute, and Chiefs: The Development of Algonquian Culture in the Potomac Valley*. Charlottesville: University of Virginia Press, 1993.

Price, Richard. *British Society, 1680–1880*. New York: Cambridge University Press, 1999.

Purchas, Samuel. *Hakluytas Posthumus or Purchas His Pilgrimes*, vols. 1–19. Glasgow: James Maclehose, 1905–7.

Purchas, Samuel. *Purchas His Pilgrims*, vol. 3. New York: Macmillan, 1905.

Quitt, Martin. *Virginia House of Burgesses, 1660–1706: The Social, Educational and Economic Bases of Political Power*. New York: Garland, 1989.

Rediker, Marcus. *The Slave Ship: A Human History*. New York: Penguin, 2008.

Rice, James D. *Nature and History in the Potomac Country: From Hunter-Gatherers to the Age of Jefferson*. Baltimore: Johns Hopkins University Press, 2009.

Richter, Daniel. *Facing East from Indian Country: A Native History of Early America*. Cambridge: Harvard University Press, 2001.

Robinson, Conway. "Notes from the Council and General Court Records, 1641–1659." *Virginia Magazine of History and Biography* 13, no. 1905–6 (1659): 389–401.

Roediger, David. *The Wages of Whiteness: Race and the Making of the American Working Class*. New York: Verso, 1999.

Rountree, Helen. "How Natural Resources Have Directly Affected Pamunkey Indian History." Paper presented at the annual meeting of the American Society for Ethnohistory, Williamsburg, VA, November 1–5, 2006.

Rountree, Helen. *Pocahontas's People: The Powhatan Indians of Virginia through Four Centuries.* Norman: University of Oklahoma Press, 1990.

Rountree, Helen. *Pocahontas, Powhatan, Opechancanough: Three Indian Lives Changed by Jamestown.* Charlottesville: University of Virginia Press, 2005.

Rountree, Helen, ed. *Powhatan Foreign Relations, 1600–1722.* Charlottesville: University Press of Virginia, 1993.

Rountree, Helen. "Powhatan Indian Women: The People Captain John Smith Barely Saw." *Ethnohistory* 45, no. 1 (Winter 1998): 1–29. http://dx.doi.org/10.2307/483170.

Rountree, Helen. *The Powhatan Indians of Virginia: Their Traditional Culture.* Norman: University of Oklahoma Press, 1989.

Rountree, Helen, and Thomas Davidson. *Eastern Shore Indians of Virginia and Maryland.* Charlottesville: University Press of Virginia, 1997.

Rountree, Helen, and E. Randolph Turner III. *Before and After Jamestown: Virginia's Powhatans and Their Predecessors.* Gainesville: University Press of Florida, 2002.

Rowe, J. G., ed. *Aspects of Late Medieval Government and Society: Essays Presented to J. R. Lander.* Toronto: University of Toronto Press, 1986.

Sahagun, Bernardino. *The Conquest of New Spain: 1585 Revision.* Salt Lake City: University of Utah Press, 1989.

Salisbury, Neal. *Manitou and Providence: Indians, Europeans and the Making of New England, 1500–1643.* New York: Oxford University Press, 1982.

Schmidt, Ethan A. "The Well-Ordered Commonwealth: Humanism, Utopian Perfectionism, and the English Colonization of the Americas." *Atlantic Studies* 7, no. 3 (September 2010): 309–28. http://dx.doi.org/10.1080/14788810.2010.495219.

Scott, James. *The Moral Economy of the Peasant.* New Haven, CT: Yale University Press, 1976.

Scott, James. *Weapons of the Weak: Everyday Forms of Peasant Resistance.* New Haven, CT: Yale University Press, 1985.

Sharp, Buchanan. *In Contempt of All Authority: Rural Artisans and Riot in the West of England, 1586–1660.* Berkeley: University of California Press, 1980.

Sharpe, J. A. *Crime in Seventeenth Century England.* New York: Cambridge University Press, 1983.

Simmons, William S. *Spirit of the New England Tribes: Indian History and Folklore, 1620–1984.* Hanover, NH: University Press of New England, 1984.

Smith, John. *The General History of Virginia, New England, and the Somer Isles.* In *The Complete Works of Captain John Smith,* ed. Philip Barbour. Chapel Hill: University of North Carolina Press, 1986, 2:33–478.

Smith, John. "A Map of Virginia." In *The Complete Works of Captain John Smith*, ed. Philip Barbour. Chapel Hill: University of North Carolina Press, 1986, 1:131–80.

Smith, John. "The Proceedings of the English Colony in Virginia." In *The Complete Works of Captain John Smith*, ed. Philip Barbour. Chapel Hill: University of North Carolina Press, 1986, 199–282.

Smith, John. *Travels and Works of Captain John Smith: President of Virginia and Admiral of New England, 1580–1631*. Ed. Edward Arber and A. G. Bradley. Edinburgh: John Grant, 1910.

Smith, John. *A True Relation of Such Occurrences and Accidents of Note, as Hath Happened in Virginia since the First Planting of That Colony, Which Is Now Resident in the South Part Thereof, Till the Last Return*. In *The Complete Works of Captain John Smith*, ed. Philip Barbour. Chapel Hill: University of North Carolina Press, 1986, 23–297.

Stannard, Mary Newton. *The Story of Bacon's Rebellion*. Washington, DC: Neale, 1907.

Steele, Ian, and Nancy Rhoden, eds. *The Human Tradition in Colonial America*. Wilmington, DE: Scholarly Resources, 1999.

Stith, William. *The History of the First Discovery and Settlement of Virginia Being an Essay*. Williamsburg, VA: William Parks, 1747.

Stone, Lawrence, and Jeanne Fawtier Stone. *An Open Elite? England, 1549–1880*. New York: Oxford University Press, 1984.

Strachey, William. *The Historie of Travel into Virginia Britannia*. London: Hakluyt Society, 1953.

Strachey, William. *For the Colony in Virginia: Lawes Divine, Morall and Martiall, etc*. London: Walter Burr, 1612; reprinted Cambridge: Da Capo, 1972.

Strange News from Virginia. London: William Harris, 1677.

Sutton, Mark Q. "Warfare and Expansion: An Ethnohistoric Perspective on the Numic Spread." *Journal of California and Great Basin Anthropology* 8, no. 1 (1986): 65–82.

Thompson, E. P. *Customs in Common: Studies in Traditional Popular Culture*. New York: New Press, 1993.

Thompson, E. P. "Eighteenth-Century English Society: Class Struggle without Class?" *Social History* 3 (1978): 133–65.

Thompson, E. P. *The Making of the English Working Class*. New York: Vintage Books, 1966.

Thompson, Peter. "The Thief, the Householder, and the Commons: Languages of Class in Seventeenth Century Virginia." *William and Mary Quarterly* 63, no. 2 (April 2006): 253–80.

Tomlins, Christopher. *Freedom Bound: Law, Labor, and Civic Identity in Colonizing English America, 1580–1865*. New York: Cambridge University Press, 2010. http://dx.doi.org/10.1017/CBO9780511778575.

Townsend, Camilla. *Pocahontas and the Powhatan Dilemma*. New York: Hill and Wang, 2004.

Trigger, Bruce. "Ethnohistory: The Unfinished Edifice." *Ethnohistory* 33, no. 3 (Summer 1986): 253–67. http://dx.doi.org/10.2307/481814.

Tyler, Lyon Gardiner, ed. *Narratives of Early Virginia, 1606–1625*. New York: Barnes and Noble, 1946.

Underdown, David. *Revel, Riot and Rebellion: Popular Politics and Culture in England, 1603–1660*. Oxford: Clarendon, 1985.

Virginia State Historical Society. "The Family of Nathaniel Bacon, the Rebel." *Virginia Magazine of History and Biography* 14 (1907): 411–19.

Virginia State Historical Society. "Governor West and the Council to the Privy Council, March 4, 1628." *Virginia Magazine of History and Biography* 7, no. 3 (January 1900): 259–60.

Virginia State Historical Society. "Mr. Bacon's Account of Their Troubles in Virginia by the Indians, June 18, 1676." *William and Mary Quarterly* 9, no. 1 (July 1900): 6–8.

Virginia State Historical Society. "Virginia Colonial Records (Continued)." *Virginia Magazine of History and Biography* 15, no. 1 (July 1907): 38–43.

Virginia State Historical Society. "Virginia in 1629 and 1630." *Virginia Magazine of History and Biography* 7, no. 4 (April 1900): 368–86.

Walsh, Lorena S. *Motives of Honor, Pleasure and Profit: Plantation Management in the Colonial Chesapeake, 1607–1763*. Chapel Hill: University of North Carolina Press, 2010.

Walsh, Lorena S., and Russell R. Menard. "Death in the Chesapeake: Two Life Tables for Men in Early Colonial Maryland." *Maryland Historical Magazine* 69 (1974): 211–27.

Walter, John, and Keith Wrightson. "Dearth and the Social Order in Early Modern England." *Past and Present* 71 (May 1978): 22–42.

Waselkov, Gregory, Peter H. Wood, and Tom Hatley, eds. *Powhatan's Mantle: Indians in the Colonial Southeast*. Lincoln: University of Nebraska Press, 2006.

Washburn, Wilcomb. *The Governor and the Rebel: A History of Bacon's Rebellion in Virginia*. Chapel Hill: University of North Carolina Press, 1957.

Washburn, Wilcomb. *Virginia under Charles I and Cromwell, 1625–1660*. Williamsburg: Virginia 350th Anniversary Celebration Corporation, 1957.

Webb, Stephen Saunders. *1676: The End of American Independence*. New York: Alfred A. Knopf, 1984.

Webb, Stephen Saunders. *The Governors-General: The English Army and the Definition of the Empire, 1569–1681*. Chapel Hill: University of North Carolina Press, 1979.

Wells, Robert V. "The Population of England's Colonies in America: Old English or New Americans?" *Population Studies* 46, no. 1 (March 1992): 85–102. http://dx.doi.org/10.10 80/0032472031000146026.

Wertenbaker, Thomas Jefferson. *Torchbearer of the Revolution: The Story of Bacon's Rebellion and Its Leader*. Princeton, NJ: Princeton University Press, 1940.

Wertenbaker, Thomas Jefferson. *Virginia under the Stuarts, 1607–1688.* New York: Russell and Russell, 1959.

West, Elliot. *The Contested Plains: Indians, Goldseekers, and the Rush to Colorado.* Lawrence: University Press of Kansas, 1998.

Whitaker, Alexander. *Good Newes from Virginia.* London: Felix Kyngston and William Welby, 1613.

White, Richard. *The Middle Ground: Indians, Empires, and Republics in the Great Lakes Region, 1650–1815.* New York: Cambridge University Press, 1991. http://dx.doi.org/10.1017/CBO9780511584671.

Williamson, Margaret Holmes. *Powhatan Lords of Life and Death: Command and Consent in Seventeenth-Century Virginia.* Lincoln: University of Nebraska Press, 2003.

Winfree, Waverly K., ed. *The Laws of Virginia: Being a Supplement to Henings the Statutes at Large, 1700–1750.* Richmond: Virginia State Library, 1971.

Wright, Irene, ed. *Documents Concerning English Voyages to the Spanish Main, 1569–1580.* London: Hakluyt Society, 1932.

York County Court. "Proceedings in York County Court." *William and Mary Quarterly* 11, no. 1 (July 1902): 34–43.

Young, Alfred F. *The Shoemaker and the Tea Party: Memory and the American Revolution.* Boston: Beacon, 2000.

Index

Page numbers in italic indicate illustrations.